Invitations, Celebrations

Ideas and Techniques for Promoting Reading in Junior and Senior High Schools

Revised and Enlarged Edition

By Fay Blostein

Neal-Schuman Publishers, Inc.

New York   London

T 78982

Published by Neal-Schuman Publishers, Inc.
100 Varick Street
New York, NY 10013

Printed and bound in the United States of America

Library of Congress Cataloging-in-Publication Data

Blostein, Fay.
   Invitations, celebrations : a handbook of ideas and techniques for promoting reading in junior and senior high schools / Fay Blostein. -- Rev. and enl. ed.
      p.   cm.
   ISBN 1-55570-202-3
   1. High school libraries--Activity programs--Canada. 2. High school libraries--Activity programs--United States. 3. Junior high school libraries--Activity programs--Canada. 4. Junior high school libraries--Activity programs--United States. 5. Teenager--Canada--Books and reading. 6. Teenagers--United States--Books and reading. I. Title
Z675.S3B617 1993
027.8'223'097--dc20   93-36976
                                                                                      CIP

For David
with gratitude and love

CONTENTS

PREFACE TO THE REVISED EDITION

The library is a place of celebration,
for it contains within it,
in the concentrated form of literature,
that celebration of life which the writer of books
perpetually and inevitably creates.
But if no invitations are sent out,
students and teachers may well be unaware
that there is anything to celebrate.

So began the first edition of *Invitations, Celebrations.* Thirteen years later, I am more convinced than ever that the tasks of the librarian must include actively welcoming students and teachers into that great place of celebration in which it is our privilege to work. But for all the gratifying feedback I have received about the approaches and techniques suggested in my book, I have come to be convinced equally that something extra is needed for these methods to work – *really* work.

Have you ever gone to a party in which the hosts had done all the correct things but it was clear that their hearts were not in it? You won't find "Keep Your Heart In It" among any of the section titles that follow, yet consider it the implied subtitle for all of them. To do this might require reviving a part of you that you'd thought you had well outgrown.

For the more analytical, mature and "adult" we may have become, the more, I think, we must cultivate our ability to take "childish" and "adolescent" emotions seriously, generously, unpatronizingly. The authors of these novels have done so. Whatever creative itch impelled them to publish their fiction, all of them share the imaginative gift to keep in touch with their younger selves – to recall, indeed to relive what it was like to be young. When you ask many of them how they thought up their ideas, they reply, "It's what I felt, so it's what I did."

A similar capacity for imaginative emotion can be drawn upon by the school librarian. When we accommodate, encourage, stimulate the young people who answer our invitations, we can call upon both the overview afforded by adult experience and the immediate contact of personal involvement. Mere expertise thus becomes enriched by trustworthy instinct. And we too can say, with confidence, "It's what I *felt,* so it's what I *did.*"

ACKNOWLEDGEMENTS

My heartfelt thanks go to:

    Larry Moore for bringing his values and generosity to the editing,

    Theresa Lung for her dependability and steadfastness in the preparation of the manuscript,

    Jefferson Gilbert for his creativity and design,

    Toni Porter and David Payne for their continuing support throughout the project.

And to the many librarians and teachers who over the years have urged me to celebrate again.

Fay Blostein,
Autumn 1993.

The invitation
is a way
of bringing students
into the world
of fiction
through what
is familiar
and important
to them.

1

Still
Inviting

You and your students have all seen invitations to parties, special dances, weddings, or civic celebrations, with their quotations and their often humorous exhortations. The invitation can be just as potent a device for the librarian.

It can be intriguing, projecting a tone to which the students can respond. How you word the invitation will ensure that the reply arrives. The reply, needless to say, consists of the sound of feet marching in to the library to give me the chance to make the magic link between these flesh and blood human beings and the rich treasures on my shelves.

I have found that students respond to the people who live in books more than to the plots in themselves. Concentrate in your preparations, therefore, on identifying and getting to know the fictional people who can "live" for your students. As you develop strong feelings for these characters, you will discover themes and ideas upon which your exhortations can be based.

For example, I both admired and disapproved of 17-year-old Billy in Russell McRae's *Going to the Dogs*. I smarted at his well-aimed barbs at teaching methods and was uneasy with his contempt for the mediocre. I admired his loyalty to friends and could envy his confidence. His need for chemical stimulants was worrisome as was his active social life.

But then there was Jon, an elderly seventeen year old in my school who affected a world weariness, practiced a doubting left eyebrow, and tossed off outrageous statements as though they were the final word. Stories circulated in the school about his challenges of curriculum, marks, teaching styles and education in general.

I really wanted to introduce Jon to Billy because what I learned from Billy was that the need to challenge authority amounts to no less than a desire to change the world. Did Jon know this already? Would this knowledge take shape as he read *Going to the Dogs*?

How would I introduce the two to each other? Directly as in,

> "Jon, I'd like to introduce you to Billy MacKenzie,
> > a rebel with a cause."

Or could I find the opportunity to show Jon page 33 and to ask him if he thought Billy had gone too far? Or should I gather together some more "rebels" and issue an invitation to Jon's class, most of whom were his informed colleagues or followers?

For thoughts on keeping notes, see p. 148.

I chose to invite Jon's class to the library. Who could they meet and what might they learn from them? This required thought. I leafed through my reading cards and browsed at the spinners and the shelves. My thinking developed the more I looked. I finally made my choice, collected the books together, wrote annotations for a hand-out, by which time I was ready to make my introductions. Here are the "rebels" I chose for them to meet:

> Billy MacKenzie who knows how to flourish amidst the monotonous mediocrity of school.
> > (*Going to the Dogs*. Russell McRae.)
>
> Celine, 16-year-old, who wryly observes the assignment change as the teacher gives in to whining.
> > (*Celine*. Brock Cole.)
>
> Lorne, a 17-year-old who leads a school strike.
> > (*Thirty-Six Exposures*. Kevin Major.)
>
> Louisa, big and bossy. Some people don't want to change her.
> > (*Roadside Valentine*. C.S. Adler.)
>
> Margaret, who makes up her list: Things I Would Most Like To See Changed In My Life and then another: Things To Do To Make Those Changes. To begin the latter, she changes her name to Harriet - as in Harriet Tubman, a leader.
> > (*Harriet's Daughter* . Marlene Nourbese Philip.)
>
> Daniel who proudly calls himself 'a problem child'. "Only provide the means of expression, only give wings to the imagination, and social harmony will prevail." How will a school that believes in freedom for young people handle him?
> > (*Daniel And Esther*. Patrick Raymond.)
>
> Bullet, who doesn't believe in compromises: "You've got to honour the differences, or what's similar will be useless to you."
> > (*The Runner*. Cynthia Voigt, p. 151.)

Weetsie, a skinny girl with a bleached blonde flat-top, feathered
headdress, moccasins, a pink fringed mini-dress, and who is
looking for My Secret Agent Lover Man.
(*Weetsie Bat.* Francesca Lia Block.)

Jane, 16 "and in the slammer. But that's not the end of the story,
I can tell you that. Because I'll get out of here, and when I
do, nobody is ever going to lock me up again."
(*Running Wild.* Shirley Powell.)

Lilli, amoral, shrewd, tough, fiercely independent and willing to
battle her benefactor for possession of her soul.
(*The True Story of Lilli Stubeck.* James Aldridge.)

Cart, 17 and 3/4 years old: "My mummy loves me. I love my
Daddy. My little sister hero-worships me. I have a delightful
week-end job. And best of all I'm still desperately in love with
me."
(*Saturday Night.* Hunter Davis.)

Nik, who was accused by a teacher of being "chronically unclub-
bable" as if this were a dire ailment. Others call him a loner.
He both resents this and is proud of it.
(*NIK.* Aidan Chambers.)

Philip who is either principled or stubborn, depending on whether
you're a teacher or a student.
(*Nothing But The Truth.* Avi.)

Sarah Benjamin, a nice Jewish girl in an exclusive Christian girls
school, wearing her Elect Kennedy pin on her shepherd's
burnoose.
(*Pageant.* Kathryn Lasky.)

Janie, a 17-year-old who'd waited for 12 years to get free of her
past to make a life for herself – absolutely herself. "Be careful
what you wish for, you might get it," she told herself wryly.
(*The Solitary.* Lynn Hall.)

The preacher's son, who breaks speed limits from the city limits
to the bootleggers, swears in triplicate, lusts after Amy,
laughs insanely from the pulpit, and struggles to keep his
faith, if not his father's.
(*Preacher's Boy.* Terry Pringle.)

Dillon, the bane of Principal Caldwell's existence, who defends
what Caldwell calls his "pornographic" t-shirt, saying, "It's
grammatically correct."
(*Chinese Handcuffs.* Chris Crutcher.)

Sus5an: "The 5 is silent. It's a visual statement."

(*My Name is Sus5an Smith. The 5 Is Silent.* Louise Plummer.)

Lyddie, 13, whose strength and independence are rooted in bitter-
ness and hard pride, whose fierce love is reserved for her
family only, and of whom we and her Quaker swain can say,
"Thee is indeed a wonder."

(*Lyddie.* Katherine Paterson)

Sib who at 16 knows she is more than a musical prodigy — a
woman who belongs, by virtue of hard work and original
thinking, among the world's greatest cellists.

(*Midnight Hour Encores.* Bruce Brooks.)

I know from experience that the student responses to these books will
expose feelings and ideas that challenge authority. Their emotional responses may well result in the talk being taken out of my control.
Such is the power of fiction. And we are giving that reading power to
our students!

We are *inviting* them to take that power.

This would be my invitation:

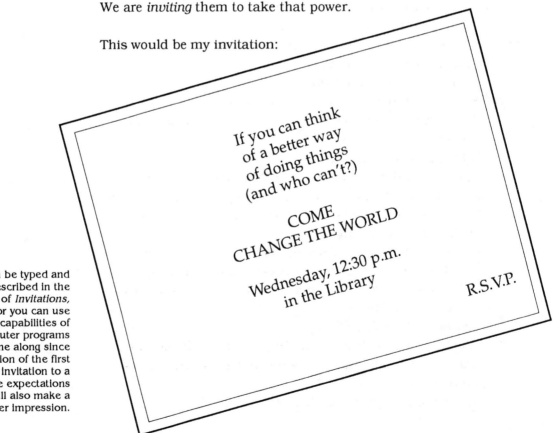

If you can think
of a better way
of doing things
(and who can't?)

COME
CHANGE THE WORLD

Wednesday, 12:30 p.m.
in the Library

R.S.V.P.

Invitations can be typed and
folded as described in the
first edition of *Invitations,
Celebrations,* or you can use
the desk top capabilities of
the many computer programs
that have come along since
the publication of the first
book. A typeset invitation to a
class will raise expectations
but will also make a
stronger impression.

To get the discussion that will lead to the books I have chosen, all I need ask is:

"What do you want to change first?"

There is a book in the list for virtually any answer I have ever received.

There are, I know, a good many teachers and librarians who are concerned about what they feel are the non-literary purposes to which students put their reading – particularly what might be called the "therapeutic" purposes. The objection is essentially that when students rush to apply incidents and characterizations of a novel to their own concerns and problems, they might trivialize it, by bypassing those features that make it art.

I have always maintained that the opposition between "literary" and "therapeutic" applications of reading is a false one. Whether we read deeply or shallowly, we read for pleasure, and the pleasures of reading add up to a celebration of human capacities:

- crafting
- imagining
- recording
- sympathizing
  and above all,
- bringing coherence to the otherwise incoherent
  experience of daily life.

You can't separate literary analysis, however rational it might be, from emotion: why and how does this poem, or story, or passage, make me <u>feel</u> this way, is basically what the critic or scholar is saying.

For a young person to recognize a parallel between her troubled relationship with her boyfriend and that of Cathy and Heathcliffe (or Finn and Seth to give a modern instance) is both a "literary" and a "therapeutic" act. And so is an academic's recognition of the human condition in the closing lines of *Paradise Lost.*

Up in Seth's Room,
by Norma Fox Mazer;
Hold Fast by Kevin Major;
A Chance Child
by Jill Paton Walsh.

When as a teacher-librarian, I would watch a young adult devouring *Up in Seth's Room, Hold Fast* or *A Chance Child*, when he or she could have been stapled to a television screen or lounging at the mall, I knew I was watching someone intuitively join in that celebration of being human that literature is all about. Was the connection analytical or emotional? The answer is far less important than the fact that the connection was made through what the student found familiar.

The invitation is my way of bringing students into the world of fiction through what is familiar and important to them personally.

By the way, Jon did meet Billy MacKenzie. It led to a long relationship with the library in which he met many, many others both real and fictional that made him one of the school's outstanding student leaders.

Talking
about one's
personal responses
in an encouraging,
non-judgmental
atmosphere
is a way of learning
about ourselves
and one another.

2

Can We Talk?

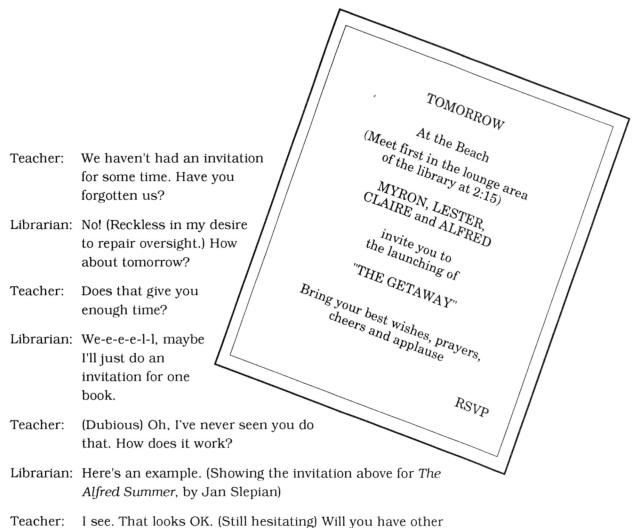

Teacher: We haven't had an invitation for some time. Have you forgotten us?

Librarian: No! (Reckless in my desire to repair oversight.) How about tomorrow?

Teacher: Does that give you enough time?

Librarian: We-e-e-e-l-l, maybe I'll just do an invitation for one book.

Teacher: (Dubious) Oh, I've never seen you do that. How does it work?

Librarian: Here's an example. (Showing the invitation above for *The Alfred Summer*, by Jan Slepian)

Teacher: I see. That looks OK. (Still hesitating) Will you have other books to offer them?

Librarian: Of course. After I finish, I will have a cart of loser/heroes for them "to applaud". Some possible titles are *Absolutely Invincible!* by William Bell and *Who Sir? Me Sir?* by K.M. Peyton or *A Question of Courage* by Irene Morck, *Probably Still Nick Swanson* by Virginia Wolff, and the sequel to *The Alfred Summer*, *Lester's Turn*, by Jan Slepian. Would that be ok?

Teacher: Good! And thank you!

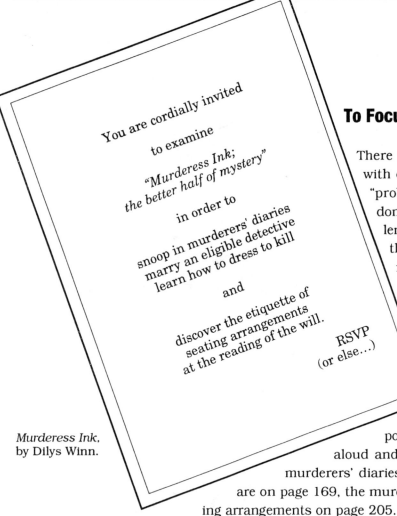

You are cordially invited

to examine

"Murderess Ink;
the better half of mystery"

in order to

snoop in murderers' diaries
marry an eligible detective
learn how to dress to kill

and

discover the etiquette of
seating arrangements
at the reading of the will.

RSVP
(or else...)

Murderess Ink,
by Dilys Winn.

To Focus on One Book

There are times when it is a good idea to deal with only one book. Is there a small group of "problem" non-readers in some teacher's domain: slow readers? behavioral problems, etc.? The invitation at left invites them to *browse* through one book. This is a non-threatening exercise, because students do not *have* to sign out a book for reading.

Gather the group around you, place the book before you on the table, and turn pages, first looking for the clues in the invitation, then just browsing, wondering and pointing out as you will, you reading aloud and the students reading as they will. The murderers' diaries are on page 98, the eligible detectives are on page 169, the murderer's dress on page 188, and the seating arrangements on page 205.

Here are some more good browsers for groups of two to ten:

Anno's Flea Market. Anno.
A cornucopia of human endeavours of long ago and today, celebrated in the author/illustrator's genius for people, feelings and humour. To begin with, an elderly couple push their cart to the centre of a town, joining others to sell, trade or buy. Legendary figures mix with the crowd: elves attract children to Christmas decorations. Simple Simon mans a stall, Santa Claus shops for sleighs. And on display are a historical range of machines, furniture of many periods, clothing, false teeth, eyeglasses, armaments, timepieces, toys, etc. Only problem: jostling for space at the table as students "read" the pages.

The Toronto Story. Claire Mackay.
Claire Mackay is not a teacher, but this social history of a city is history the way you wish it were always taught. Mackay's tone is easy, conversational, her figures of speech practical (Elizabeth Simcoe was

"a tiny woman no higher than a parking meter") her sense of humour wry and her political viewpoint firmly in place.

Notice these headings and sub-headings: "1818 or fo. Watch what happens here!" "1870 ish"; "1900 or thereabouts"; "1930 nearly"; "around 1957"; "1990 on the dot"; "Yankee go home!" "The Kids of De Grassi"; "Blind Pigs and Bullets"; "Bulldozers, BMWs and Bag Ladies"; "Hair, Hash and Hippies". In the Timelines section local trivia exists cheek by jowl with world events, e.g., "1957 Toronto radio station CHUM goes to rock and roll; Russian satellite Sputnik launches the space age." Historical personages are reduced to their essentials: "1812 – John Strachan rides into town and takes over as head of the church, head of the school and head of everything else." War is reduced to its baseness: "1756. Britain and France have a war about European real estate and North America fur."

The 13.5" by 10.5" format, wide margins, glossy pages, strong colour values, set off Johnny Wales drawings, particularly the full page maps, peopled with Anno-like characters, which introduce each chapter, e.g., In the midst of a movement of people and goods arriving and leaving by the lake, a party of settlers clears the land, a bare-bottomed diver cavorts, a recumbent figure inexplicably (a rejected caller?) lies near the main gates of Chief Justice Thomas Scott's estate. Smaller figures float freely in the margins throughout.

Old Is What You Get: Dialogues On Aging By the Old and the Young.
    Anne Zane Shanks.
Armed with tape recorder and camera, the author interviewed and photographed various men and women in various social strata, in various parts of the U.S. and England, ages sixty-six to ninety-six, and children eleven, adolescents fourteen to sixteen, and twenty-one-year-olds. The interviews are brief and the accompanying black and white photos mesmerizing. Such an accessible format invites easy browsing and commentary.

The Clue Armchair Detective. Lawrence Treat.
A series of unsolved crimes involving a small English village and the inhabitants of Tudor Close. You read each story in the police file, 26 in all, study the accompanying illustration(s), answer the questions in order, turn to the Answers and then after thinking some more (or less, if you're very quick-witted) turn to the Solutions. The illustrations, of the comic book sort, are great for perusing.

The Do-It-Yourself Bestseller: A Work Book. Tom Silberkleit and Jerry
    Biederman.
Twenty authors from Isaac Asimov to Alvin Toffler, Erskine Caldwell to
Stephen King, Steve Allen to Ken Follett have each provided a few original opening paragraphs — and a closing paragraph. Space is provided
to build your story in a coherent manner. Then after completing your
Bestsellers you are provided with a twenty-first "book", including an
author biography, space for title, name of author and co-author. You
provide the opening and closing paragraphs — and pass it along to
your friends to complete. Let students choose any one, or more, to try
on and pass around the results.

Not all book talks using a single book can or should be for
slow or difficult readers.

Here is one way to use
Kindergarten, by P.S.
Rushforth with a Grade
XI or Grade XII class (p.
56).

Librarian: What sort
            of peo-
            ple
            have

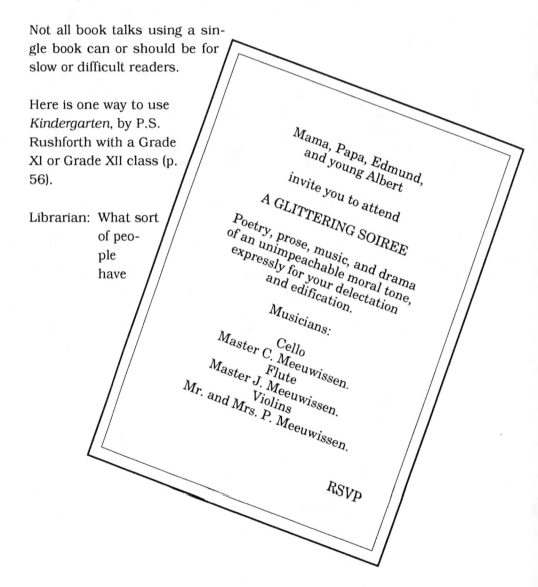

Mama, Papa, Edmund,
and young Albert

invite you to attend

A GLITTERING SOIREE

Poetry, prose, music, and drama
of an unimpeachable moral tone,
expressly for your delectation
and edification.

Musicians:

Cello
Master C. Meeuwissen.
Flute
Master J. Meeuwissen.
Violins
Mr. and Mrs. P. Meeuwissen.

RSVP

invited you into their home?

Students: Gifted. Bright. Close. Do things together. Love music, language. A cultured home. Well-off.

Librarian: That is the impression, isn't it? It is now a few years later — the mother has been killed, an innocent victim of a terrorist attack on an airport, the grandmother who looks after them now is a concentration camp survivor, and Corrie, who has always as a child loved the Hansel and Gretel story because it had a happy ending, comes upon a cache of letters written by German Jewish parents in the 1930's pleading fruitlessly with an English headmaster to accept their children into his school. The suffering of innocents in fairy tales, in Nazi Germany, in modern-day terrorism is not something the author succumbs to. He believes in a hopeful future for all families. At Christmas Grandmother Lillie lights candles, "With each child's birth, they say, the world begins again, and it is you who must use your life in trying to find a way, trying to light that darkness." (p. 148)

Here are some other titles that "light the darkness": *A Child Possessed*, by R.C. Hutchinson; *Bridge to Terabithia*, by Katherine Paterson; *One-Eyed Cat*, by Paula Fox; *The Lady is My Night Nurse?* by Gillian Rubinstein in *Landmarks*, edited by Nadia Wheatley; *Post Humus*, by Patti Tana in *When I Am an Old Woman I Shall Wear Purple*, edited by Sandra Martz.

To Focus on One Author

Concentrating on one author is another way to approach discussion. When you notice that a certain author is gaining popularity in your school, or wish that an author would be better known, or can think of an author whom you enjoy personally and therefore could be enthusiastic about, try issuing an invitation for that one writer. You are still looking for the same things in the author's books that you are looking for in all books you introduce – a revelation of powers, ideas, people that live in books.

Kevin Major

Books:

Hold Fast; Far from Shore; Thirty-Six Exposures; Blood Red Ochre; Dear Bruce Springsteen; Eating Between the Lines. Also *Doryloads: Newfoundland Writings and Art Selected & Edited for Young People.*

My invitation would read:

*Kevin Major believes that an author's work
"must be true to the small bit of earth
he writes about but also have
relevance to the general human condition
and speak to readers no matter where they live."*

*On Monday, period 4, the Library invites XI B
to speak with Kevin Major
From our small bit of earth.*

Jill Paton Walsh

Books:

The Dolphin Crossing; Fireweed; Goldengrove; Unleaving; The Emperor's Winding Sheet; A Parcel of Patterns; A Chance Child; Gaffer Samson's Luck.

My invitation would read:

*Jill Paton Walsh says that her
"preferred subjects have lain
in that large area of human experience
that adults and children have in common."
As one of her characters says
at the end of Unleaving,
"What shall we sing? O, the beauty of the world!"*

*On Friday, period 9,
the Library invites XIIC to*

Patricia Wrightson

Books:
The Book of Wirrun series: *The Ice Is Coming; The Dark Bright Water; Behind the Wind.* Also: *Balyet; A Little Fear.*

My invitation would read:

> *Patricia Wrightson*
> *sees fantasy as*
> *neither escape nor symbolism but as*
> *"that strangeness and fullness of life*
> *that spills out of the bucket of reality".*
>
> *At 1:15 Monday,*
> *the Library invites you to*
> *Keep filling the bucket.*
> *RSVP*

Suggestion:
Be ready to give an appreciative, receptive student Patricia Wrightson's article "Deeper Than You Think" in *The Horn Book*, March/April 1991.

Diana Wynne Jones

Books:
Archer's Goon; Cart and Cwidder; Castle in the Air; Charmed Life; Dogsbody; Eight Days of Luke; Fire and Hemlock; The Homeward Bounders; The Lives of Christopher Chant; Wild Robert;Wilkin's Tooth; Witch Week.

My invitation would read:

> *Diana Wynne Jones*
> *believes*
> *that fantasy stories can*
> *"lead the reader around some hidden turning*
> *of the mind into remarkable new places.*
> *Some of them have hidden turnings beyond that."*
>
> *The Library invites you to*
> *Follow some hidden turnings*
> *Monday at 1:10.*
> *RSVP*

To Focus on One Theme

*From her foreword to
Hidden Turnings.

When I read Diana Wynne Jones' words* I knew that I also had an organizing principle upon which to gather some challenging reads in which realism takes unexpected turns and possibilities. The literal-minded student could be offered the realism, a reassuring base to return to and pause at if need be. The adventurous-minded student could take off on the hidden turnings with eagerness and little guidance or reassurance.

For more on reading cards,
see p. 148.

To use Jones in this way, I would start by making a selection from her titles. I then would gather together my reading cards for other books that have some singularity, some uniqueness and search for a group of students with whom I can take a chance.

Although the theme I am pursuing is challenging, the students for whom I am looking are not necessarily the "good students". They must be a group that in the past seemed willing to listen, or that contained people who frequently visited the library, or that were just students I liked the look of, or about whom their teacher had some positive things to say.

Here are some of the books I would use:

> *Follow a Shadow.* Robert Swindells.
> 15-year-old Tim "5'3" and thin with it. Nothing special about the face, either. Zits. Nose like Concorde. Weak chin. Glasses. A mane of carroty hair" who sees "himself" reflected in a window wearing weird clothing and other glasses, and discovers disturbing similarities between himself and an ancestor, Bramwell, the ne'er-do-well Brontë brother.

> *The Return.* Barry Faville.
> Jonathan attends a two-room school in a remote village, happy to grow up unaffected by the demands of his own age group, talking and behaving as his own personality demands - until the strange boy enters his life and reads his mind.

> *Night Maze.* Annie Dalton.
> Fourteen year-old Gerald is finally reclaimed by his dead mother's family, to be greeted by "a ruined house full of dreams that have

got a separate life of their own. A witch grandmother and her apprentice. Asthma, owls and all."

Solstice. Jan Adkins.
With the angry ruins of his parents' marriage around him, Charlie and his father set out, seven days before Christmas, for their deserted summer island, and end up sharing festivities with the Filson's, so wonderful as to be — miraculous.

Other titles I would consider include
Black and White, by Jan Mark, *Break of Dark* by Robert Westall, *The Book of Kells,* by R.A. MacAvoy, *The Devil on the Road,* by Robert Westall, *Mazes and Monsters* by Rona Jaffe, and *Playing Beatie Bow* by Ruth Park.

To Focus on One Idea

The idea around which one develops a book talk can grow out of an author's philosophy, such as we have just seen with Diana Wynne Jones. Or it can grow out of a common trait of character or attitude as seen in the rebels example with which I began this book. Or it can grow out of an event or concept with which the students are familiar. It is the familiarity of the idea which will give your book talk its momentum and power.

What are your own questions about events? about life? about the way of things? If you question things, could it be that your students have the same questions? The following example comes out of just such musings.

Every spring, as our area switches from standard time to daylight saving time, I wonder about the lost hour (where did it go?) and the hour that is repeated in the fall when we go back to standard time from daylight saving time. (Could I choose any hour in time to repeat?)

I used this idea with a senior class that had grown to trust my age-groupings of titles, since these titles range from picture book to adult. But then, if your Babysitters' Corner is well-used as mine was, all grades should feel comfortable with younger selections. There is no need to explain or rationalize in any event.

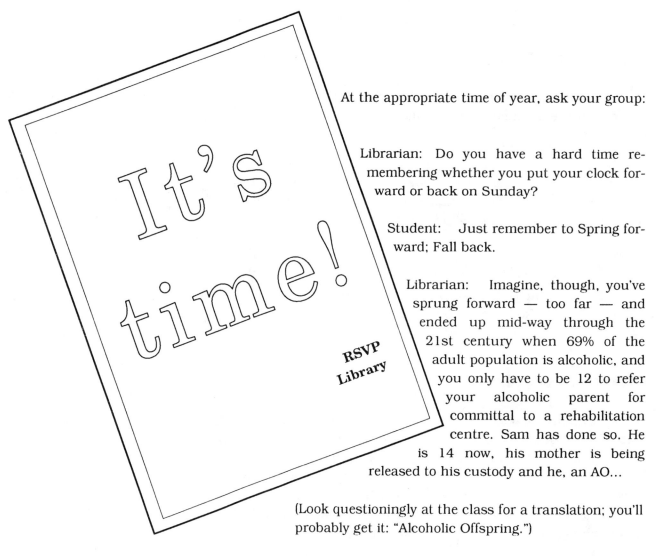

It's
time!

RSVP
Library

At the appropriate time of year, ask your group:

Librarian: Do you have a hard time remembering whether you put your clock forward or back on Sunday?

Student: Just remember to Spring forward; Fall back.

Librarian: Imagine, though, you've sprung forward — too far — and ended up mid-way through the 21st century when 69% of the adult population is alcoholic, and you only have to be 12 to refer your alcoholic parent for committal to a rehabilitation centre. Sam has done so. He is 14 now, his mother is being released to his custody and he, an AO...

(Look questioningly at the class for a translation; you'll probably get it: "Alcoholic Offspring.")

...now has the right, by law, to decide whether his kid brother, 10-year-old Ollie, can come home too or be adopted by the foster parents who have cared for him the past two years. In *No Kidding*, by Bruce Brooks.

Have you jumped too far? All right, let's try again. Put your two feet together, and jump again. Feel odd? Look down at your feet? Nothing — You're a...

(Pause – class supplies: "Ghost.")

...Do you know who? Well, either Sally or Fenella or Charlotte or Imogen — one of the sisters. And what is that grey threatening Something just beyond your sight? In *The Time of the Ghost*, by Diana Wynne Jones.

Feeling confused? uncomfortable? Want to try falling back? Here we go. E-a-s-y. Don't look at her; don't follow that furry little girl! Now you've done it! Though the place looks oddly familiar and the people are loving and protective — it's 1873 – you can't return until you fulfill an ancient family curse about a "Stranger" who will save the family from extinction. In *Playing Beatie Bow*, by Ruth Park.

Maybe you should just stand still. Now there is a pause, everything in your body stops, the way a clock stops. Then the panic. After that, the flash of pain, like lightning, cruel but quickly gone. The cold begins when the fade begins, and remains all the time you're in the fade. And you remember your uncle's words. "They will not see you but they will feel you there, know your presence." You, too, are a fader.

(Hold up *Fade*, by Robert Cormier.)

Let's try one last time; let's try moving, for happier results. Yes! For Aquilina, a circus trapeze artist, knows exactly how to follow the handsome prince who left a silver star in her hand with his kiss. She waves to her parents, seizes the trapeze, dives backward through *The Door in the Air* — the title story in an anthology of imaginative stories.

Here's a time game. The events in this book take place at different times; then again, they may all take place at the same time...

(Open *Black and White*, by David Macaulay at any two-page spread and point to appropriate places on the page as you speak).

...There are commuters waiting at a train station, cows in a meadow, some problem parents, and a boy returning home. What happens when the commuters get a big surprise, the cows get out of the field, the parents dress up in newspapers, and the boy rubs his eyes in amazement? The answers are here, in *Black and White*, by David Macaulay...

(Turn pages as you speak).

A word of caution — these answers may change every *time* you read.

PLAYING WITH TIME
the booklist

SPRING FORWARD
No Kidding.
    Bruce Brooks
The Time of the Ghost.
    Diana Wynne-Jones
The Postman.
    David Brin

FALL BACK
Playing Beatie Bow.
    Ruth Park
Stonewords.
    Pam Conrad
Time Out.
    Helen Cresswell

...AND FADE
Fade.
    Robert Cormier
The Door in the Air.
    Margaret Mahy

TIME OUT
Black and White.
    David Macaulay
*The True Story of the
    Three Little Pigs.*
    Jon Scieszka
*The Frog Prince
    Continued.*
    Jon Scieszka

KEEPING TIME
*Despite the dastardly
    efforts of the evil
"Swallowers of Time" in
Momo.*
    Michael Ende

...AND TIME NO MORE
Tom's Midnight Garden.
    Philippa Pearce

If you continue to play with time in this way, you may discover hilarious new twists to time-honoured stories — such as *The Three Little Pigs* and *The Princess Who Kissed the Frog*.

(Reading the opening lines)

"The Princess kissed the frog. He turned into a prince.
And they lived happily ever after...
Well let's just say they lived sort of happily for a long time.
Okay, so they weren't so happy.
In fact they were miserable.
'Stop sticking your tongue out like that,' nagged the Princess.
'How come you never want to go down to the pond, anymore?'
whined the Prince. The Prince and Princess were so unhappy.
They didn't know what to do....'

The answer to your bewilderment about time — passing, reverting, accelerating, fading, re-inventing — can be found when you look at the clock's inscription TIME NO MORE in the pages of the most beautifully told, time-less story of all, *Tom's Midnight Garden*, by Philippa Pearce.

(Book list at left passed out as you continue speaking)

That's what you get for playing with time.
If you're still interested, here are some more time games."

I was telling a group of librarians about this book talk and got one of those angry/frustrated outbursts from A.

"*My* kids know *nothing* about the three little pigs or frog princes. They come from *different* cultures. I could *never* try this. What *good* is it?"

Well, I suppose the answer is that while it's "good" for some kids, it's not for A's. And if I were he/she I wouldn't dream of doing the talk with that group — for now.

I wonder if A would try having her group bring its own myths, fairy tales, folk stories (written and oral) to class and sharing them. I would try to get two teachers whose teaching period follow each other to come into the project. That way you can have a relaxed double period in the library with its floor, cushion, easy chair seating where questions and explanations of cultural traditions can be aired. With the two teachers, the librarian helps draw out a pattern: creation myths, similarities, versions, etc. The three adults have come prepared with their own choices and share them too. e.g., *Baboushka and the Three Kings*, by Ruth Robbins (with bonus words and music); *The Contest*, adapted and illustrated by Nonny Hogrogian (an Armenian pronunciation guide included); *The Funny Little Woman*, a Japanese tale retold by Arlene Mosel; *In the Beginning: Creation Stories from Around the World*, told by Virginia Hamilton, with stunning transparent watercolor illustration by Barry Moser; *Strega Nona*, retold and illustrated by Tomie de Paola. This can go on for days in a row, one day a week for a few months — whatever.

In this way, lonely, alienated, fearful newcomers to our country will find their backgrounds validated, respected, honoured.

And while I bristle at Pollyanna bromides myself, I can't help wishing I could give A my favourite poster:
   "IF THERE IS NO WIND, ROW".

The familiar,
the commonplace –
the things everyone
knows about or does
but for one reason
or another still finds
interesting,
involving,
arresting.
A relaxed, recognizable
and comfortable
entrance to reading,
a natural medium
for non-reader and
reader alike.

3

What Are You Doing Today? Oh, Nothing.

GOING SHOPPING

Librarian: Dinky has picked up this shopping instruction when she
comes home from school:

*Dinky:
Please
pick up
my order for
four pies at
Woerners.*

Mom

J CORNSI

From *Dinky Hocker Shoots
Smack*, by M.E. Kerr,
p. 19- .

Now, I
can tell you
that Dinky's mother
works with dope addicts. So
this can't be a dangerous errand for
her to send Dinky on, can it?

Students: (Puzzled – or perhaps very sharp)

Librarian: Well, there are addicts and then there are addicts. Dinky,
who is 5'4", weighs 165 pounds. She is a food addict!
(Reading)

> 'Tucker should have known that Dinky would still be at Woer-
> ner's, eating. To ask someone like Dinky to go into Woerner's
> Restaurant just to pick up pies for her mother was to ask a
> wino to drop in at a vineyard just to watch the bottling process.

Oh, Nothing.

... Dinky was sitting at the counter finishing a plate of hot roast beef with home fries and fresh peas. She acknowledged Tucker's presence with little more than a raised eyebrow, and went right on eating and reading a book ... He ordered a piece of chocolate pie with whipped cream when he sat down, and Dinky told Agnes, the waitress, "Make that two, with a side of chocolate ice cream on mine."

... After Tucker left Woerner's with Dinky, they walked down to Court Street on their way to the library. In front of Chock Full 'O Nuts, Dinky said, "Do you want to try out their new barbecue sauce? It has onions in it, and it's really neat."

"You try it out," Tucker said. "I'll come with you."

"I'm not going to sit at the counter if you're just going to take up space beside me. They don't like that in Chock Full 'O Nuts."

"I don't know what I'd order," Tucker said.

"All right!" Dinky said, as though she were going to have to make a big sacrifice on account of him. "I'll order two franks and you can pretend one is yours." ... Tucker didn't say anything. "Three franks," Dinky told the waitress, "and a heavenly coffee."

Shopping lists whether they actually appear in a given book or not can tell everything about the characters who make them up and be a good base for discussion. The shopping lists need not always be for food either. Here is a different kind of shopping list that I have used and that worked very well.

Librarian: Do you ever get asked to go shopping for your mother after school? Here is a list. What do you think the shopper is going to make?

Students: (Various guesses.)

Oh, Nothing.

Librarian: I'll give you some clues. When you think what is going to be made, interrupt and tell me.

> (Reading)
>
> "This is supposed to be justice for Uncle Otto for all the mean things he's done."
>
> "Right," said Debbie, handing over the half-sewn tee-shirt to Verna, along with the needle and thread.
>
> When Verna was through, Iris mixed a green colour from the yellow and blue food coloring to dye the shirt. Adele finished the lanyard, which was really cute, and we even had a tiny whistle from a Cracker-Jack box to hang from the end of it. The moccasins were perfect. We made them out of the soft brown clay, and an extra touch was a tiny piece of string which we made to look like it was laced through the sides of each shoe and tied in front, like the real thing.
>
> The clay mold of the doll looked terrific ... so much like Uncle Otto it was almost scary.

From *In Summertime It's Tuffy* by Judie Angell, p. 157.

Uncle Otto, as the girls call him, is Camp Director; the girls think he's been mean, and want to punish him. So, using Iris's knowledge of magic, they've made a clay image of Uncle Otto. What is the next step?

Students: (With enthusiasm) Stick pins in the doll.

Librarian: (Mixture of amusement and shock) How fiendish! Will that work?

Students: (Various replies: increased fiendishness, contrition, reluctant denial, virtuous non-participation)

Librarian: *In Summertime It's Tuffy* is filled with the craziness, the boredom, the bad food of camp life. You'll recognize a lot of your own experiences.

You don't always have to rely on the direct text for your list, but you should list items carefully, as in the following, so that students will pick up clues.

For *I.O.U.s.* Ouida Sebestyen.
> To Stowe:
> > At health food store:
> > > 1 lb whole wheat flour
> > > 1 lb oatmeal
> > > 1/4 lb wheat germ
> > At Buy-Save Market:

Oh, Nothing.

> 1/2 dozen eggs
> 4 oranges
> 1 bag 2% milk
> small bottle ketchup — no-name brand or on special if
>   cheaper
> 1 box cereal that crunches, sparkles and rots your teeth
>   — *(only if enough money left after other purchases).*
>   Love, Mom

Will students recognize Mom's health and thrift-minded habits?

For *Pick-Up Sticks.* Sarah Ellis.

> 6 pounds cold cuts,
> assorted cheeses, 1 lb each: Feta, Camembert, Brie,
>   Provolone, Roquefort
> couple dozen jars of pickles – sour, bread and butter,
>   gherkins, mustard
> couple cases of bottled juice – apple, orange, etc.

Is this family's carelessly wealthy style obvious?

For *Pick-Up Sticks.* Sarah Ellis.

> 4 tubes white glue, large size
> 4 packages toilet paper
> 2 aerosol cans whipping cream
> 2 aerosol cans shaving cream
> 4 cans coke
> 4 large containers of yoghurt

Will the students notice that these items and their quantities denote, not use, but mischief-making?

For *It Happened at Cecelia's.* Erika Tamar.

> 2 lbs raw scallops
> 2 lbs ham
> 2 lbs raw baby shrimp
> 2 large bunches dill
> 2 lbs each Hungarian imported medium and hot paprika
> 6 boneless chicken breasts
> 1 gallon jar apricot jam

Will students be surprised that Cecelia's is a restaurant with a schizophrenic menu?

For *Walking Up a Rainbow.* Theodore Taylor.

Oh, Nothing.

Purchase at

Lazenby's Dry Goods and Ladies' Emporium

      India rubber raincoats

      woolsack coats, wool pantaloons, buffalo robes

      sheet iron stove, two Dutch ovens

      600 pounds flour

      50 pounds pilot bread

      150 pounds bacon

      50 pounds ham

      dried fish, lard, coffee, rice, raisins, oats

      2 dozen bottles medicine for sheep screwworms

      800 pounds licking salt

      2 quarts lime juice

Surely the clues to this historic trek adventure are clear.

Oh, Nothing.

CALENDARS

* This idea was first described in slightly different form in *Strategy*, vol. 3, no. 1 / January/February 1983. Libraries & Learning, Inc.

I first used the device of the calendar* as a means of avoiding The Deadly Skills Lesson taught in anticipation of a need, in which one talks at the students, reminding them of the usefulness, the life-saving potential of almanacs, yearbooks, etc., setting an exercise at the end of the "lesson". Boring. Ineffective. Inefficient. And when it comes time to use the almanacs and yearbooks for an assignment, they have forgotten all I've "taught".

Librarian: How many calendars do you have in your home? Your room? My office? (I'm prepared and show them three — one a desk model used to keep track of circulation statistics, and phone calls; one which records scheduled and pre-arranged class visits; one which is anecdotal — to record student questions (my favourites are the garbled and humorous variety) student comments on books, book-talks, my lessons, etc.)

Then I showed them the *Mary Ellen's Helpful Hints Calendar*, with all its household hints on the top illustrated half of the calendar, the bottom half the actual calendar. I took this calendar apart, distributing the months, so that students could examine the model more closely. They noted the format, that the hints were assembled under categories, e.g., Food Tips, Stain Removers, The Laundry, etc. Then I suggested we could create our own helpful hints for a social studies calendar, beginning with the categories of addresses for associations, and inviting them to add more categories for factual information. Very quickly we listed statistics, embassy addresses, monuments, government agencies, awards, records of highest, lowest, biggest, smallest, oldest, etc.

Next I directed the students to the mound of almanacs and other research guides I had placed on a table and invited them to browse through them looking for information. They worked singly, in pairs, and in groups of three. As soon as a student found a likely fact, he/she printed it on a small slip of paper (p-slips cut up into four pieces) gave it to me, and I started pasting it over the Mary Ellen hints. You can re-assemble the calendar as the students work, or use possibly a second copy, or another similar calendar, or make up one of your own. Very quickly you can cover twelve

1 Fonzie's birthday is October 30, 1945.

2 of Oz Club, 1957 and as of 1982, having a membership of 1850, can be written to at Box 95, Kinderhook, IL 62345

3 Singapore separated from Malaysia in 1965. It is not the size of Quebec; it is the size of Toronto!

4

5 Timothy Hutton won his Academy Award for Ordinary People when he was still in his teens.

6 The largest drum in the world is at Disneyland.

10'6" across and weighs over 450 pounds.

7 Did you know an elephant is pregnant for 11 months?

7 The National Hockey League

can frames and leave one day on a When the sun n, remove the rec- should be good as

"THE BEST WAY TO START PAINTING IS TO GET PLASTERED FIRST."

sheet of heavy-duty aluminum foil large enough to cover your grill completely. Press foil, shiny side down, on grill and fold sides under, covering as tightly as possible. When coals have nearly reached their hottest point,

Food Tip
• Thaw fish in milk for a fresh-caught flavor.

Stain Remover

THAT'S WHAT IT SAYS IN: 1. Current Biography. 2. World Almanac. 3. Statesman's Yearbook. 4. The Everyday Almanac. 5. Information Please Almanac. 6. Guinness Book of World Records. 7. World Book Encyclopedia Yearbook. 8. Canadian Almanac.

MAY

SUNDAY	MONDAY	TUESDAY	WEDNESDAY	THURSDAY	FRIDAY	SATURDAY
					1	2
3	4	5	6	7	8	9
10	11	12	13	14	15	1
				21	22	

APRIL 1981
S M T W T F S
        1 2 3 4
5 6 7 8 9 10 11
12 13 14 15 16 17 18
19 20 21 22 23 24 25
26 27 28 29 30

JUNE 1981
S M T W T F S
  1 2 3 4 5 6
7 8 9 10 11 12 13
14 15 16 17 18 19 20
21 22 23 24 25 26 27
28 29 30

Oh, Nothing.

months. The work looks something like the illustration on the previous page. It's amazing how much the students will learn from this activity about the purpose, organization, format and usefulness of almanacs — and without a "lesson", lecture, repetition and an "exercise" to make sure the students have mastered the skill.

There are many other variations in which students can create personalized calendars.

Why not use the calendars as a means of acknowledging and recording student tastes in reading genres, e.g., mystery, romance, science fiction; subjects, e.g., movies, motorcycles; favourite authors, etc.?

Librarian: Did you ever give anyone a calendar as a gift? Did you ever receive one? What was the reason for giving the calendar as a gift?

How many specialty calendars are there in your home? Our library? What are their themes?

I showed them my own favourites: *Baryshnikov Dances* (its delectable pull out poster), *The Peace Calendar* (with its moving quotations and the pictures of their authors), *Louis L'Amour* (as an example of an author calendar), and the *Baking Bread* calendar (as an example of the how-to-do-it type).

Librarian: If you could make and give a calendar as a gift for someone, or yourself, what would it be?

Students: (A variety of responses.) Are we going to do that?

Librarian: Would you like to? I can provide the scissors, paste, paper and a box of discarded magazines, and posters and pictures.

Teacher: And I...
            (Here the teacher can outline the requirements, guidelines, time lines etc. that you and he/she have worked out beforehand.)

In the planning stage both you and the teacher agree on the goals: a validation of reading tastes; a respect for process as a value; the value of peer recommendations. You try to think of all the possible developments, preparations, logistics, e.g.,

1. What will you do about the non-reader who wants to do motorcycles? and preferably pictures only?

    Decision: Require the inclusion of factual information, culled from the 700's, the encyclopaedia (e.g., *Canadian Encyclopaedia* article, "Motorcycle Racing" in Volume II, p. 1169), directories, yellow pages, etc.

    Decision: Minimum fiction to be referred to — one novel (e.g., *Into the Road*, by Adrienne Richards, *Collision Course*, by Nigel Hinton) and one short story from a collection or magazine.

    Decision: Quotations from books or peers or teachers.

    Decision: Number of pictures: maximum of twelve.

2. The student who wishes to create a favourite author calendar will be

    ▲ invited to use the *Judy Blume Diary* (Dell, 1981) its quotations and illustrations from the novels as a model.

    ▲ encouraged to verbalize why he/she has chosen that author, what she/he consider his/her best novels, e.g., *A Fuzzy Warm Calendar* for Patricia MacLachlan to celebrate her world of innocence and beauty.

    ▲ provide at least one example each of an excerpt, a re-telling, a rhetorical question, an illustration, a newspaper clipping appropriate to one of the novels.

3. In general the sources for the top portion of the calendar, apart from the student's expertise, can be culled from browsing at the shelves, inspecting a Dewey section of the library, mulling over a pre-selection (teacher's and/or the librarian's) of materials at a table.

4. The librarian provides the work space, temporary storage space probably for several days, scissors, paste, colour felt tip pens, encouragement, direction, support.

These calendars can help the student see reading as a multi-faceted process: conceptualizing, selecting, gathering, creating. If you do this project in November, you will see some amazing productions for Christmas presents. Do provide an opportunity for display with an acknowledgement that "All these calendars were created by Ms. A's Grade IX Social Studies Class using the following library materials: (List them)"

I wonder whether some of the calendars could be reproduced and sold to support a school project?

Oh, Nothing.

THE AWARDS CEREMONY

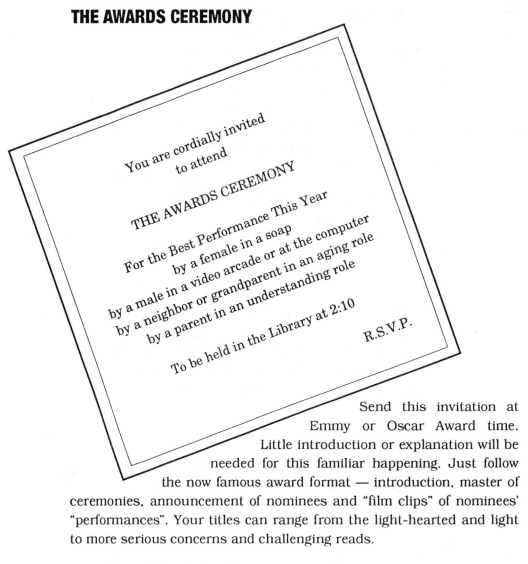

You are cordially invited
to attend

THE AWARDS CEREMONY

For the Best Performance This Year
by a female in a soap
by a male in a video arcade or at the computer
by a neighbor or grandparent in an aging role
by a parent in an understanding role

To be held in the Library at 2:10   R.S.V.P.

Send this invitation at Emmy or Oscar Award time. Little introduction or explanation will be needed for this familiar happening. Just follow the now famous award format — introduction, master of ceremonies, announcement of nominees and "film clips" of nominees' "performances". Your titles can range from the light-hearted and light to more serious concerns and challenging reads.

Librarian: Welcome to the annual Award Ceremony. I am your host and here are the nominees...

(Hand out the book list now, so students can follow.)

In the category
Best Performance by a Female In A Soap:

●   Samantha Sonnheim in *The Young and the Soapy*

(Turn slightly to pick up and show book or read excerpt as if showing the movie clip. Don't worry – your class will "get it".)

Oh, Nothing.

Here is a poem for Diamond Savoy by Samantha Sonnheim (p. 24)

> 'You were just a mild-mannered housewife,
> having a couple of extramarital affairs,
> when he came to you,
> Dressed all in black,
> and smelling of cappuccino,
> he took you away
> to his world of dreams
> and illusions.
> And you found you were
> a different person
> and would never be
> the same.'

Samantha wants to prevent a TV producer from killing off her favourite soap character – and when the star of the soap and her producer-husband move into her building, she and a friend put their minds to work.

● Sue Sudley in *Suds*

> (Reading p. 1.
> Try to capture the "impending" tones
> of a soap announcer)

'As you remember...
We left Sue Sudley in a deep emotional decline, staring at the canopy above her bed at Suddenly, the family mansion, with only old Nanny Grossup in attendance, and nightmares of the ghastly accident haunting her. That June day that began as a happy celebration and ended so tragically replayed itself over and over in Sue's mind in a catastrophic kaleidoscope:
— Her mother deciding to surprise her father on Sue's fifteenth birthday by flying herself and Sue in the family's Cessna 182 Skylane to his corporate convention on the west coast.
— Her father deciding to surprise Sue and her mother for Sue's fifteenth birthday by flying himself home in his Lear jet.
— The midair collision...
— Sue, hanging from her birthday present — a multicolored designer parachute — watching in horror as her parents' plane fragments fall to earth...
— The double funeral.
   Then, finally
— The silence of Suddenly, the soft blue drapes blotting out the harsh July sun, and except for the quiet patience and sympathy of old Nanny Grossup, Sue was all alone.'

THE LIBRARY AWARDS
the booklist

FEMALE IN A SOAP

The Young and the Soapy.
   Jamie Callan

Suds.
   Judie Angell

Soaps in the Afternoon.
   Lavinia Harris

The Agony of Alice.
   Phyllis Reynolds Naylor

Love Letters to My Fans.
   Jackie Parker

MALE IN A VIDEO ARCADE OR AT THE COMPUTER

Love Byte.
   Helane Zeiger

Switching Tracks.
   Dean Hughes

The Gadget Factor.
   Sandy Landsman

Computer Nut.
   Betsy Byars

Oh, Nothing.

THE LIBRARY AWARDS
the booklist

NEIGHBOR OR GRANDPARENT IN AN AGING ROLE

The 79 Squares.
  Malcolm J. Bosse

*Sweet Bells Jangled
  Out of Tune.*
  Robin Brancato

Leave Me Alone, Ma.
  Carol Snyder

Grace.
  Liesel M. Skorpen

Daphne's Book.
  Mary Downing Hahn

PARENT IN AN UNDERSTANDING ROLE

Cracker Jackson.
  Betsy Byars

*There's a Girl in My
  Hammerlock.*
  Jerry Spinelli

*Memo: To Myself When
  I Have a Teen-aged
  Kid.*
  Carol Snyder

Pick-Up Sticks.
  Sarah Ellis

Fourteen.
  Marilyn Sachs

The other nominees:
- Celia in *Soaps in the Afternoon*
- Sylvia in *Over the Hill at Fourteen*
- Alice in *The Agony of Alice*
- Penny in *Love Letters to My Fans*

In the category
Best Performance by a Male in a Video Arcade or at the Computer:

- Mark in *Love Byte*

  Mark is a whizz at every video game there is. Amy is a computer nut who needs a date for the prom. The solution? Go where the boys are. And that's how she meets Mark. Every thing seems slated for success, when Amy's mother starts a citizens' campaign against video arcades.

- Mark in *Switching Tracks*

  Mark is obsessively committed to playing Space Invaders; the only problem is money . So he reluctantly takes on a job of helping 80-year-old Willard put his collection of electric trains into order. Is it only money that ties these two unlikely people together?

The other nominees:
- Mike in *The Gadget Factor*
- BB-9 in *Computer Nut*

In the category of A Neighbor or Grandparent in an Aging Role:

- Mr. Beck in *The 79 Squares*, who teaches Eric from 79 squares staked out in his garden.

- Ellen's grandmother Eva in *Sweet Bells Jangled Out of Tune*, who reminds Ellen that unacceptable social behavior doesn't mean you lack feelings or human rights.

The other nominees:
- Jamie's grandma in *Leave Me Alone, Ma*
- Grace in *Grace*
- Daphne's grandmother in *Daphne's Book*

Oh, Nothing.

In the category of A Parent in an Understanding Role

● Mrs. Jackson and Mr. Jackson in *Cracker Jackson*

Mr. Jackson phones every Thursday night and Mrs. Jackson steps in to provide crucial help when Cracker suspects that his beloved former sitter Alma is being abused by her husband.

● Maisie's mother in *There's a Girl in My Hammerlock* (p. 31)

When Maisie's mother learns her daughter wants to try out for the wrestling team, she confronts the coach: "Mr. Capelli, maybe Maisie won't even make the team. I can only tell you that if she doesn't, it won't be because she quit. When you talk about boys being stronger, you may be right about arms and legs. But nobody" — she squeezed me — "nobody is as strong in the heart as this girl right here."

The other nominees are:
● Karen's mother in *Memo: To Myself When I Have a Teenaged Kid*
● Polly's mum in *Pick-Up Sticks*
● Catherine Cooper in *Fourteen*

Who do you think should win the awards? Here are your 'votes'.

(Indicate books on cart, or stand or whatever, from which students then make their selections).

The Awards Ceremony may remind you of the number of times your students have told you enthusiastically of a book they just **loved**.
"This was the **best** book I ever read."
"**Fantastic!**" "**Cool!**" (or the latest 'in' accolade).

Why not use the award format to enable the students to do their own awarding? Start this off on the day you have just decorated a bulletin board with *We're Proud of Our Award Winners.*

Librarian: We have all read books we thought deserving of awards, and if not the book itself, at the very least, some character

Oh, Nothing.

in the book. So from a book you have read recently, choose an admirable character whom you think worthy of an award. Give your award a name. You may design the award also, if you wish. Write the citation. We'll show you some samples. Then announce your award. Have your character give his/her acceptance speech.

Students enjoy reading each other's work. Perhaps some artistic souls in the class can help decorate a bulletin board with the results. The class effort is always acknowledged. e.g., This bulletin board prepared by the students of _____ English.

This activity should encourage critical thinking, literary appreciation, awareness, sensitivity, as well as drawing out creative writing abilities.

An example of your own to get the class started:

The Waltzing on Water Award
this year goes to
Meribah Simon of
Beyond the Divide, by Kathryn Laski

Thank you. I accept this award on behalf of Serena Billings who because of false notions of womanhood held by men and women can never now be courageous, independent, can never be what she hoped. It is in her name that I accept the *Waltzing on Water Award* and vow to carry on the struggle to **be**.

THE WALTZING
ON WATER
AWARD
to the female
most exemplifying
courage
in the face of
overwhelming
odds

Waltzing on Water is a collection of poetry by women, edited by Norma Fox Mazer and Marjorie Lewis.

Oh, Nothing.

THE YELLOW PAGES

Does your neighborhood have a telephone directory? Mine does. It calls itself *Your Neighbourhood Yellow Pages Directory* and covers businesses and services in a local area. Why not a *Your Library Yellow Pages Directory*? It's amazing how many of the original's headings can apply to your own library's collection. Use it to get yourself started. You can fill up your bulletin board quite quickly, and take care of several weeks of displays (our library policy stated that displays stayed up for one week only) before you finish the alphabet. You may want to start off with special sections, e.g.,

Map Of Your Neighborhood Paperbacks
(i.e. in the library... see illustration at right)

Assaulted Women's Help Line...
Cracker Jackson. Betsy Byars.
How can Cracker rescue his beloved babysitter Alma from her brutalizing husband?

Telecommunications Centre
For Special Needs (Disabilities)
Gideon Ahoy! William Mayne.
Will Gideon's loving family be able to ensure an independent future for this deaf and brain-damaged 18-year-old?

Senior Citizens' Organizations
Memory. Margaret Mahy.
An outcast himself, can Jonny provide care for Sophie, suffering from senile dementia, a brain disorder marked by loss of memory and disorientation?

Then proceed to the alphabetical listings:

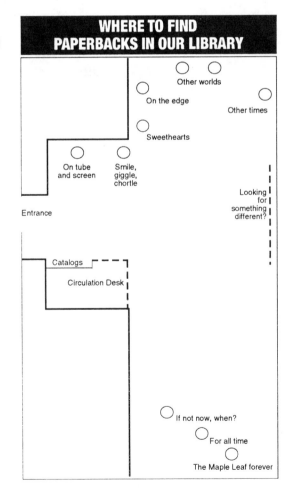

Oh, Nothing.

Baby Sitters

Taking Care of Terrific. Lois Lowry.
How do you entertain a four-year old who has never had a popsicle, bubble bath or dirty hands?

Bakeries

M.V. Sexton Speaking. Suzanne Newton.
Bradley's Bake Shop could use M.V.'s get-up-and-go. But first she has to learn to make change, bag chocolate brownies, and wear sensible shoes.

Pizza

Eating Between the Lines. Kevin Major.
"MASTERPIZZA — It's Too Much a For Words"
Mrs. Landsberg, M.L.S., prop.

Students could create their own directories of a year's reading, couldn't they?

THE BACKPACK

Backpacks are everywhere. You do not have to be on the wilderness trail to use one. Every kind of person seems to use them at one time or another. There are people on virtually every main street in North America with one. The idea of using the backpack in booktalks makes more sense than ever; it has become so versatile.

My original use of the device was more traditional, coming as it did out of a library research strategy lesson I was asked to do for a Grade XII class doing a unit on wilderness survival. I noticed the Geography teacher in the staff room filling a backpack with some items, and it came to me that I was in a sense filling a backpack, too – with research skills: observation, application, analysis, deduction, summary, etc. Some of these are personal skills, I thought. So, I went off at a tangent, thinking of reading experiences that exemplified the development of coping skills.

Never fear, I returned to the research task for the class.

Of course, there were some obvious ones, such as the Paulsen stories, and *The Island Keeper*, obvious in that the settings were wilderness. A young person reading these stories might think, "What would I do if I were in this situation?" and experience the luxury of thinking of strategies, savouring the satisfactions of success, realizing the significance of self-reliance.

by Harry Mazer

Expanding on the meaning of survival, the reader of *The Vandal* learns the coping skills of trusting one's instincts, of developing independent thinking. Surely the reader of Thomas' *The Secret* grows in appreciating differences, develops a sensitivity to the hurt beneath anti-social behavior? Isn't the subtle message of *Face the Dragon* and *Coloured Pictures* that we are all capable of acts of bravery, however small they may be? And *Bingo Brown* teaches us the power of humour which can provide balance and proportion in our lives.

by Ann Schlee

by Joyce Sweeney, Himani Bannerji, Betsy Byars respectively

Indeed all these additional titles, so varying in literary style, tone and subject matters, teach us that we can discover help in fiction – something to pack into our backpacks of daily life.

Oh, Nothing.

Survival Skills On My Own...

Hatchet. Gary Paulsen.
> After the plane crash 13 year old Brian survives 54 days in the wilderness with only the aid of a hatchet given by his mother.

The River. Gary Paulsen.
> It was to be a controlled, scientific project – recreating those 54 days in the wilderness. Who could believe it could happen again? (Sequel to *Hatchet*)

The Island Keeper. Harry Mazer.
> How could a wealthy teenage girl survive on a deserted island, with all communication cut off and winter setting in?

Cave Under the City. Harry Mazer.
> Blanket, candles, tinned goods, knife, matches, hammer, nails, saw, Bubber's rabbit.

Survival Using The System...

The Burning Questions of Bingo Brown. Betsy Byars.
> "In the future," the principal stated, "no one will be allowed to wear t-shirts that have any words on them." So they decide to hold a wear-in.

The Secret. Ruth Thomas.
> 1 sweater, 1 slice birthday cake, stale biscuits, 1/2 loaf bread with the mould cut off, half empty box of cornflakes, 2 cold potatoes, 4 bits of cold chicken, 1 pint milk.

The Vandal. Ann Schlee.
> He would forget. He must. But he did not want to. He did not want the Drink and the Toast to the Future.

Harry & Hortense at Hormone High. Paul Zindel.
> The secret for survival whether you're sane or insane is the ability to change.

A Hunter in the Dark. Monica Hughes.
> Mike is just 16 and determined to live. So he runs away to the hills to hunt, and alone in the wilderness faces his darkest fears.

Oh, Nothing.

Survival With A Little Help From My Friends...

The Goats. Brock Cole.
　　Victims of a cruel practical joke, stripped and marooned on an
　　island for the night, Laura and Howie decide to get their revenge –
　　and disappear.

The Foxman. Gary Paulsen.
　　Sent to live on a remote wilderness farm, the boy forms a friendship
　　with an elderly, disfigured man who teaches him through story and
　　skills how to live his life.

Coloured Pictures. Himani Bannerji.
　　When the Ku Klux Klan moves into the neighborhood, Sujata and
　　her friends under the guidance of a teacher discover the power of
　　collective action.

Face the Dragon. Joyce Sweeney.
　　The group faced their fears, their dragons, for bravery is like a
　　virus. When it's done with you, it'll pass to somebody else.

The Runaways. Ruth Thomas.
　　Two unhappy, unlikable kids, the object of ridicule and rejection,
　　run away together, reluctant partners with an unattainable goal.

Oh, Nothing.

THE GRUDGE MATCH

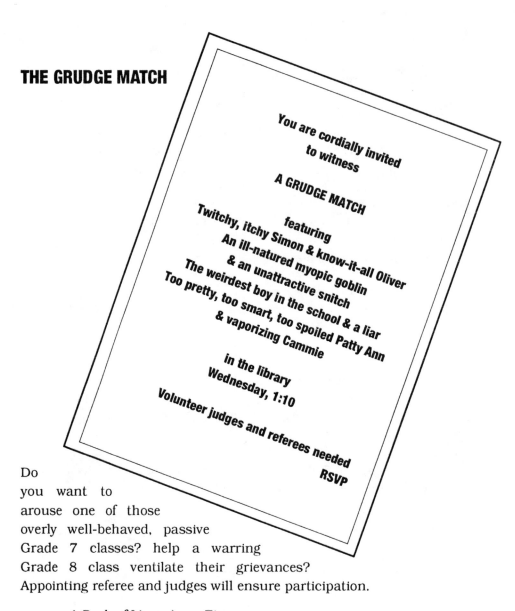

You are cordially invited
to witness

A GRUDGE MATCH

featuring
Twitchy, itchy Simon & know-it-all Oliver
An ill-natured myopic goblin
& an unattractive snitch
The weirdest boy in the school & a liar
Too pretty, too smart, too spoiled Patty Ann
& vaporizing Cammie

in the library
Wednesday, 1:10
Volunteer judges and referees needed
RSVP

Do
you want to
arouse one of those
overly well-behaved, passive
Grade 7 classes? help a warring
Grade 8 class ventilate their grievances?
Appointing referee and judges will ensure participation.

> *A Pack of Liars.* Anne Fine.
> *The Runaways.* Ruth Thomas.
> *Next-Door Neighbours.* Sarah Ellis.
> *Cousins.* Virginia Hamilton.

You have to be prepared to describe the situation and character's point-of-view in as brief and succinct a manner as possible. Then the student volunteer judges and referee offer their judgments. In the voice of either or both of the book characters, the librarian then can offer a rebuttal, or if the judgments are so true to the book or so inventively different, the librarian can say so, commending the wisdom or creativity of the judges.

Oh, Nothing.

SHOPPERS' GUIDES... JUNK MAIL... MERCHANDISING FLYERS...

We get all this stuff in the mail. Don't automatically pitch it out. Use it for some ideas; it might lead to an unusual format.

For example, a grocery chain in our city distributes a chatty newsletter periodically, extolling its products, lines and specials. It gave me the idea to produce a library newsletter focusing on books as food, promoting the taste and style of certain kinds of reading, e.g., mysteries, romance, series, etc.

Obviously this takes some time to execute and probably an artistic partner to design it. If this is beyond your library's expertise, you could still use the food analogy in a simpler bulletin board display.

And what of the hardware store flyer? the drug store promotion? Do these suggest other directions, other possibilities?

Ms. BLOSTEIN'S
Reader's Report

A Long Standing Tradition in Our Library

VOL. XXVIII
Fall, 1993

Unless otherwise stated, books are always effective.

PLAN AHEAD FOR THE PAST — THANKSGIVING

Warm thoughts and pungent memories
The Cookcamp. Gary Paulsen

A Gathering of Days. Joan Blos

FOR THE FUTURE — CHRISTMAS

Cheer and a rainbow of tastes
Solstice. Jan Adkins

Other Bells For Us to Ring. Robert Cormier

Tasters' Choice —
Sauces for discerning palates

FOR THE SUBTLE: *Redwork.* (Michael Bedard)

FOR THE FIERY: *David and Jonathan.* (Cynthia Voigt)

FOR THE SWEET: *The Mole and Beverley Miller* (Allan Jones)

FOR THE EXPERIMENTAL: *Nothing But the Truth.* (Avi)

MEMORIES...

OF MINNESOTA
For those *Popcorn Days & Buttermilk Nights!* Another winner from the Paulsen label!

OF MISSISSIPPI
At 1940's prices! Mildred Taylor's 3 prize winning labels
Roll of Thunder, Hear My Cry
Let the Circle Be Unbroken
The Road to Memphis

"MATURE POTABLES"

Cold Sassy Tree (from the vineyards of Olive Ann Burns)
In Country (from the vats of B.B. Mason)
Annie John (from the cellars of Jamaica Kincaid)

READY FOR BREAKFAST WITH SISTERS IN CRIME?

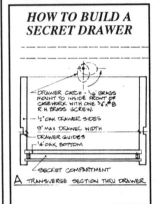

HOW TO BUILD A SECRET DRAWER

DRAWER CATCH - 1¼" BRASS MOUNT TO INSIDE FRONT OF CASEWORK WITH ONE 3¼"×#8 R.H. BRASS SCREW.
½" OAK DRAWER SIDES
9" MAX DRAWER WIDTH
DRAWER GUIDES
¼" OAK BOTTOM
SECRET COMPARTMENT
A TRANSVERSE SECTION THRU DRAWER

You Asked For It!
A new Douglas Adams!!

The inimitable flavour, the rich texture, the boundless energy of our Douglas Adams products have proved to be our all time best sellers. So here in answer to your requests. *Mostly Harmless, The Fifth in the Increasingly In-accurately Named Hitch Hiker's Guide to the Galaxy Trilogy* (still in stock at the old prices): *Hitch Hikers Guide to the Galaxy*; *The Restaurant At the End of the Universe*; *Life, the Universe and Everything; So Long and Thanks for All the Fish.*)

Murderess Ink: the Better Half of Mystery offers a choice of juices or fruit to begin with.

V.I. Warshawski provides a no-nonsense, filling, hot cereal guaranteed to leave *Burn Marks.* Paretsky label.

Charred bacon from P.D. James. Beverages range from the bitter brew of Ruth Rendell to old fashioned dependable tea from Agatha Christie.

Splendid condiments to accompany your finest dishes.

Piquant: Brian Doyle's latest, *Speed Sweetgrass*

Pungent: Jerry Spinelli's award winning *Maniac Magee*

Lingering aftertaste: Phyllis Reynolds Naylor's medal winner, *Shilo*

MANAGER'S SPECIAL RECIPE

Our manager shares an original recipe for those sad, grey days. Let Taylor stew over the move and the loss of her old friends. Grill her over the future. Before she reaches the boiling point, sprinkle in a new friend, a pet goose, and control over 10-x. Chop up BOMB, SUNSET, STORM, GARBAGE until mixture is 100%. Simmer until smooth. If mixture turns to liquid because Taylor wants to forget, toss in some strong talk, a pinch each of re-gret and common sense. Watch carefully as mixture returns to normal because Taylor has found it easier to remember. Playing some Beethoven will settle everything into a smooth rich batter ready for maturing in the oven. Suitable for a HUM on bright days too.

(The Revolt of 10-x. Joan Davenport Carris.)

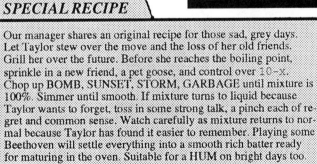

Liberate Your Taste Buds.
Box of Tricks in *Here Tomorrow, Gone Today.* Tim Kennemore

Please see the next page for many, many more great 'products' you can savor.

TOO GOOD TO BE TRUE PRODUCTS

prices frozen until further notice

NEWBERY'S CHOICE
Shiloh. Phyllis R Naylor. 1991.
Maniac Magee. Jerry Spinelli. 1990.
Distinguished contributions to children's literature.

CALDECOTT'S CHOICE
Black and White. David Macaulay. 1990; *Tuesday.* David Wiesner. 1991.
Distinguished picture books.

IODE CHILDREN'S BOOK CHOICE
Voices on the Wind: Poems for All Seasons. David Booth. 1990.

CORETTA SCOTT KING'S CHOICE
Road to Memphis. Mildred D. Taylor. 1990. For text
Aida. Leo & Diane Dillon. 1990 for illustration

JANE ADAMS' CHOICE
A Long Hard Journey: The Story of the Pullman Porter. P & F McKissack. 1990.
Promoting the cause of peace, social justice, world community and the equality of the sexes and all races.

CARNEGIE'S CHOICE
The Ghost Drum. Susan Price. 1987.
Outstanding merit.

MR. CHRISTIE'S CHOICE
The Covered Bridge. Brian Doyle. 1991.
For English text.
Le Zamboni. Francois Gravel. 1991.
For French text.

EDGAR'S CHOICE
Incident at Loring Groves. Sonia Leviten.
Best YA Novel, Crime Writers of America. 1990.

RUTH SCHWARZ FOUNDATION'S CHOICE
Forbidden City. William Bell. 1990.
Awarded by Grade 6, 7, 8 students from St. Francis Xavier School in North York, Ontario.

YOUR CHOICE OF 4
Any combination, Lowry label

- *Anastasia Again!*
- *Anastasia And Her Chosen Career*
- *Anastasia, Ask Your Analyst*
- *Anastasia At This Address*
- *Anastasia At Your Service*
- *Anastasia Has the Answers*
- *Anastasia Krupnik*
- *Anastasia On Her Own*

Romantic Valentine confections

Individually wrapped by Marianne Gingher in her distinctive *Teen Angel* label.

And tastes to touch your heart from the highly popular Byars label
Bingo Brown And The Language of Love.
Bingo Brown, Gypsy Lover.
Bingo Brown's Guide to Romance.

Meouw!

FELINE FLAVORS FROM MASTER CHEF ROBERT WESTALL

Three distinct flavours:

Yaxley's Cat

The Cats of Seroster

A Walk on the Wild Side
(in 7 miniature sizes)

Guaranteed to satisfy that special cat or your money back.

CRUNCHY COOKIES

Double the nuts! Available in bulk!
Maniac Magee,
by the Spinelli.
Easy Avenue,
by the Doyle.

★ ★ ★
★ ★

SHOPPER'S BLEND –
MYSTERY PROCESS BEVERAGES
Regular blend: *The Haunted House Joke Book* (Hegarty)
Fine grind: *The Sandman's Eyes* (Windsor)
Extra-fine grind: *Mote* (Reaver)

NEW! DOUBLE THE PLEASURE
Extra strength for swimmers:
Alex Archer in Lane 3
Alex in Winter
As recommended by Olympic expert Tessa Duder who promises two new items for our next newsletter.

BULK BIOS
Irish imports
Starry Night
Frankie's Story
The Beat of the Drum
(Courtesy of cooking expert Catherine Sefton)

IMPORTED CONTAINERS!!
A first rate duplicate of turn-of-the-century coal tubs
Two Pence A Tub (original design by Susan Price)

FISH FRY TAKE-OUTS
fried perch
cole slaw
french fries
Available on *Fish Friday* at our Gayle Pearson counter

SPECIALS | SPICES!!

2 for 1 Newton: Available in An *End to Perfect* and *A Place Between*
Buy 4 Blossoms get 1 free:
The Not-Just Anybody Family
The Blossoms Meet the Vulture Lady
The Blossoms and the Green Phantom
A Blossom Promise
Wanted — Mud Blossom
(Byars label only)

Guaranteed to keep you wakeful and alert
A King dash of danger: *The Sound Of Propellers*
A Banks soupcon of terror: *Melusine*

LAUNDRY DETERGENT BREAKTHROUGH
For all colors, races, religions. On display throughout our Fiction section

---

COMFORT FOOD FOR SPLIT LEVEL MINDS!
A Game of Dark. William Mayne; *Red Shift.* Alan Garner; *Breaktime.* Aidan Chambers.

Being drawn into
contemporary
dilemmas
can give
the young person
an opportunity
to provide
sense, order
and justice
in our
chaotic world.

4

Did You See
Today's
Headline?

RUNAWAYS

I wish that the alarming statistics on teen-age runaways had lessened since I last wrote about this book-talk. Alas, they have increased. When I pass a well-known teen-age counselling drop-in centre in my city, I look at those drawn or blank or hostile or frightened faces and I wonder, "Whose child are you?" "Why are you here?" "Will you stay?" "Will you be saved?" "What if..."

What if — what? I think that students reading stories about runaways and then writing their notes to be left behind are capable of empathizing and offering comfort and strategies that are fresh and less predictable than that of family members and even professionals. I think they will absorb the complicated personal, economic and social factors that lead to such numbers of disaffected youth.

Librarian: The Children's Aid Society received 2,758 telephone calls last December concerning runaway kids. Why are these numbers so great? What are the reasons for so many runaways?

Students: Parents hassle them.
They want more freedom.
Unhappy homes.
Adventure.

Librarian: Do these notes runaways left behind them give you any further clues?

These notes are my adaptations of passages in the books. Actual passages may be used, even if lengthy as in Pete's letter to his parents as he leaves that evening because "God has called me to help this preacher" (*A Fine White Dust*, by Cynthia Rylant, p. 83-85).

After each letter, students conjectured as to the personality and problems of the writers, the possible motives of the adults around them,

① Dear Pop,
Bubber and I are all right. We are not far away. We have a place to sleep and we are waiting for you to come home. I will sneak back to check the mail every few days.
Your son, Tolley

② Dear Pop, where are you? Send me some money. We're all right. Bubber is hungry all the time and I am, too. If you don't come soon, maybe I should let him go to the orphan home and let somebody take care of him.
T.

③ Momma:
I have taken with me whatever memory can carry.
Bullet

1, 2. *Cave Under the City.* Harry Mazer.
3. *The Runner.* Cynthia Voigt.

the nature of the threats to the young person's equilibrium. If a class seems receptive, you could go on with further speculation. For example, if the runaway packed or might pack a suitcase he or she could take with him or her, what would go in the suitcase (real things, ideas, feelings, etc.)? Would the runaway send a postcard home? How would it read?

If you have an opportunity for a follow-up session after the students have read their books, try asking them to think again about the young runaway and write their own notes which the runaway might have left behind. To whom would the note be addressed?

Other books that you can use that

1. Deal with actual runaways:
   The *Boll Weevil Express*. P.J. Peterson.
   The Runaways. Ruth Thomas.
   The Secret. Ruth Thomas.
   Mr. Nobody's Eyes. Michael Morpurgo.
   No Promises in the Wind. Irene Hunt.
   A Season for Unicorns. Sonia Leviton.
   The Freedom Machine. Joan Lingard.
   Coming Back Alive. D.J. Reader.
   Maybreak. Frances Usher.
   The Carnival in My Mind. Barbara Wersba.

2. Describe situations from which running away seems understandable:
   In the Castle of the Bear. Steve Senn.
   A Place Called Ugly. Avi.
   Bobby Baseball. Robert Kimmel Smith.
   Night Riding. Katherine Martin.
   Pick-Up Sticks. Sarah Ellis.
   Back Home. Michelle Magorian.

NO MORE CAUSES?

I first did this as a bulletin board. I have always appreciated the intensity with which students responded to it and the titles it recommended. One Grade 10 English teacher liked this display so much, she asked her class to do book reports on each of the issues that I had featured. I took pride in the passion, partisanship, advocacy they demonstrated in their reports. The results were a salute to their idealism.

When they become parents, spouses, social workers, nurses, doctors, lawyers, judges, teachers, artists, psychologists, playground supervisors, pharmacists, therapists, police, will they still be able to identify with, show compassion, become activists for the victims, unenfranchised, dispossessed and unfortunate of our society? I believe so.

There are many ways in which these themes can be presented. You will want to use your own imagination. Rather than a bulletin board this time, how about a display that is a "garden" of picket signs? Or...

Here are new "causes" I have been thinking about and titles that lend themselves to discussion.

Save Our Homes

Never Walk Alone. Gareth Owen.
They were confident their picketing would make a difference. But "Remember Grace Park" was all, and it was a lot, they could finally do.

Home Free. Kathryn Lasky.
"I tell my grandson the sad tale of how, fifty years before... the engineers with fancy degrees...came up here and did their planning to quench the thirst of city folk... that resulted in our losing homes, farms and businesses — and dug up our dead."

Pick-Up Sticks. Sarah Ellis.
Polly is an unwilling participant in her mother's efforts to save the co-op from being torn down and a high rise condominium erected.

A Very Small Rebellion. Jan Truss.
Metis children putting on a play at school about Louis Riel attempt their own rebellion to protect their homes from government appropriation.

No to Nukes

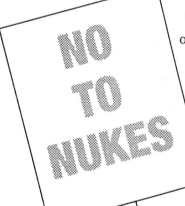

The Guilty Party. Joan Lingard.
We're here because we're worried about a nuclear plant on our doorstep. We don't want another Chernobyl.

Matt's Crusade. Margot Marek.
Matt intends to join the demonstration against the projected stockpiling of nuclear missiles outside his town. Complications? 1. His father, a wounded Vietnam vet believes a strong defence will prevent war. 2. The big football game in which he is to be key player coincides with the time of the demonstration.

Sentries. Gary Paulsen.
The common theme of nuclear disaster and human vulnerability interweaves the lives of four young people, an Ojibway, an illegal Mexican itinerant worker, a rock musician and a rancher's daughter with the lives of three veterans of past wars.

Shelter for the Homeless

Secret City, U.S.A. Felice Holman.
Against all odds, 13 year old Benno and his friends turn "The Space" into a refuge for the homeless children and families he sees every day on the street.

A Very Touchy Subject. Todd Strasser.
"Warm cozy beds. Free for teenaged runaways and their friends."

Mr. Kneebones' New Digs. Ian Wallace. (From my Babysitters' Corner.)
April Moth and her friend Mr. Kneebone can't afford even their grungy one room — and set off to find shelter.

Monkey Island. Paula Fox.
He was a truant. His mother was a runaway,
and his father had disappeared.
His own face would show up on a milk carton.

End the Abuse

Mac. John Maclean.
"Everybody talks about sex. I don't want to talk
about sex. I don't want to talk about anything.
Something's wrong with me and nobody cares." (p. 71)
It is a long time before Mac can believe the therapist: "I
just feel so strongly that for a kid to get sexually assaulted is bad
enough without all this guilt. Just remember it wasn't your fault. It's
never the youngster's fault." (p. 129)

Everything Is Not Enough. Sandy Asher.
Saturday night in Braden's Point and Traci has another bloody nose.
And then Pete will tell her how much he loves her.

Gillyflower. Ellen Howard.
"You're my baby girl," Dad would say to me in the evening when Mom
was at work.

Hildy Ross. In *Class Dismissed! High school poems* by Mel Glenn.
"Yeah, I know there are agencies for this sort of thing, but I can't see
turning him in. He's still my father."

Racism Stops Here!

Coloured Pictures. Himani Bannerji.
What happens when the Ku Klux Klan comes to a multi-cultural
neighborhood.

The Murderer. Felice Holman.
The year of Hershey's Bar Mitzvah is marked with name-calling,
brutality and prejudice.

Prank. Kathryn Lasky.
Out of an ingrained religious intolerance and a casual racism,
Birdy's brother vandalizes a synagogue.

The Eternal Spring of Mr. Ito. Sheila Garrigue. p. 73.

"Well, as you know, all Japanese men between the ages of eighteen and forty have already been shipped out. Today, we received authorization from Ottawa to ship the rest of them. Everyone of Japanese background is to go, every man jack of 'em."

"Good heavens!" said Aunt Jean. "There are thousands in Vancouver alone. You don't mean all of them? Not the Canadians?"

He nodded. "The whole bunch, Canadian-born or not, citizens or not... We're getting camps ready — up in the mountains. There are places up through there that have been virtually ghost towns since the mining petered out. It will keep them properly isolated."

Death with Dignity

Shadow and Light. Katharine Bacon.
Emma looks forward to spending the summer on her beloved grandmother's Vermont farm, but is devastated to learn she is fatally ill and wants Emma to help her live her last months in peace and dignity.

The Bumble Bee Flies Anyway. Robert Cormier.
Barney believes he is different from the terminally ill kids around him.

One Green Leaf. Jean Ure.
Friends since childhood, the four are forced to confront their mortality and the meaning of their lives, when one of them is diagnosed with cancer.

Sheila's Dying. Alden R. Carter.
What can you do for a dying young friend to help her face the end with courage and dignity? "Listen to the silence with her. There are no things to say."

House Keeping Is a Non-sexist Activity

Anastasia On Her Own. Lois Lowry.
When Mrs. Krupnik goes to California on a ten-day business trip,

Anastasia draws up Krupnik Family Nonsexist Housekeeping Schedule (on page 17). It gets revised on page 31 and 32. Version 3, page 44, Version 4 page 59, Version 5, page 75 and so on to pages 93, 107 and the final one — 2 lines.

Borrowed Children. George Ella Lyon.
Twelve year old Amanda is forced to act as mother and housekeeper during mama's illness — with no help from Ben, 14 and David, 16 – who aren't forced to leave school either.

House-keeping is a NON-SEXIST activity

Support Services for the Handicapped

Izzy Willy-Nilly. Cynthia Voigt.
"The only thing I wanted was not to be in the hospital, not to have my leg amputated."

Absolutely Invincible! William Bell. p. 41.
"We oughta form a group so we can help each other out a bit, you know? I mean, all of us missing *something*, right?" There's George with no memory, Hook without legs and a hand, Annie without sight, Heather without hearing.

Probably Still Nick Swanson. Virginia Euwer Wolff.
Sixteen year old learning-disabled Nick endures the humiliation of his date for the prom making an excuse not to go with him, and the memory of his sister drowning while he watched, not understanding.

Ernest Mott. In *Class Dismissed! High School Poems* by Mel Glenn.
"Now after years of special classes,
Years of Thorazine and therapy,
They want to put me back into a regular class.
I don't know if I want to go back,
Back to people who still have fear in their faces."

If you have time or the place, cite the final word from Ellen Stafford's *Was That You at the Guggenheim?*

Please help finance research for a bigger, better bomb, to kill people more efficiently

During a discussion of all the diseases supported by charities and fund-raising drives, Marie "remembered thinking once that someone should write a play about a world turned around: a world in which research into cures for these terrible ailments was financed to the full by the governments of all nations, while donations were solicited on street corners for armaments, people holding out collection cans: 'Please help finance research for a bigger, better bomb, to kill people more efficiently.' "

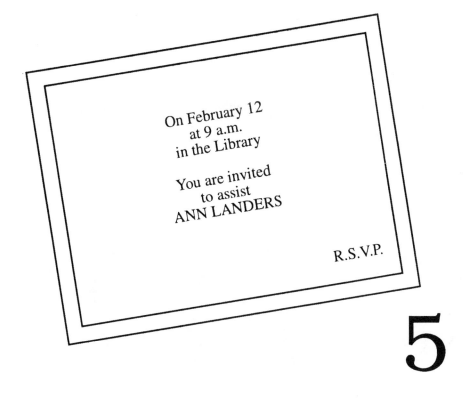

On February 12
at 9 a.m.
in the Library

You are invited
to assist
ANN LANDERS

R.S.V.P.

5

Right Now...
Always...
The Real Thing!

THE AGONY COLUMN

Household words... Pepsi-Cola... Coca-Cola... and Ann Landers.

Never have I met students who didn't know of, or who denied reading, "agony columns," or who didn't feel they could give good advice too.

The "Agony Column" in the daily newspaper can do much more than appeal to the familiar and recognizable depending on how it is applied. It has emotional attraction for adolescents, eager to identify themselves with the problems of others. And it can be helpful in developing self-awareness through the adoption of roles. It's one thing for a student to write a "Dear Ann..." or a "Dear Abby..." letter for a character with whom he identifies closely. But what happens if he must find words for someone who is quite different, someone he is not even sure he likes? And what if he is asked to take on the role of the advisor-columnist? Another style must be assumed, and another attitude.

Two students could be encouraged to engage in a written or oral exchange, maintaining the assumed fictional character roles under the eyes of their classmates. The exercise could even be extended to cover a sizable period of time and the writing of several letters. The discussion which results from using the "agony column" as a book talk device involves everyone in the class, the characters in the books come alive, and books circulate.

Librarian:　Did you read Ann Landers, or Dear Abby last night? What do you think of the advice they give?

Students:　(A mix of sophisticated, naïve, jaded, enthusiastic replies.)

Librarian:　What most of you seem to suggest is that a lot of plain common sense advice is given. That means you could do as well. What would your advice be to this letter:

'Dear Ann Landers,'
　　Can a person who is mentally ill be crazy and know it?

'Pepsi-Cola" is a registered trade mark of PepsiCo Ltd.

"Coca-Cola" is a registered trade mark of Coca-Cola Ltd.

Ann Landers is a column syndicated by Creators' Syndicate.

"Dear Abby" is a column syndicated by Universal Press Syndicate.

The Real Thing!

My friend Lisa keeps saying she's crazy and to tell you the truth her behavior is becoming so peculiar, even violent, that I'm beginning to agree with her. She says her parents won't listen to her, and our teachers think she just wants attention. How do I get help for Lisa? I'm frightened for her.

Betsy.

Students: She should go to a psychiatrist.
A minister. A rabbi.
Can't her friends help her?

Librarian: Well, they try.
(Reading from *Lisa, Bright and Dark*, by John Neufeld, p. 36, slightly edited.)

"That's it!" she said. "We'll just have to do it!"

"What?" Betsy asked.

"Help Lisa ourselves, of course. Obviously no one else is going to. Her parents don't believe anything is wrong. Most of the teachers are chicken. We can't set Lisa up with doctors. We have to convince Lisa's family that she's in real danger. We'll go to her house and tell her parents what's happening in school, and that Lisa wasn't kidding, after all. They can't help but be upset and they'll have to get some professional help for her."

Librarian: Betsy and Lisa are characters in *Lisa, Bright and Dark*. Do you think their plan should work?

(Hand the book to anyone who looks interested.)

Are you ready with more advice for troubled young people?

(I hand out more letters. Each letter is numbered.)

Really, no instructions are needed now. The kids read and murmur to each other. Just ask any student what problem he or she is dealing with; or someone may simply venture a comment. Have someone read a letter, and then the advice and discussion goes on as long as you or the students want. You should be ready to read an appropriate passage, summarize an incident, explain background from whatever book they are discussing.

Cover as many titles as you have time for or the students care to discuss. If the class seems to be breaking into small groups and discussing among themselves, I leave them alone and comment only when asked to. Just before the end of the period, I hand out the "Replies" (the list of corresponding titles).

The letters to "Ann Landers" are not arbitrarily or accidentally culled from novels. In a sense they throw themselves up and out at me. The voice of the fictional adolescent in the novel speaks strongly, aching to be heard, comforted, strengthened. As I find myself increasingly sensitive to these voices, so do I find it natural to write letters in these voices.

As I read Jan Slepian's *The Alfred Summer*, I was touched by the unhappiness of those children. I wondered whether I would be patient with Myron were he my student. Who do the Myrons of our classes reach out to? What would they say if they had a ready listener? How would the listener respond? I noted passages where Myron's plight is best captured, e.g., the passage on page 21 (hardcover edition) reproduced in the margin.

It seemed to be the most familiar situation in the world for him to be doing something he didn't want to do. "Myron, do this, Myron, do that," from his mother, his sisters, even his grandma. And so he was always looking away from where he happened to be, only part of him there. That was why if there was a glass of milk to be spilled, he spilled it. If there was a door to be walked into, he did. "My son, the *shlemiel*," was his mother's summation. He gave the most pleasure to his younger sisters because they knew how to tease him into a frenzy and then escape his rage with delighted screams. Myron was inarticulate, shy, clumsy; his sheer bulk got him into games but not to parties.

The Alfred Summer. Jan Slepian. p. 21.

You'll notice I changed the wording slightly so that Myron speaks directly — to other Myrons who may feel validated, encouraged — and to non-Myrons who may be challenged to look at the Myrons of this world more compassionately.

> Dear Ann Landers,
> I guess I am absent minded. I'm always looking away from where I'm going to. So if there is milk to be spilled I will spill it. If there is a door I will walk into it. My mother calls me "My son, the shlemiel" and my sisters tease me until I lose my temper. Here is my problem. I am shy and clumsy and don't know what to say to people. I am big enough to get into games, but I want to be invited to parties. Can you help me?
> Love
> Myron

As I read Susan Beth Pfeffer's *The Year Without Michael*, I felt a surge of commiseration as Jody's friends offered her well-meaning advice, as

Dear Abby,

Everybody's after me to do all the normal things, even though my 16 year old brother is missing. So here, for everyone to see, is my final word: I'll start eating more sensibly later when Michael comes home. I'll concentrate on my homework when Michael comes home. I'll straighten out my room when Michael comes home. I'll eat more sensibly, brush my teeth more regularly, jog every day, watch less TV, stop biting my nails, my lips, my tongue, when Michael comes home. I'll start sleeping again, and breathing again, and laughing again, when Michael comes home. I'll be alive again when Michael comes home.

Satisfied?

J.C.

though, in such a terrible situation, one thinks and behaves in a common sense manner, as though there is a time-table for grieving.

Junior high

Will young students gain understanding of grieving? My letter at left is from page 42, almost word for word.

Grade 11 or 12

Sometimes we're fortunate enough that an author provides the letter, as Norma Fox Mazer does in *When We First Met*. (p. 119). After your students discuss the letter you can read out the answer Jenny provides for Dear Abby.

"Dear Abby,"

I'm in love with a boy that my parents refuse to be civil to. Their only response to him is to tell me to give him up. Abby, he is eighteen, responsible, polite, and thoughtful. He loves me, too. This is not a teenybopper crush, Abby. We're both serious about each other and our future. We love each other tremendously, but making out is far from all we have on our minds. He's looking for work, I hold down a part-time job, we both get respectable marks in school and have plans for the future, which include college. We are not acting foolishly or immaturely. His "crime" is that he is the son of a woman who caused grief and hurt to my family. I know this has made it difficult almost beyond words for my family but, still, don't you think they should at least try to see him for himself, and to give us a chance?
Signed,
Deeply in Love

And the answer? Jenny could write that, too (p. 120):

Dear in Love,

If you two are the kind of kids you describe yourselves to be, I think your parents should definitely give you a chance. Go to them and tell them Dear Abby approves.

Grade 7   *Bathing Ugly* by Rebecca Buselle, *Laura Upside-Down* by Doris Buchanan Smith, and *There's a Girl in My Hammerlock,* by Jerry Spinelli.

"Dear Ann Landers,"

I've been chosen to compete in the camp's Bathing Ugly Contest. That's right, *Ugly.* I guess I didn't get selected for the Beauty Contest because I'm 5'5" and weigh 142-1/2 lbs. Well, I'll show them ugly — and maybe they'll rethink their ideas about the importance of outward appearances. I'll let you know how successful I've been.

Betsy

"Dear Abby,"

I don't have any religious upbringing. My best friend Anna has The Bible. My other best friend Zipporah has the Torah. When I ask my father, "What do we have?" he answers, "We have ourselves." Lately that doesn't seem like enough for me, although I think I should tell you my parents are fine people, and I think I am basically a good person. Do you have any thoughts about my life?

Yours truly,
Laura

"Dear Mrs. Thompson,"

The capital of Canada is Eric Delong. Twelve times twelve equals Eric Delong. The action word is Eric Delong. Yes, I, for 13 years a boy-hater, have a mega-sized crush on E.D. The catch is, I failed to make cheerleader (E.D. is the football hero). But come to think of it, he's also on the wrestling team. Tryouts are Monday. So what do you think?

Maisie

Grade 8   *Afternoon of the Elves,* by Janet Taylor Lisle, *Taking Sides,* by Gary Soto, and *If You Need Me,* by C.S. Adler.

"Dear Ann Landers,"

I'm just a little sick of all these "help-you" columns where you suggest we speak to counsellors, doctors, ministers, etc. Regular people don't like us. They don't like other people who live different from them, other people who are sick. Help is the last thing you want to ask for when you're somebody like me. People like *you* can ask for help. People like *me* have to steal it.

S-K.C.

"Dear Abby,"

When I first moved here from the barrio, I loved the peace and beauty of the neighborhood but, you know, this place is dead. No one ever comes out of the house to check out the world. And worse, there are no other brown faces like mine. But worst of all, my basketball team is going to play my old high school. I really miss those *vatos.* I'm not sure I can play my best, and I also feel guilty at my *hermanos* wearing K-mart sneakers while I squeak about the court in Air Jordans. This is the better life?

Call me Vendido

"Dear Ann Landers,"

You must be tired of people writing to you about divorce — but here goes anyway. I have always admired my father because he seemed to have such values and taught me to have them too. So of course I've always trusted him to do what was right. How could I have misjudged him? All he really cares about is himself — and appearances. How do I tell him I'm not moving to Boston with him and his "beautiful lady." Who needs him! I am 13 years old.

Lynn

Grade 9 *Taking Care of Terrific*, by Lois Lowry (p. 2), *Switching Tracks*, by Dean Hughes and *M.V. Sexton Speaking*, by Suzanne Newton.

"Dear Ann Landers,"

No advice please; I just want to get something off my chest. Murmuring "There now, this will perk you up" to a 14 year old girl does not encourage independence. That is why my mother says that only to small droopy plants suffering from aphids or root rot. To me, when I look, feel, and am droopy, discouraged, depressed, and about to throw myself out of my bedroom window, my mother says, "Enid, , you have to learn to solve your own problems. And for a start, do something about your hair." Sometimes I wish I were a philodendron.

E.

"Dear Dr. Smith,"

I've just come from another argument with my son, ending in the usual way. I say he's changed since his father's died. He says he doesn't want to talk about it. But he's quit studying, he won't make friends, he talks to me as though I'm his enemy, he screams at his brother no matter what he says. The only thing he wants to do is play that space game at the arcade. Is it normal to care about nothing at all except playing a silly game?

Yours in sadness,
Mark's mother

"Dear Mrs. T."

I probably shouldn't be writing when I'm so upset, but I can't wait till I'm calmer. No wonder none of my classmates knows what to make of me. The truth is I don't know what to make of myself. Aunt Gert's everlasting do's and don'ts encircle me like a fence. I hate living in this house. I hate the dullness and rigidity. I hate feeling that anything fun or exciting is bad. I hate not even knowing what question to ask you. ????????????????

M.V.

Grade 10 *People Like Us*, by Barbara Cohen, *Just One Friend*, by Lynn Hall (p. 1) and *Missing Pieces*, by Sandy Asher.

"Dear A.L.,"

G was my first real date, a guy I was crazy about. How lucky I thought — until I told my family. He's not Jewish and the difference this has made to my family has caused the most bitter disagreement. Judaism is very important to me — as is G — as is my family. I feel as though I'm being torn to pieces. Any words of strength for me?

Dinah

Dear Friend

My social workers used to ask me sometimes if I had imaginary friends and I told them no, that was silly. I still know that. But nobody listens when I try to tell them why I did what I did. They keep asking me and pretending like they want me to tell them, but they get in a hurry and interrupt me before I can get it all out. You won't interrupt me, will you? Well, you can't very well, if I just made you up. I didn't mean to do it to her. I would never do something that terrible. It was just, well, it was partly her fault. It was because of the car.

Dory Kjellings

"Dear Ann Landers,"

My dearest father died 3 months ago, and the remaining pieces of my family, my denying mother, my soon-to-be-delinquent brother and I just don't seem to fit together anymore. Because one piece, the dearest one, is missing. Or are we all missing? My mother says she doesn't want to be a burden. But shouldn't there be a place between a burden and a missing piece? Please. Help us.

Heather

Grade 11 *Supercouple*, by Mary Towne, *Remembering the Good Times*, by Richard Peck, and *Amber*, by Jacqueline Wilson.

"Dear Abby,"

Today Piers asked me to a school dance, and I guess there's a certain irresistible logic about the whole thing — the football star and the cheerleader. But I hate people making assumptions about us on this basis. I don't want to start letting other people's opinions dictate what I do or don't do. So do I assert my independence or follow the path of least resistance? I should tell you that Piers is good looking and a nice person.　　　Binky

"Dear A.L."

Why didn't I notice? Understand? Put two and two together? Tell someone? A beautiful, gifted, 16 year old has taken his life. All I can do is remember and wish I had noticed, understood, put two and two together and most important, *TOLD SOMEONE*.
　　　　　Buck

"Dear Dr. Smith,"

Just a few words of background. When I was sent to a special unit for the Educationally Subnormal, they showed me some pictures and I couldn't recognize pyjamas, tooth-brush, a birthday cake and candles, an iron, a rocking-horse, monkeys, giraffes and lions in a zoo. I couldn't name them because I'd never set eyes on them. I could have named all the *homes* I've ever had, though — communes, mobile homes, sea-side chalets, squats, attic rooms. Every morning millions of mothers help their children find their socks, and wake them for school. In our room, the rules are reversed. Well, I'm not going to get up, ever. I'm not. And I'm not going to think about IT either. Because I can't blame any one else. Just myself. I must be mad. Don't you think so?
　　　　　A.

Grade 12 *The Giver*, by Lynn Hall and *Permanent Connections*, by Sue Ellen Bridgers (p. 6).

"Dear Ann Landers,"

I look down the rows at Mary's dear face with all its ingredients for beauty, knowing all that's needed is the confidence that another twenty years will bring. I know, for I am 35, her teacher, and she is 15. I feel as though I'm poised on the brink of some great happiness — or betrayal. Shall I speak? Shall I act?
　　　　　J.F.

"Dear Ann Landers,"

It's the middle of the night and I want to write something — about how it feels when you wake up because your folks are arguing about you, about how lousy it is to never be left alone, about what a pain in the butt your 12 year old perfect sister is, about how you're already messed up. Already at 17 boxed in with no way out. Not enough guts to scramble, never enough bucks to float. Sinking, always sinking. It is 3:45 a.m.
　　　　　Rob

The Real Thing!

Grade 12 *Alex in Winter*, by Tessa Duder (2 letters).

"Dear Dr. Smith,"

I am writing as a teacher in a high school noted for its support of sports, seeing the negative aspects as well, principally in the person of a promising young athlete who has recently lost a friend. I have watched her reaction to success, to pressure from all sides. To a grief as profound as any I've seen and only two months along its course. She needs very careful handling, reinforcement of her social role, understanding of her anger and loneliness. Recognition that a girlfriend ostensibly outside the family can grieve as deeply as someone inside it. Encouragement to think about something else other than swimming. Let us bear in the mind the necessity of keeping these young athletes on an even keel.
            A Concerned Educator

"Dear Dr. S."

Instead of saying this out loud to my gifted athletic daughter who has recently suffered a loss and sounding like a nagging Mom, I'll put it all down on paper: "We know it's hard, it's hard on us too, please eat some breakfast, please stop cutting your hair in that awful way, please tidy up your room, please stop picking at the quicks of your nails, please stop swearing at your brother, please put your jeans out for a wash, please wear something normal for a change, like a dress, please try to meet your teachers half-way, please try to forget Andy, please...

Thank you for letting me get this off my chest.
            A Concerned Mother

When students come to read these stories, they recognize feelings: "Oh, yes, I know that's true." "How could someone feel as I do about that?" "I never thought of that before, but that is exactly what I've been trying to express." "Oh, how I sympathize." "Life oughtn't to be like this." "That's just like me, him, her." "If I could only..."

If you give students the opportunity to speak out in answer to these pleas, you involve them in a growing process, a means of stirring their thinking and empathizing. You can cover about five or six letters in this way in half an hour. Much discussion is generated, and students come to feel a proprietary interest in the stories' outcomes.

It was in stories like these, as I read them, that I saw the possibilities for students to explore their relations with others, identify their own anxieties, resolve problems, or at least perceive a range of possibilities for solutions. In fact I didn't find the books; they found me. Can we say the same for our students?

The community
in which
the dreadful, painful,
funny, provocative,
curious, surprising
co-exist gives
the reader
permission
to manage
human experience.

6

What Else Did You See in the Paper Today?

THIS CHILD

Many local newspapers carry a column devoted to describing children who are eligible for adoption. Pictures are usually included and the descriptions are candid and moving.

I changed the idea of adoption to that of the foster home, the idea of taking a child into your home for an indefinite but temporary period of time. Students are given the opportunity to empathize, to be constructive, supportive and just.

At least that is what I had intended. Yet one Grade 11 class seemed obdurate in its hardened attitude to the children in the Today's Child column. I detected a note of anger towards the victims in their responses. Why were they angry? Was it really fear? frustration? powerlessness?

I let them talk about each case and had them try to envisage a home and family for the fictional child. It enabled the students to absorb, modify, and reconstruct the unhappy circumstances. We talked about the social programs and institutions, the family services appropriate for these children. By this reassuring exercise they started to surrender their fears, and moved on to more rational, positive and caring attitudes.

On the next two pages are the "children" we discussed.

Nathan

Nathan is the middle child in a large, noisy and somewhat un-sympathetic family. If he looks angry and ill-natured it is because he badly needs a breathing space and some peace. He does fairly well in school and excels in spelling and loves reading. His energy, stubbornness and temper could be channeled if he were the only child, or else had responsibility for someone or something helpless. Patience and understanding are necessary for this youngster who is his own worst enemy.

From *The Runaways*, by Ruth Thomas.

Lilac

Lilac is 10, and as you can see is an angry and suspicious child. She comes from a large, unstable family with little time for affection. At first unfamiliar with showers, pizza, credit cards, how to ride a bicycle or swim, Lilac has stubbornly made progress in getting along with people. She requires a patient, loving, but unsentimental family who will not attempt to repress her energies, but rather re-direct them. Lilac responds beautifully, if slowly, to affection.

From *The Potato Kid*, by Barbara Corcoran.

Ada

Labelled "problem child" Ada won't speak, can barely read, and is prone to use her fists when ridiculed. Under a patient and wise teacher she has revealed a gentleness and response to discipline when it is combined with respect. Who knows what she can accomplish in behaviour and scholastic capability when encouraged and loved?

From *Kool Ada*, by Sheila Solomon Klass.

Nicky 11, and Roy 9, are looking at each other only, not the photographer as you see. This is typical of the brother and sister whose reliance on each other and hostility towards the rest of the world has led them into a remarkable if threatening adventure. It is still not certain what their future arrangements will be, but whatever they are, the arrangement must respect their fierce loyalty to each other and their hopes for eventual reunion with their mother.

From *The Secret*, by Ruth Thomas.

Nicky, Roy

David's past has been an unhappy and unusual one. He has experienced loss, a confusing array of foster parents, some time on the street, and the worst that bureaucracy can do. David doesn't need a "nice stable family" so much as someone who'll treat him as though he likes him. It will take a lot of love to replace his negative view of life, and make him feel like David again.

From *Family Pose*, by Dean Hughes.

David

Mary Faith desperately wanted to present a happy face for our photographer, but her anxious smile and sad eyes betray her. She has experienced incredible hurt and betrayal in her 14 years and needs a supportive family, preferably one where there is a younger child whom she can protect and love. Mary Faith has a good heart and deserves a chance for a good life.

From *Night Riding*, by Katherine Martin.

Mary Faith

HOROSCOPES

I continue to use the horoscope book talk as an easy way to make friends with a class. I think it's because I am making a personal contact, albeit a very simple one:

> "Would you like to hear your horoscope for today?"
> "I'd like to introduce you to a fellow [Aries]."
> [a character in a book]

It's a way for the class to make friends, too, craning to see who has the same sign. In a sense they also have a connection with their sign fellows in the books. I believe that seeing a common bond with a fictional person is part of the process (started in the "protection" of the library discussions) of making some kind of meaning in our lives.

> "Here is someone like me – neurosis, strength, experience and all."

There is life in books.

On the basis then of my successes with this methodology, the fun I have using it, the echoes of spirited responses, I've included some more horoscopes, first for a junior class, and then for a senior. They make good bookmarks. Students will not only take their own, they will take them all.

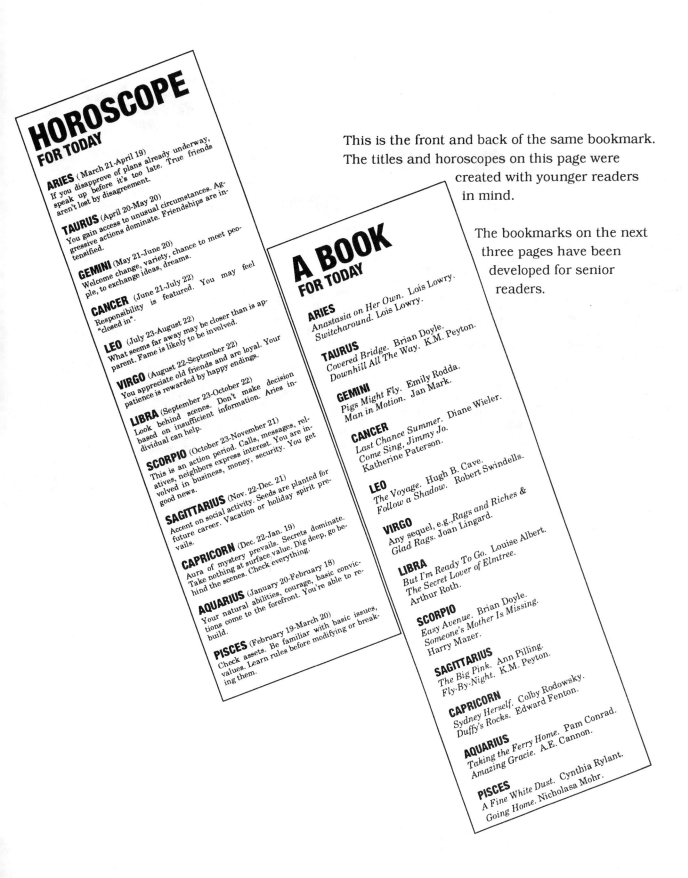

HOROSCOPE FOR TODAY

ARIES (March 21-April 19)
If you disapprove of plans already underway, speak up before it's too late. True friends aren't lost by disagreement.

TAURUS (April 20-May 20)
You gain access to unusual circumstances. Aggressive actions dominate. Friendships are intensified.

GEMINI (May 21-June 20)
Welcome change, variety, chance to meet people, to exchange ideas, dreams.

CANCER (June 21-July 22)
Responsibility is featured. You may feel "closed in".

LEO (July 23-August 22)
What seems far away may be closer than is apparent. Fame is likely to be involved.

VIRGO (August 22-September 22)
You appreciate old friends and are loyal. Your patience is rewarded by happy endings.

LIBRA (September 23-October 22)
Look behind scenes. Don't make decision based on insufficient information. Aries individual can help.

SCORPIO (October 23-November 21)
This is an action period. Calls, messages, relatives, neighbors express interest. You are involved in business, money, security. You get good news.

SAGITTARIUS (Nov. 22-Dec. 21)
Accent on social activity. Seeds are planted for future career. Vacation or holiday spirit prevails.

CAPRICORN (Dec. 22-Jan. 19)
Aura of mystery prevails. Secrets dominate. Take nothing at surface value. Dig deep, go behind the scenes. Check everything.

AQUARIUS (January 20-February 18)
Your natural abilities, courage, basic convictions come to the forefront. You're able to rebuild.

PISCES (February 19-March 20)
Check assets. Be familiar with basic issues, values. Learn rules before modifying or breaking them.

A BOOK FOR TODAY

ARIES
Anastasia on Her Own. Lois Lowry.
Switcharound. Lois Lowry.

TAURUS
Covered Bridge. Brian Doyle.
Downhill All The Way. K.M. Peyton.

GEMINI
Pigs Might Fly. Emily Rodda.
Man in Motion. Jan Mark.

CANCER
Last Chance Summer. Diane Wieler.
Come Sing, Jimmy Jo. Katherine Paterson.

LEO
The Voyage. Hugh B. Cave.
Follow a Shadow. Robert Swindells.

VIRGO
Any sequel, e.g., *Rags and Riches & Glad Rags.* Joan Lingard.

LIBRA
But I'm Ready To Go. Louise Albert.
The Secret Lover of Elmtree. Arthur Roth.

SCORPIO
Easy Avenue. Brian Doyle.
Someone's Mother Is Missing. Harry Mazer.

SAGITTARIUS
The Big Pink. Ann Pilling.
Fly-By-Night. K.M. Peyton.

CAPRICORN
Sydney Herself. Colby Rodowsky.
Duffy's Rocks. Edward Fenton.

AQUARIUS
Taking the Ferry Home. Pam Conrad.
Amazing Gracie. A.E. Cannon.

PISCES
A Fine White Dust. Cynthia Rylant.
Going Home. Nicholasa Mohr.

This is the front and back of the same bookmark. The titles and horoscopes on this page were created with younger readers in mind.

The bookmarks on the next three pages have been developed for senior readers.

What Else Did You See

In The Paper Today?

HOROSCOPE
FOR TODAY

ARIES (March 21-April 19)

"He will look you straight in the eye, with un-abashed honesty and touching faith. You're his friend, aren't you? You like him, don't you? No? Then the tears will start, but inside."
Linda Goodman's
Sun Signs

All summer he'd been in a fever of indecision, afraid to make a move for him-self, focusing everything on Mary. Wanting her had been easier than figuring out what to do with his own life.
Hey, Kid! Does She Love Me? Harry Mazer

Eight stories about people who feel looked down on because they're different — they're misfits.
The Misfits.
Peggy Woodford

Perhaps Marianne is denying Abe his indepen-dence, and they'd be happier apart?
After Thursday.
Jean Ure

HOROSCOPE
FOR TODAY

TAURUS (April 21-May 21)

The truth is that Taurus is as stubborn as a human can be and not actually turn into solid stone. Taurean men and women seem to be glued to both their seats and their opinions."
Linda Goodman's
Sun Signs

Dicey struggles to make a go of a boatbuilding business, neglects Jeff, her family (even Gran) and in her youthful arrogance puts her trust in the wrong person.
Seventeen Against The Dealer.
Cynthia Voigt

You can do anything if you don't try to explain it.
Ivy Larkin.
Mary Stolz

Everything in Chato's life in the L.A. barrio is stacked against him, but he's out to beat all those odds.
Famous All Over Town.
Danny Santiago

HOROSCOPE
FOR TODAY

GEMINI (May 22-June 21)

"Just remember that Gemini is the sign of the twins, and there are two distinct sides to his changeable personality."
Linda Goodman's
Sun Signs

Because he is the Baptist minister's son, groomed for public consumption, Neal feels he must hide his absorbing interest in jazz music.
I Will Call It Georgie's Blues. Suzanne Newton

Boring job — motorcycle stolen — best friend gone domestic — trouble with father — girlfriend closing in. It's time for France and sunshine.
Nick's October.
Alison Prince

After his mother's death Simon gives family, friends, neighbors the cold shoulder. But it's harder shaking off a complete stranger — especially when she's someone like Charlie.
The Charlie Barber Treatment.
Carole Lloyd

HOROSCOPE
FOR TODAY

CANCER (June 22-July 23)

"Cancerian's moods are so intense, they can make you feel them too. They seize joys and despair, horror and compassion, sorrow and ecstasy and hold each emotion fast with a retentive memory."
Linda Goodman's
Sun Signs

Chip's loyalty to his mother, and love for baby sister are put to the test when a long-time family friend turns out to be the baby's father.
A Kindness.
Cynthia Rylant

An ill-fated romance between 16 year Mildred from the wrong side of the tracks and Powell, son of the richest man in town affects three generations.
I Stay Near You.
M.E. Kerr

The only thing I wanted was not to be in the hospital, not to have my leg amputated.
Izzy Willy-Nilly.
Cynthia Voigt

HOROSCOPE
FOR TODAY

LEO (July 24-August 23)

"Leo, the lion, rules all other animals. Leo, the person, rules you and everybody else. Notice the commanding air and stately bearing. That is why so many Leos end up as educators, politicians and psychiatrists."
Linda Goodman's
Sun Signs

When Colette got the chicken-pox, she refused to let Ma put Calamine on her spots... "Calamine's pink," she said, "and I'm black! When they start making black Calamine, you can put it on me."
Rainbows of the Gutter.
Rukshana Smith

Louden lives his life as though he's invincible. How about some sympathy for the strong?
Vision Quest. Terry Davis

Umberto's learning experience puts him in the care of an army deserter and Eunice Tichenor, the library's most passionate and eccentric librarian.
Dr. I.R.T. Louise Tanner

HOROSCOPE
FOR TODAY

VIRGO (August 24-September 23)

"The first thing you'll notice about the typical Virgo is the definite impression he gives that there's a serious problem he's struggling to solve, or that he's secretly worried about something. He probably is. Worry comes naturally to him."
Linda Goodman's
Sun Signs

Life is what happens to you while you're busy making other plans.
Other Plans.
Constance C. Greene

Life without friends? Yes, if your feelings of guilt tell you you don't deserve them.
Life Without Friends.
Ellen Emerson White

You were too desperate, too needy. And you depended on Arnold to make you thin.
Love Is the Crooked Thing.
Barbara Wersba

HOROSCOPE
FOR TODAY

LIBRA (September 24-October 23)

"Her sweet manners and smooth ability to cool your fevered brow can lead you to think she's weak and helpless. But that dear womanly little creature is composed of nine parts steel."
Linda Goodman's
Sun Signs

Marcia finds her strength in bluegrass music when she needs to break away from her overprotective mother .
Face the Music.
Barbara Corcoran

Obese 15-year old Bo is shocked when heartbreak Howard returns to school after his mother's death, an unrecognizable blimp.
A Lot Like You.
Judith Pinsker

Kate endures a summer with her overpowering artist father, gaining the courage to pursue her own artistic goals.
In Summer Light.
Zibby Oneal

HOROSCOPE
FOR TODAY

SCORPIO (October 24-November 22)

"It's quite an experience to see a Scorpio operate under adversity's black clouds. While others are mumbling and crumbling, he is at his forceful, courageous best. He seldom wallows in envy or self-pity."
Linda Goodman's
Sun Signs

"People like you can ask for help. People like me have to steal it."
Afternoon of the Elves.
Janet Taylor Lisle

The week-long endurance training the four high school athletes undergo teaches them to face the Dragon.
Stotan!
Chris Crutcher

"Lord, your sea is so large and my boat is so small — have mercy."
Voyage of the Frog.
Gary Paulsen

HOROSCOPE
FOR TODAY

SAGITTARIUS (Nov. 23-Dec. 21)

"Rebellion against authority and stuffy society is common for the Sagittarius personality. The male's temper can flare like a sky rocket; he will never run away from a fight or call for help. The women can lose their normally pleasant dispositions and let go with a barrage of unexpected plain talk that puts troublemakers right where they belong."
Linda Goodman's
Sun Signs

Rosa survives her mother's 60's activism, her obsession with clothes and style, assorted crushes, friends in need — to win the brass ring!
The First Time.
Aisling Foster

Denis takes his beloved philosophy teacher's dictum to heart: "I believe in questioning everything because everything is relative."
The New Aristocrats.
Michel De Saint Pierre

Claudia's aggressiveness and sharp tongue often attack her friends, the grown-ups are sure she's a survivor, and Claudia herself isn't certain she can ever come first with anyone.
All Ends Up. Gina Wilson

HOROSCOPE
FOR TODAY

CAPRICORN (Dec. 22-Jan. 20)

"You may bump into a Capricorn who has open contempt for his relatives, or who has bitterly cut family ties and never looked back - but scratch the surface of his independence and you'll find a deep emotional wound."
Linda Goodman's
Sun Signs

What Natty sees in his sadistic father's eyes first imprisons him in fear, then frees him from the tyrant forever.
The South African Quirt.
Walter D. Edmonds

Ozzy's bitter quarrel with his brother over his mother's funeral arrangements leads him to New Orleans and Maysie's healing.
Ozzy on the Outside.
R.E. Allen

Bitter, angry, deeply hurt at his father's defection, David pours out his feelings on page 4 of his college application form.
Page Four.
Sheila Solomon Klass

HOROSCOPE
FOR TODAY

AQUARIUS (January 21-February 19)

"Look for a strange, faraway look in the eye, as if they contained some kind of magic mysterious knowledge."
Linda Goodman's
Sun Signs

The dream and the ancient skull bring peace to Coyote Runs' spirit and Brennan's struggle for self-knowledge.
Canyons.
Gary Paulsen

Separated by misunderstandings from his mother, Charlie and his father spend Christmas on a remote Maine island with a family that has at long last been re-united in unconditional love.
Solstice.
Jan Adkins

Shona has always had a strong belief in the impossible and magic, though that belief is stored in a body that can hardly walk and a tongue that cannot speak.
The Flawed Glass.
Ian Strachan

HOROSCOPE
FOR TODAY

PISCES (February 20-March 20)

"He has no prejudices. He'll understand and not pass critical judgment. He possesses a rare sympathy of spirit."
Linda Goodman's
Sun Signs

Mina's deep love for preacher Tamer drives her to seek a way to give him an unforgettable gift, restoration of his faith (and help the Tillerman's too).
Come a Stranger.
Cynthia Voigt

On this holiday 17 year old Joe gathers insights, experiences, friends to last a lifetime.
French Leave.
Wendy Robertson

Tormented by the memory of his best friend's suicide, 17 year old Gideon struggles to realize their shared dream of making it in Nashville.
Singin' Somebody Else's Song.
Mary Blount Christian

When I was working on some new "horoscopes" in the new year, I remembered something I'd clipped and placed in my Idea File. It was a full page explanation with illustrations of the Chinese zodiac. You had to look for the year of your birth to find out which animal sign you were born under. Your year comes around every 12 years in the Chinese zodiac. Under each sign was a personality profile and a prediction.

You have fewer choices to work with in a booktalk, since every student in a grade would be in one of three signs at the most. Still, it's a fascinating variation; students may want to try out their teachers' and parents' signs as well as their own. I think I'd read out the personality profile first, then the prediction, and then the books that match (or contradict) the prediction. This idea could work for a bulletin board – lots of browsing potential here!

For example:

DRAGON

    1916, 1928, 1940, 1952, 1964, 1976, 1988

PERSONALITY: Not to put too fine a point on it, you're
    something of an eccentric. You're full of health and
    energy and yet you tend to worry. You're honest,
    sensitive and courageous but that goes
    hand-in-hand with stubbornness and a quick
    temper. You're capable of devoting yourself to
    good...or bad.

PREDICTION: Try not to be too stubborn this year. You
    may lose a friend or worse. When advice is offered,
    listen to it. Don't expect too much too soon or you
    could hit trouble. Patience, on the other hand,
    should pay off.

Julie's Daughter, by Colby Rodowsky, fits well here:
three strong-willed women, each from a different
generation, all surely Dragons. And how about
Moonkid, a true original, whose coming to terms
with his humanity is a moving experience for the
reader in Paul Kropp's *Moonkid and Liberty*.

WANT ADS

Spend a few days looking at the want ads in your daily newspaper, and collect unusual ones that arouse curiosity as to the nature of the job, its difficulty, pay, etc. This will be part of the motivation of your talk. Think of some books in which characters might advertise for help, or jobs.

Librarian: I've just been looking at the want ads in The Daily News. Have you ever done this? So many of the HELP WANTED ads ask for specialized help, for example:
           (Reading)
           claims processor, person Friday, electro optics engineer, chat operators. Do you know what these people actually do? And over here in the PERSONAL columns, people seem to express their goals, hopes, dreams, even desperation. I should put in an ad myself.

Students: Yeah?
           What for?

Librarian: My ad would read – 'Wanted. All the time in the world to read.'

Young cynic (eyes heavenward): Figures.

Librarian: What would your ad say?

Students: (Various replies)

Librarian: Look at this ad. Who do you think wrote it and why?

It's been a while since I've tried this book-talk. I remember how the groups huddled together figuring out the "ads". I remember how they took their clues from language, tone. I remember how the discussions became more intense as students took sides on issues.

I'm ready for more but I think I'll expand on the Classifieds to be found in newspapers, e.g., Personals, Messages, etc. The want ads here were created to look like the real thing using desk top publishing. Type-written ads, although less polished, work well, too.

THE CLASSIFIEDS

102 WANTED

MONUMENTS

Artist specialist in war monuments. I will give you the kind you truly want but just need to be shown. References: Town square, Bolton, Kansas. Reasonable. Write Mick, Westfalia, Texas (for now).

The Monument.
Gary Paulsen.

A large church organ pipe

Will provide a good home in snug attic bedroom, well-organized, with lots of good company. Leave message for Henry at 272-1487.

Henry's Leg. Ann Pilling

THE RELEASE of words
  stored in my head,
Others who have the
  patience to wait.
To be up to my elbows in
  flour.

The Flawed Glass.
Ian Strachan

UNPAID POSITION

Man from Reading requires position as sales clerk in used furniture store, preferably antiques and collectibles, e.g., beds, roll-top desks, umbrella stands, lead soldiers, clocks, etc. Willing to accept a bite of lunch, free run of books, and a bed for the night in lieu of pay.

Contact MCC Berkshire c/o Public Library, reading room.

A Pack of Lies.
Geraldine McCaughrean

PARENTS WANTED

Calm parents wanted for sensitive, artistic fourteen-year-old. Applicants must be loving without being suffocating, patient, and most of all pleasant to each other. Also able to impart a knowledge of drawing in perspective. André 978-5678.

Laurie Loved Me Best.
Robin Klein

A MOTHER

- who doesn't care so much about the world
- doesn't think about future generations
- or atrocities in Asia
- who comes to school on Parents' Night
- makes cupcakes for Hallowe'en

Write Warren, Box 101, The Star

The Two-Thousand-Pound Goldfish. Betsy Byars

103 ANTIQUE CARS

OVER 200
EXOTIC & CLASSIC
CAR AUCTION
CALL ABC, 725-1171

WANTED — old books that libraries and people don't want any more. Can only pay 5¢ or 10¢ each for ancient, back-broken math books, flaking travel books, warped spellers, mangled mysteries, biographies, music books, astronomy books, cookbooks. 101 Band Shell Blvd.

Maniac Magee.
Jerry Spinelli

107 PERSONALS

HANDYPERSON AVAILABLE

17 year old student with experience in lawn-mowing, baby sitting, selling auto-parts, delivery person, etc. Willing to handle all light and heavy odd jobs. Available after school absolutely every day, and week-ends. Ask for Jane. 962-6959

The Solitary. Lynn Hall

Mom: Come back. You can't hide from me. Let's live for Teddy's sake, so he will always be alive for us. Travis.
Changes in Latitude.
Will Hobbs.

104 LOST

DADDY, things like a television set, a refrigerator, cushions and frying pans, a private bathroom, a telephone, a place of one's own, a private place among millions of people. Leave message for Clay at entrance to Monkey Island.

Monkey Island.
Paula Fox

105 ROOMS

ROOM FOR ELEPHANT

I want to live where I can have any kind of pet. A piece of land that no one can take away from me. Ever. To dig holes in, rearrange, grow trees on. No stupid landlord to tell us what to do, how long we can live there, or say move because we like dogs. If you can accommodate, contact Stowe, Box 133, The Globe.

I.O.U.'s.
Ouida Sebestyen

106 SITUATION WANTED

ALL MY CLOTHES clean at the same time; no lugging horn to school in the rain; no busing home from the library; no dishes; no cleaning out the bath-tub; one princess phone with re-dial button.

Pick-Up Sticks.
Sarah Ellis

TO PLACE AN AD CALL 683-3222

PROFESSIONAL PACKRAT

Have you lost a valuable in the town dump? Are you looking for spare parts for appliances? broken toys to fix? I will do the rummaging for you. Will provide my own crescent wrench, pliers, wire cutter and tin snips. Reasonable rates. Call George 922-1234.

The Night of the Bozos. Jan Slepian

162 MESSAGES

WOLFGANG: Concerning K.157. You know that hard part? You wrote it. So — a hint please, the tiniest wiggle of a vibrato. Just one week to go! Minna.

Facts & Fictions of Minna Pratt. Patricia MacLachlan

Sam Gordon, Mr. Jenks of Montpelier, Vermont; Nancy Rudolph, Daryl Carpenter of Logan, Utah; Margot Rose, Artie, Lionel Winter of Venice, California; Laurel Mendenez of Brooklyn, New York: If you think you know a person named Nina Lewis or Margot Carpenter, I am sorry I didn't say good-bye to you. You were real friends, and I miss you. I am someone else now. But I'm not certain who.

Where It Stops Nobody Knows. Amy Ehrlich

MARCELINE: I'm no racoon killer. I'm a good kid. My stepfather says so. And I won't be short forever. Jason.

Space Station Seventh Grade. Jerry Spinelli

CHARISMATIC CHRIS: If you attended all boy's school in 1967, "dieted" to study Latin, and were expelled, please call Danny 485-1234. Let's renew our friendship. It meant a great deal to me.

Only Birds and Angels Fly. Joshua Horwitz

TICKETS FOR THE HALLOWE'EN DANCE ON SALE NOW

OLIVIA: Remarkable opportunity. Return trip paid. Come if you can. Your father.

Rear View Mirrors. Paul Fleischman

Contribute to *The Reader's Report!* See the librarian.

HAVE YOU HAD
an out-of-body experience?

Are you fond of pizza and the classics?

Am interested in forming a club of like-minded persons.

Only serious replies invited.

Privacy guaranteed.

Ask for Jackson 345-6789.

Eating Between The Lines. Kevin Major

173 FOR SALE

Monday, March 2

Yard sale: Household items: including

1 parrot answers to name of Sidney;

1 potted plant, thriving, needs TLC

1 Book of Spells, copyright 1887, rare edition, handle with extreme caution.

115 Cantle Rood, 8 am — 4 pm

Time Out. Helen Cresswell

SET OF WEIGHTS, almost new (used 2-1/2 months); 10 lb dumbbells; tin of Pro/Gain (unopened); back issues of 'Muscles' and 'Body Beautiful' — mint condition — cheap. Box 6003.

Who Put That Hair In My Toothbrush. Jerry Spinelli

Your Library Has The Answer!

182 HOMES FOR SALE

Northern England

Once thriving coal mining centre. Suitable for peaceful country living. Accessible by charming, winding country roads and lanes. Historical slate roof, stone block walls, ballroom, parquet flooring, marble fireplace, high ceilings, greenhouse, kitchen garden, extensive grounds and wild woods. Handy man and gardener's delight. Extremely reasonable. Owner willing to negoti-ate mortgage. Immediate occupancy. Call agent 9-4 Am3 4892; evenings Am9 4913.

The Coal House. Andrew Taylor

169 RENTALS

JUNIOR APARTMENT: Career girl's dream: minimum of upkeep, suitable for scaled furniture; efficient kitchen; no-nonsense bathroom. Reasonable urban rate. Call 227-4811 day or evening. Martine.

Babyface. Norma Fox Mazer

PERSONAL REPLY SERVICE

219 INVESTMENT PROPERTIES

COUNTRY PROPERTY

POWER OF SALE: Unworked rabbit farm. House has combined kitchen/living room, fireplace, 1 bedroom, loft, outhouse. Two acres include barn, stream, underground spring, rolling, rocky grounds. Extensive basic repairs needed. Any reasonable offer welcome. Call Agent ME3 1749 day or evenings.

The Solitary. Lynn Hall

WILD CHILDREN?

Researcher looking for Russian adults who were "bezprizorni", (wild children) homeless, desperate, criminal, running in packs and terrorizing city and country in the years following the Revolution. Working on book. Please write Alexi's son c/o Box 427.

The Wild Children. Felice Holman

SPONSOR NEEDED

To fund construction of Freeze-Dried Grandmother Launch Pad. Project based on scientific principles of speed, space, time and one trip around a star. Phone Jason.

Space Station, Seventh Grade. Jerry Spinelli.

MARCELINE: I'm no racoon killer. I'm a good kid. My stepfather says so. And I won't be short forever. Jason.

Space Station Seventh Grade.
Jerry Spinelli

301 PROJECTS AND CAUSES

BLOOD TRANFUSIONS BEFORE 1987? WORRIED?

Support group of Aids, HIV infected sufferers, and their families, friends. Meet twice monthly for information and support. Privacy guaranteed. Call ABC 1234.

Good-Bye Tomorrow.
Gloria Miklowitz

CELEBRITIES NEEDED

Researcher requires participants for in-publication study: How Prominent Americans Perceive Angels. Respondents must consent to interviews and questionnaires. Address answers to Sarah Benjamin, Stuart Hall c/o Box 320.

Pageant. Kathryn Lasky

"UMU AYA BINFRA"

Were you born in Nigeria in the years between 1964 to 1967? Are you "babies born around the civil war" and the creation of the nation of Biafra? Interviews needed on growing up in politically unstable environment. Write History Department, Box 354.

The Wrestling Match.
Buchi Emecheta

PERSONAL DEVELOPMENT

NEVER too late to be happy. Educational opportunities, entertainment careers, family counselling.
Dodger 244-9738.

Dodger. Libby Gleeson

GENETIC TINKERING?

Who owns your memory and brain patterns? Persons interested in raising moral and ethical questions concerning human and animal medical experimentation are asked to attend a public forum, Monday 8 p.m. at Town Hall. Guest speaker: Director of Primate Zoology, U of S; Doctor J. Pradesh, Researcher; Giorgo Kennedy, animal rights activist; Eva/Kelly.

Eva. Peter Dickinson

PERSONAL weight loss plan — Food and loneliness and sex and emotional starvation are completely within your control. For free information write to Rita Formica. Box 742.

Fat: A Love Story.
Barbara Wersba

CULTURAL AFFAIRS

Opportunity to hear world premiere of Serenade which could only have been written by a young man of sixteen with a bountiful gift. Complimentary tickets to graduates of Dartington School. Call school for reservation 011-44-8237.

Daniel and Esther.
Patrick Raymond

Do you know how to write a resumé? The library does. Ask.

THE COMICS

For Better or for Worse

I'm sure a lot of people pinned up this strip from *For Better or For Worse*. It's by noted cartoonist Lynn Johnston, recently awarded the prestigious Order of Canada. Makes you think doesn't it?

If you can get permission, enlarge the cartoon, and place it on a bulletin board as the centre of a display about books for the disabled. Here are some suggestions:

THINK ABOUT IT!

Izzy Willy-Nilly, by Cynthia Voigt.
Absolutely Invincible! by William Bell.
Wheels for Walking, by Sandra Richmond.
Come Back Mr. Magic, by Harriet May Savitz.
Head Over Wheels, by Lee Kingman.
The Alfred Summer, by Jan Slepian.

I also clipped this strip from *Walnut Cove*, as it put me in mind of a lot of macho swaggering that, alas, one sees.

Walnut Cove

Watch the reactions to the strip and to the book list. Do students look on an individual basis? or in groups? couples? Do they discuss openly? Do you get a reaction from staff? Do any requests for book-talks or curriculum planning come about as a result? Be prepared! Here's a list to start off your preparations.

NOW YOU KNOW...

Jason and Marcelline, by Jerry Spinelli.
A Very Touchy Subject, by Todd Strasser.
Bad Boy, by Diane Wieler.
Sex Education, by Jenny Davis.
Up in Seth's Room, by Norma Fox Mazer.
NIK, by Aidan Chambers.
The Fat Girl, by Marilyn Sachs.
Running Loose, by Chris Crutcher.
The Girl of His Dreams, by Harry Mazer.
Circles, by Marilyn Sachs.

These titles contain a healthy mix of male characters' attitudes to dating, sex, female needs, male needs, self-knowledge, self-respect, responsibility. Many present the female viewpoint effectively. There is also a range of style and literary value. Most are explicit about feelings and a few are explicit about love-making. There is enough variety to cover the immature and mature reader. Take courage.

To that state of mind
and feelings in which
the confused
and unsure
adolescent
seeks the core of
his/her identity,
the book says,
"I know just
what you're
going through.
It'll be all right."

7

Show Me
Your I.D.

THEY FOUND THE RIGHT WORDS TO SAY

The insights that fictional characters have into relationships, concepts, and the style with which their creators have expressed those insights make for some memorable quotations which I like to publicize by means of a bulletin board display.

The quotations that are on the next three pages are spoken by fictional young people about themselves, about members of their families, about their opinions, feelings. They are the right words in the sense that they express what many adolescents feel and think. Once again, we see how imaginative literature can reach out to assure the adolescent that he or she can "Come to me. I acknowledge your presence and your essence."

Why do these kinds of topics catch students' interest? I have watched them at the display, intent, re-reading, then moving on to other subjects. Are they thinking, "I never knew any one else felt this way." "I never thought of that." "What does that *mean*? Ah, I see." Quite a few copy the words that seem to have connected to something inside them. And they ask for "the book this came from."

When I began browsing through my reading cards to prepare this bulletin board, I was so thankful that I had continued to note my topics, themes and methodologies with page numbers.

For more on reading cards (see p. 148)

In no time at all I gathered many quotes and could contemplate a second display and even a book talk using them.

If you do decide to integrate a book talk into the decorating of the bulletin board, you will quickly realize what an undaunting way this is to get students to discuss freely some moral, ethical, behavioral and personal issues in an unselfconscious manner. (More on this on page 95.)

I offered some of the quotes to my fellow-librarians at our next meeting. Of course I provided copies for every one, and we decided to hold a regular Swap Shop at each meeting. In that way, we all provided something and received something in return.

They found the right words to say about...

WAR

"The nineteen year old soldier looks at the faces of his platoon, "Alive and happy in the face of death... You live, they bury you. And then it's as if you had never existed, as if you had never lived under the sun, under this eternal blue sky where a plane was humming now. Would unspoken thoughts and pain disappear without a trace? Or would something remain, floating invisibly, and when the right time came, find an echo in someone's heart? Who would divide them up into great and non-great when they hadn't time to live yet? Maybe the greatest — a future Pushkin or Tolstoy — were left unknown on battlefields and would never say anything to the world. Would the world feel that emptiness and loss?"

From *Forever Nineteen*, by Grigory Baklanov (p. 36).

"I think I understand, now," he said, "at least a little, about the things that happened in the war."

Matthew drew in a gigantic breath, as though he had been weeks without enough air. "Do you really, Steve? Do you know how I feel?"

Steve nodded. "It just gets started. You don't really know how, but it does. And there you are ... doing things. Terrible things. And other people, too. But it's like there's no way to stop."

"And when it's all over.." Matthew's voice faded away.

"You don't want it to happen again. Not in a million years. So you've got to tell people what it was like ... even if they don't want to hear."

From *Rain of Fire*, by Marion Dane Bauer (p. 153).

MUSIC

"In music there can be no mess. There can be no misunderstanding, no pretence, only an exquisite order... you have heard the best that men can do in a tormented world." *Joachim Schulz one of the finest composers in Europe talks to Daniel who may want to study composition.*
From *Daniel and Esther*, by Patrick Raymond.

"Jeff sang the song, all the way through. Her presence affected his voice, which had settled down over the summer: she listened so intently he was confused; she stood so still he barely dared look at her. Or maybe it was her eyes he didn't want to look at, because he had seen the way the music coiled around her and drew her to him, in her eyes, seen something helpless in her against music and melody. She stared at his hands playing and soaked in his song in a way that made him think — for the first time in a long time — of the island, of solitude and space and the waves tumbling up on to the broad white beaches. He finished the song and looked up at

her. she had her hands jammed awkwardly into her pockets; the song still played behind her eyes, he was sure of it."

From *A Solitary Blue*, by Cynthia Voigt (p. 137).

"Why the sounds of life around him meant so much to him, he didn't know. They interested him. They were the building blocks of a kind of music alive only in his head or in his inspired fooling, like just now. That kind of music wasn't to be heard on his record player or in what he played on the piano. Once in a long while on the radio, he heard something called electronic music which came close. What he knew was that the sounds he could wring from ordinary things were not unchangeable, but were like clay or plastic, his to bend and shape as he wished, his to play with. The world was full of things to feed his fascination, from the sweet clunk of a hammer on car springs to strange sounds locked up in electricity. All his—and let the rest go hang. "

From *The Night of the Bozos*, by Jan Slepian (p. 24).

READING

"Are you a mystery fan?"

"No", said Travis flatly. "I hate it when the only reason to read something is to know what happens next."

"But that is a good reason to read something."

"Yeah. But it shouldn't be the only one."

From *Taming the Star Runner*, by S.E. Hinton (p. 112).

"Stories and books help. Some help you with the living itself. Some help you to just take a break. The best do both at the same time.

From *Goggle-Eyes*, by Anne Fine (p. 139).

SEX

"When it came to girls, there was always a certain cynical way guys talked. You didn't want to express emotion or show that you really liked a girl, or that you could be hurt or unhappy or vulnerable. Emotion was for girls. Guys were macho, impregnable. Iron forts. Any guy was superior to any girl. On higher ground. Judging. Commenting. Ruling. Handing down the final verdict"

17 year old George is only at the beginning of his wisdom about himself — and women.

From *City Light*, by Harry Mazer (p. 45).

"I stayed in my room all night, trying to figure out how my father could be queer. I mean, historically, queers are not fathers."

From *Jack*, by A.M. Homes (p. 21).

SPORT

"Fakes" I said. "Got to learn some moves...."

"No fakes," he said

"Come on, man! What's the big deal? You can't be any kind of hoops player without fakes!..."

"No", he said, booming it...

"Then you won't play basketball for beans," I said.

"Yes I will," he said... "I do not spend all my time teaching my body to trick people like you do. Part of the game you tell me. Well, if that's so, this game is not a game at all. Not for me. If this game is worth playing it is worth playing straight, clean, no cockamamy mumbo jumbo in it. And if it is a good game, then the player who takes it straight will be the best player."

From *The Moves Make the Man*, by Bruce Brooks (p. 179).

"He ran because it was what he did, what he was. He didn't run to win races, or to beat anybody. He ran because his body was built for it. He ran for himself. Simple as that."   From *The Runner*, by Cynthia Voigt (p. 97).

BRINGING UP YOUR PARENTS

"The main thing I have to say is I love my mom and dad very much. I know they love me and Jenny, but stuff just got too much for them, or so they thought. I think if they could just realize that they do love each other and they do know how to be good parents, and that they have responsibilities, and that they can live up to them and be happy doing it, then everything's going to be okay. They're about to hurt a little kid very much, and they don't need to. They can stop themselves, so I think they should."

When Chris Mills sees his family starting to fall apart, he takes charge.

From *Necessary Parties*, by Barbara Dana (p. 303).

"You think your parents are a part of you like an arm or a leg. Then you're shocked when you realize they're separate people and you're strong enough to know you're separate, too."

From *Camilla*, by Madeleine L'Engle (p. 141).

"Everybody needs to raise their parents. Time comes when you have to kiss them goodbye and trust them to be OK on their own."

From *Good-bye and Keep Cold*, by Jenny Davis (last page).

"He is a pretty cagey little person. Usually Mom is on his back as soon as he walks in. It's 'Tell me what you did at school,' or 'sit down and do your homework right now,' or 'why did you do what I specifically told you not to?' Georgie is infinitely patient with her, but the more patient he is the more irritated she gets."

Seven year old Georgie.

From *I will Call it Georgie's Blues*, by Suzanne Newton (p. 8).

"My criticisms — spoken or silent — had little outward effect on my mother, except to make her a little more quiet, a little more sad.

This was worse than the still and mysterious dignity that I was used to, and it infuriated me. I did not want to hurt her. I even loved her. But what I really wanted was for her to change. Why couldn't she. Or why wouldn't she? I couldn't understand it. To me it seemed so simple."

From *My Mother and My Father*,
In *The Leaving*, by Budge Wilson (p. 72).

"The worst thing about my mom is that she understands me. Do you know how awful it is to have someone hanging over you all the time, understanding you?" *Sixteen year old Casey wants to break away from her possessive mother* .

From *Letting Go*, by Lynn Hall.

POVERTY

"Mom says I'm not to worry about money. 'It's my business, Sarabeth,' she tells me at least once a day. I don't worry about money, but I admit I do think about it quite a bit.

Mom has a bunch of little envelopes that say things like RENT, FOOD, GAS, CAR REPAIRS, DENTIST that she keeps in a shoe box. Everyday when she comes home from work, she takes the money she earned from cleaning houses and divides it up. She tries to put something in every envelope. If there's any money left over, she puts it in the envelope that says WE NEED.

'What do you need?' Leo said one day, watching Mom put five dollars in that envelope.

Mom gave him a look. 'Everything.'"

From *Silver*, by Norma Fox Mazer (p. 1).
(I hope the discussion gives me an opportunity to interject with the many calls on that envelope (page 2) or with how a man paid her with a tin of pennies, short changed her by $3.57 and then accused her of lying when she protested.)

"Money might not make you happy, but perhaps it makes being miserable easier to bear."
From *Henry's Leg*, by Ann Pilling (p. 33).

"It was the most matched room she had ever seen. Curtains, chair covers, throw cushions, sheets, even the towels hanging on the back of the door. They must have bought everything at the same time, thought Polly. Imagine going into a store, walking right past the sale tables, ignoring the displays of seconds, picking out piles of everything, and not caring how much it cost... When she and Mom went shopping, it was usually more of a case of crisis management — replacing underwear that had lost its elastic or the toaster that had blown up."

From *Pick-Up Sticks*, by Sarah Ellis (p. 63).

SCHOOL

'I like the excitement'

Mr. Lockett, headmaster of the villages two-room school, has the pleasure of watching his pupils grow up unaffected by the demands of their own age group. His pupils talked and behaved not as their friends did, but as their personalities demanded.

From *The Return*, by Barry Faville (p. 15).

"It was a testament to his strength of character that he had not only survived the monotonous mediocrity but also had continued to flourish. In a triumphant tour de force of manipulation, hypocrisy, and impenetrable cynicism, he comported himself like Miss Copper's postage stamp. And, as every June rolled round at last, he was licked once more by the long tongues of authority, stuck to the empty envelope of his own packaged future, and shipped upward like a piece of heavily insured, special delivery mail. He was always post marked as the top-ranking flunky in his class."

17 year-old Billy MacKenzie is bright enough to play the education game and shrewd enough to know that what he really needs are loose ends.

From *Going To the Dogs*, by Russell McRae (p. 34).

"Life begins when school ends - if it's not too late." From *Mondays Will Never Be the Same*, by Martin Elmer (p. 2).

"The Meyerhoff Association for Behavioral and Emotional Education — We're all basically in our own private galaxies here."

From *The Year It Rained*, by Crescent Dragonwagon (p. 28).

LOVING

"It's like dying of thirst in the middle of a huge lake filled with sparkling fresh water. We're surrounded by it but we can't touch it."

This summer Scott's libido is particularly healthy, but he decides not to move on Paula, despite her reputation, when clearly she sleeps around to gain attention, affection.

From *A Very Touchy Subject*, by Todd Strasser (p. 87).

"Being close with someone isn't easy, he thinks. It's not just a matter of saying I love you. When you're with somebody else, when you like that person and love that person, you have to think about them as much as you think about yourself. If easy is what you want, he says to himself, then be alone and all you'll have to think about is you."

From *The Girl of His Dreams*, by Harry Mazer (p. 183).

"I'm so sick of the words used to describe sex these days. I never paid much attention to them until now, words like the ones I heard all day: turn on, turn off, screw, do it.

What I want to know is, has sex, or rather, has making love, become nothing but a mechanical act described by mechanical words?

Isn't there anything beautiful in it, anything tender and loving? Because if there isn't, if sex is just the conquest of one person by another, then it's not for me.

I'll wait until somebody who thinks the way I do comes along."

Mimi ponders the meaning of loving .

From *If It's Not Funny, Why Am I Laughing?* by Philippa Greene Mulford (p. 138).

LIBRARIES

"'I need everything you have on grief and fat.'

He didn't even look up but continued to sort papers. He mumbled, 'Card catalog,' and pointed an elbow toward it.

'Excuse me,' she said fairly loudly, 'I'm in a rush. Where would I find the books on grief and fat?'

He looked up at her, met her eyes, gave a little smile. 'Under G,' he said precisely. 'And under F. Over there.' And he pointed again to the area of the card catalog. 'You could also try D for death or deceased or defunct or O for obesity or obscene...' He looked mean and pleased with himself.

Bo... spoke slowly and deliberately. 'Could you tell me, so that I can save some time, what areas of the shelves have those topics — so that I can just go and scan the titles?'

'I could,' he said. 'Sure I could. My mind is a veritable computer full of library trivia. But I'm told our sacred mission here is not to lead the unenlightened through the intricacies of the system, but to produce library users capable of independent research.'

'In the time you took to say that you could have told me.'"

From *A Lot Like You*, by Judith Pinsker (p. 64).

"Our library was still pretty low-tech and trusted in the innate honesty of the bookworm."

From *No More Cornflakes*, by Polly Horvath (p. 99).

DIVORCE

"Family life is over. You're just not worth it."

From *Celine*, by Brock Cole (p. 86).

"Whoever invented divorce never thought about kids. Parents split away from each other to make themselves happy. But all the happiness they get is taken right out of their kids."

From *The Squeaky Wheel*, by Robert Kimmel Smith (p. 141).

(*Please go on to read pages 165-171 in which Mark confronts his father and they work out a deal.*)

Consider using these "right words" in a book-talk. First, gather together some of the themes (don't try to use them all; leave some surprises) and copy the quotes on separate slips of paper, enough to distribute, one each, to each group of three to four students. Set up your bulletin board with the heading: "They Found the Right Words To Say About..." Just that much; the rest of the bulletin board remains blank.

Librarian: You see that I've just started to prepare a new bulletin board display entitled: "They Found the Right Words To Say About..." The subjects are wide-ranging. But I thought I should check with you first, to see if you approve of the subjects and what the books have to say about these subjects. So — here are the quotes. Will you read the quote, and discuss what you think the subject is, and whether the author's comment is appropriate? Shall we share your deliberations in about 15 minutes?

Distribute the quotes, one to each small group of students. Have the books ready, in order to answer any questions, or to give to someone who wants to start reading. Move around the room with the teacher who has accompanied the class. If the students seem very involved in discussion or have already slipped into reading, just leave them to it.

You and the teacher can confer about how to proceed. Another period in the library? in the classroom? (To avoid the confusion of trying to collect the slips of paper at the end of the period – I think this kind of housekeeping ruins the spirit of the book talk – use only duplicates with the class.)

When the students start to give their impressions and reactions at the end of the 15 minutes, be ready to respond with: "You certainly approve of including that subject and its quotation, so that goes up on the bulletin board," or "There's a lot of dissension on this one. Shall we pool the class opinion?" And so on.

Thank the groups for their thoughtful analysis. Can you express your gratitude by telling them you will post an acknowledgement on the bulletin board, something like "This bulletin board was prepared with the contribution of Mrs. G's Grade — Health Class."

Announce to the class at the end of the period, that you will complete the display at the end of the day, and hope they will return to read all of the quotes.

Perhaps out of this experience of validating your display for you, you will find that students are eager to play this role again (Invite them!) or to do an entire display for you (Sign them up!).

A variation on the last bulletin board:

THEY FOUND THE "WRITE" WORDS...
Writers tell us why...

Many authors explain why they wrote sequels, or what the genesis of the book was. Many authors give themselves and their characters away in their dedications, and students are intrigued by this insider's information. I'd like to share some of my finds with you:

Harry Mazer   On why he wrote *The Girl of His Dreams*,
the sequel to *The War on Villa Street:*
"I never stopped thinking about [Willis] What had become of him after high school? How was he making out? In the back of my mind was the thought that if he had someone — the right person, a girl — he'd be all right. It was a romantic thought. So shoot me. I suppose that makes this a romantic book."

Gary Paulsen   On *The River:*
"*The River* came into being for two primary reasons. First and foremost, it was demanded — I received thousands of letters (sometimes fifty or sixty a day) from readers interested in Brian who did not want him to end with *Hatchet...* This became so strong that Brian seemed to take on a life of his own — not as a fictional character but the true life of a real person. On top of this feeling was my personal belief that Brian was not...done... in some way. He learned so much in *Hatchet*, became so much of a different person that I wanted to see him be more, see him use what he had become, see him as the new Brian under new circumstances and these two drives kept pushing at me until I decided to write a second book about him."

Diana Wieler   On *Bad Boy:*
"For my husband, Larry, who relived his moments of hockey glory for me, over and over."

Zilpha Keatley Snyder
Dedication to *Libby on Wednesday:*
"To all of you who said, 'I write too.'"

William Bell
For *The Cripples' Club,* now titled *Absolutely Invincible:*
"To a considerable extent, *The Cripples' Club* was inspired by two of my former students, Shelley and Darin and by the late Terry Fox."

Brock Cole
Dedication to *Celine:*
"For Amy Hosler. 1967-1987"

Walter Dean Myers
Dedication to *Fallen Angels:*
"To my brother, Thomas Wayne "Sonny" Myers, whose dream of adding beauty to this world through his humanity and his art ended in Vietnam on May 7, 1968."

Norma Fox Mazer
About *Summer Girls, Love Boys:*
"This book is in memory of my father. He lived his life among women: mother, sister, wife, daughters. To them all he was fiercely loyal and devoted."

Robert Cormier
A note by the author in *8 Plus 1:*
"My memory may falter when it comes to facts and figures, but I have almost total recall of my emotions at almost any given moment of the past. Thus, I began to write a series of short stories, translating the emotions of both the present and the past — and finding they were the same, actually — into stories dealing with family relationships, fathers and mothers, daughters and sons. I wrote about growing up, and the parents in the stories grow up, too, in the knowledge, often bittersweet, that the passing years bring."

Brian Fairfax-Lucy & Philippa Pearce
Prologue to *The Children of the House:*
"No children have lived here since before the First World War, since the time of Laura, Thomas, Hugh and Margaret Hatton. This is their story."

Gary Paulsen
About how he came to write *The Monument:*
"Ten or more years ago I read what Katherine Anne Porter once said: 'Art is what we find when the ruins are cleared away.' Since then this book has worked at me. I wanted to show art, show how it can shake and crumble thinking, how it can bring joy and sadness at the same time; how it can own and be owned, sweep through lives

and change them — how the beauty of it, the singular, sensual, ripping breath-stopping wondrous frightening beauty of it, can grow from even that ultimate ruin of all ruins: the filth of war."

Jo Carson   On *Stories I Ain't Told Nobody Yet,* her collection of first-person poems taken from the actual conversations of Appalachian people:
"I can say to students 'write about what you know' till I'm blue in the face. Sharing these pieces in a writing workshop is a kind of permission for them to really do it: they know people like these."

M.E. Kerr   Author note in *Mememememe: Not a Novel:*
"This is an answer to many letters from kids wanting to know if the things I write about really happened to me."

Ian Strachan   Dedication for *throwaways:*
"The poor don't count, so don't count the poor."
A comment on the exclusion of 5 million Americans from the 1990 Census.
"The sort of people you step over when you come out of the opera."
A comment on London beggars, 1991
Naturally, nobody really knows how many street children there are, but UNICEF believe a minimum of one hundred thousand million earn some sort of living on the streets of the world and at least half of those will have no form of shelter to sleep under. But, they add, these figures may be greatly under-estimated.
This book is dedicated to them.

Robert Cormier   About *Fade:*
"...the key to all my writing: what if?"

I am aware that these displays are almost *all* print. Yet the bold headings stopped students initially, and once they started to read, they were caught up. The principal who *always* stopped at the latest display on his shortcut through to the cafeteria, poured over each one. We changed the displays each week, almost always in the last two periods on Friday, when interruptions for last minute week-end requests didn't make a difference to our task. We always got a lot of queries, advice, commendations, etc. as students passed by or stopped to observe. When I noticed the same people week after week, I asked for suggestions for themes, or recommended books to get me going on new displays.

A student's enthusiastic 'ALL RIIGGHT!" in response to my single ex-
clamatory "AAARRRG!" display for horror stories prompted me to use
his exclamation for a display of books with intriguing titles (Zindel and
Danziger are good starting points). If you collect statistics on circulation or can break down circulation on specific titles, use this exclamation for a display of the library's most heavily read titles.

GRAFFITI

I'm looking at the graffiti sheet of thanks that a Grade 8 class I've visited recently gave me, to match the graffiti sheet we'd been examining in my book-talk. The comments all had to do with the *choice of books* I'd provided them, and they'd read. I'd like to think that the strong feelings and opinions expressed in their graffiti were a reflection of the connection between the students' own emotions and the books'. Graffiti continues to be an intriguing "hook".

So I've written some new graffiti (numbers 1 - 16) to add to some of the ones I did for the Grade 8 class (numbers 17-20).

1. Celine Morienval SUCKS. But can Celine fly? *Celine.* **Brock Cole.**
2. Being is what counts. *The Wrong Way Home.* **Liza Fosburgh.**
3. I am in a mental institution because it is the sanest place I have found in this world. *Sex Education.* **Jenny Davis.**
4. It isn't that our parents care that bothers us. It's what they care about. *Year of the Gopher.* **Phyllis Reynolds Naylor.**
5. Ours is an era in which people are proud of machines that think and suspicious of any student who tries to do likewise. *Mondays Will Never Be the Same.* **Martin Elmer.**
6. Chance favours the prepared mind. *Catalogue of the Universe.* **Margaret Mahy.**
7. Charity is: Neighbors sitting on the edge of every spoon. *Borrowed Children.* **George Ella Lyon.**
8. Use it up, wear it out, make it do. I'll have another. *Borrowed Children.* **George Ella Lyon.**
9. Toby lived here! October 16, 1977 *Toby Lived Here.* **Hilma Wolitzer**
10. On the great board game of Romance, I am still at square one. *The Girl Who Invented Romance.* **Caroline B. Cooney**
11. Do unto others, then split. *Beyond the Chocolate War.* **Robert Cormier**
12. You can never hold anybody as long as you want. *Two Moons in August.* **Martha Brooks**
13. People don't have to be the way they worry they might turn out to be. *Two Moons in August.* **Martha Brooks**
14. The three powers of the soul: memory, understanding, will. *Duffy's Rocks.* **Edward Fenton**
15. Better a NIKEL than a knuckle. *NIK.* **Aidan Chambers**
16. Life is what happens to you while you're busy making plans. *Other Plans.* **Constance C. Greene**
17. Welcome to Mariasburg. Population 18 years of age and under. *The Taking of Mariasburg.* **Julian F. Thompson.**
18. Shakespeare loves Legs *Shakespeare and Legs.* **Norah McLintock.**
19. KING KONG LIVES. *Would You Settle for Improbable?* **P.J. Peterson.**
20. Sue your parents! *Necessary Parties.* **Barbara Dana.**

T-SHIRTS

What is more omnipresent and celebratory than t-shirt slogans! Students wear them to exhort, intrigue, flaunt membership, ownership, prowess, attitude, etc. Let's involve these young people creatively by getting them to provide slogans for fictional characters. Not only will this give the students a sense of owning the book, but also a sense of pride in their creations.

I have included an assignment that evolved from the t-shirt book talk. Also I think it's possible to have a contest to decide what the best three are (students can vote) and have actual t-shirts made up and sold as a library project.

Librarian: The principal of Bingo Brown's school has passed a ruling that no one may wear t-shirts to school with words on them. So the junior high students resolve to have a protest wear-in. Each student will wear a t-shirt with a slogan on it — and no one will enter the school until the principal cancels the rule. Next day, they wear their t-shirts:

'If you can read this you are too close'
'Weird but loveable'
'Shud uppa u face'
'I are a genius'
'In a world full of copies, here's an original'
'Have you thanked a plant today?'
'Smash computers and let the chips fall where they may'
'Reality is for those who can't face science fiction'

Bingo's is simple:

In
*The Burning Questions
of Bingo Brown,*
by Betsy Byars

(holding up the cardboard cut-out
illustrated at left)

Librarian: How many t-shirts do you own that have words on them?
             Tell us about them. What are your favourites?

As the students give their answers, I listen carefully, hopeful that
someone will mention a genre I can match with one of my prepared
't-shirts'.

Student: My favourite is one my uncle gave me because he was an
            official. It's:
                        'Winter Olympics, Calgary 1988'

L:ibrarian: How wonderful to have a t-shirt marking such an
             occasion. Here is Chris' occasion...

(holding
up my
cardboard
cut-out)

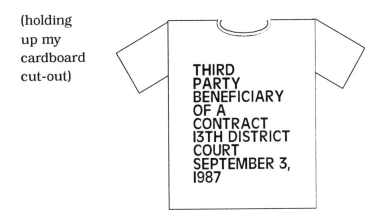

THIRD
PARTY
BENEFICIARY
OF A
CONTRACT
13TH DISTRICT
COURT
SEPTEMBER 3,
1987

Determined to prevent his parents' impending divorce, and
his sister's increasingly disturbed behaviour, Chris has
hired a brilliant lawyer, the persuasive Corelli, whose
t-shirt might be.. "Oratory is persuasion, not the truth." It
is Corelli who comes up with the idea that since Mr. &
Mrs. Mills entered a marriage contract, their children who
are beneficiaries of that contract are now suffering
irreparable damage, Chris is suing on those grounds to
prevent the divorce. This is from *Necessary Parties*, by
Barbara Dana.

Student: 'Save the whales'.

In *The Gadget Factor,*
by Sandy Landsman.

The computer is the ultimate gadget!

Librarian: You're an activist, then. Good for you. So is Mike, college freshman at age 13, a brilliant mathematician, and now computer whizz. He is about to invent an incredible computer game, which he will call Universe Prime. He believes that... (holding up Mike's "t-shirt")

...because it is the ultimate mind against which to test his own."

Librarian: [In response to one of the more cynical slogans.] That slogan sounds like something Archie would like. You remember the battle of wills between good and evil in *The Chocolate War*, by Robert Cormier. The battle continues in *Beyond the Chocolate War:*
          Do unto others, then split.

Student: My favourite t-shirt is this school's – I'm on the swim team.

In
Who, Sir? Me, Sir?" by
K.M. Peyton.

GASWORKS
TETRATHALON

Librarian: I'll bet you're proud of that. I've got another one for athletic affiliation.

Do you know the events in this competition? It's for all round athletics — running, swimming, shooting and riding cross-country. The four boys at Hawkwood Comprehensive (they call it The Gasworks because of its highly progressive architecture which featured a lot of ventilation pipes) chosen by their teacher to enter this event are the sorriest lot of apathetic, undersized, unco-ordinated, unathletic (one of them can't swim at all) — Oh — there's one exception, a good runner, not surprisingly considering how often the police are after him.

Student: Mine is one I bought at a bookstore.
                     'Think, Inc.'

Librarian: Oh I love that store! Here's one for my favourite
                   restaurant. 'The Restaurant at the End of the Universe'
                   Aha, I see you've been there too, and possibly have t-shirts
                   for *The Hitch Hiker's Guide to the Galaxy,* and *Life, the Uni-*
                   verse and Everything, also *So Long, and Thanks for All the*
                   Fish (holding each title up in turn). And as an added
                   pleasure, the latest, *Mostly Harmless, the Fifth Book*
                   in the Increasingly Inaccurately Named
                   Trilogy, by Douglas Adams. Mrs. G.
                   loved all the t-shirts I showed her,
                   and she has an idea —

Ms. G.:   How about creating a t-shirt saying and/or
                   drawing for your next book report. It can be
                   for any character, situation, issue, etc. in the
                   book — and yes, you can use the author's own
                   words. The librarian is offering us "t-shirts" in
                   any colour you want, and promises to make a
                   display of them here in the library when we are finished.
                   (Enthusiastic, pleased responses)

Restaurant at the End of the Universe

Of course you will encourage students who wish to decorate their own
real t-shirts!

My preparations for the book talk:
         The t-shirts are easy to prepare. Cut out the shape on bristol
         board. Make it large enough for students to see the lettering
         easily, but not so large as to overcrowd a display.

If you can station yourself and the class comfortably near a bulletin
board, you can tack up each t-shirt as you talk about it, and create a
display as you go along.

You might consider a variation for this same class' next book report —
a bumper sticker. You'll have to discuss what differences you'd have to
accommodate for this new format, e.g., number of words, size of letters, etc.

BUSINESS CARDS

Librarian: I had a visitor in the library recently who left me his business card. It reads:

He was selling books. And now I can add his card to about twenty others I have which read exactly the same way:

> Name of company, person's name, person's occupation.

How could John W. Bloor's identity be made more unique? What information might be added to his business card to make us more interested?

Students: His university degree.
Awards he's won.
He could put some
  special accomplishment.
Or describe himself.

Librarian: Now that would get my attention, and if the description were intriguing enough, I might just tell the office secretary to send in this person. (Read card at right)

Patrick Pennington

- ■
- RELUCTANT STUDENT
- ■
- DISHWASHER
- ■
- CHAMPION SWIMMER
- ■
- PIANO MEDALIST
- ■
- SUSPENDED SENTENCE
  FOR ASSAULT
- ■

Based on *Pennington's Seventeenth Summerr*, by K.M. Peyton.

Student:　　　No way.

Yeah, Let's have a look at him.

Librarian:　　Then through the doorway comes Patrick. He's about 17, good looking, except for the sullen look on his face. His hair is really too long, and although he's got on a jacket, he's left off a tie. He lounges up to you, stares you in the eye as if daring you to knock the chip off his shoulder. For the hero of *Pennington's Seventeenth Summer* is his own worst enemy. He's got all those talents and awards, but he can't control his temper. The assault charge is for hitting a policeman.

Would you like to see any one else? Here are the business cards. You're in charge. Who do you want to see?

BILLY KENNEDY, the shrimp

GOOD GRADES, GOOD OUTSIDE SHOOTER,
FAIR SHORTSTOP, SENSE OF HUMOUR,
OKAY GUY IN GENERAL

VIRGIN

1.

Imelda

Fact Gatherer

Data Harvester

Bundler Of
Useless News

2.

Knox Lionel
(Opportunity Knox)

DWARF IS beautiful

3.

a little patience please.

4.

Henry
Maximillian
Ledniz

Dinosaurs
Limited

5.

We will do
anything,
cheerfully
$1.00 hour

**Jackson (Cracker) Hunter
Ralph (Goat) McMillan**

6.

TIRED OF DOING
YOUR OWN LAUNDRY?
Rebecca

FOUR LOADS AND FOLDING
OUR SPECIALTY

7.

McGrew Pratt
The Hummer

Answers to teachers' questions.
Observations and newspaper headlines a specialty.

8.

JENNY
Horse Handler

Reliable –
not clever
or sharp
or polite
or promising, but
RELIABLE

9.

★

MICK

★

★

Cheeky, talks back,
insolent lout,
and undisputed
musical star.

★

10.

SIMPLE-WAYS-TO-GET-WHAT-YOU-WANT, INC.

John D., President

Potential re-marriage our specialty

11.

EARL GRAYSON

I am not what you see.
I am not a line-laying, pick-up driving,
live-at-the-Y, bean-brained parkhand.
I am not rickety, whiskered worm chow.
I AM A PITCHER
(printed by Maniac Magee, on Earl's behalf)

12.

DANIEL

An anarchic mind governed by a sense of order

14.

MANIAC MAGEE

No knot untied,
no race not won,
no pitch struck out.

BLACK/WHITE RELATIONS A SPECIALTY

13.

I have distributed the cards throughout the class, so that two or three kids are looking over one card, and wait for questions and remarks. As we deal with each card, I give that book to the group who dealt with it. When enough discussion has gone on, I put up the poster, entitled "Who Shall I Say Is Calling?" with a duplicate set of the business cards on it and point out the list of numbered titles corresponding to the cards.

I like the business card book-talk because it celebrates achievements and strengths. The achievements may be minor, the strengths not always socially approved – but they are there. And I think adolescents can claim them as sustenance for the journey. I haven't forgotten the enthusiasm with which Mrs. L's Grade 10 class wrote calling cards for their next book report, nor their pride when I added their cards to mine on the "Who Shall I Say Who Is Calling?" bulletin board. It was a "feel good" exercise.

KEY TO THE BUSINESS CARDS

1. *The Arizona Kid.* Ron Koertge.
2. *The Facts and Fictions of Minna Pratt.* Patricia MacLachlan.
3. *Little, Little.* M.E. Kerr.
4. *The Alfred Summer.* Jan Slepian.
5. *A Begonia for Miss Applebaum.* Paul Zindel.
6. *Cracker Jackson.* Betsy Byars.
7. *Fourteen.* Marilyn Sachs.
8. *The Facts and Fictions of Minna Pratt.* Patricia MacLachlan.
9. *Darkling.* K.M. Peyton.
10. *Dodger.* Libby Gleeson
11. *The Animal, The Vegetable and John D. Jones.* Betsy Byars.
12. *Maniac Magee.* Jerry Spinelli.
13. *Maniac Magee.* Jerry Spinelli.
14. *Daniel and Esther.* Patrick Raymond.

FAMOUS FIRST WORDS

These are all great openings to books – written to grab the attention. But you have to open the book first, don't you? I thought about openings – and decided to feature some.

The passages can stand alone on individual bookmarks or collectively on a bookmark or in a book list.

Or you could do a book talk on first impressions, using the list or bookmark that you have created. If you do a book talk, start by reading aloud the first two paragraphs of *Dear Shrink*, by Helen Cresswell. Then ask the group to judge the effectiveness of some of the following opening words. Are they compelled to read on? What sort of story do they expect? You are there as a restrained (don't give it all away) advocate for the book.

Here are some of my choices for a book list or book mark:

> *The True Confessions of Charlotte Doyle.* Avi.
> "Not every thirteen-year old girl is accused of murder, brought to trial, and found guilty."

> *Two Moons in August.* Martha Brooks.
> "Our Angel Mother who art in Heaven, flapping around with both sets of grandparents used to say my hair is just like Lucille's."

> *Journey.* Patricia MacLachlan.
> "Mama named me Journey, Journey as if somehow she wished her restlessness on me."

> *I Capture the Castle.* Dodie Smith.
> "I write this sitting in the kitchen sink."

> *We Have Always Lived in the Castle.* Shirley Jackson.
> "I have often thought that with any luck at all I could have been born a werewolf."

The Secret Diary of Katie Dinkerhoff. Lila Perl.
> "On Tuesday, March 5, Katie Dinkerhoff wrote another big fat lie in her diary... She didn't write in her diary everyday, only when she needed a lift. And the lie she'd written today wasn't that terrible."

Such Nice Kids. Eve Bunting.
> "What happened was my fault and Meeker's and Pidge's too... I wish I could stop going over it and over it the way I do, trying to find excuses for myself, because there aren't any. Not for this."

The Year It Rained. Crescent Dragonwagon.
> "I have the mother everyone wants."

Round the Bend. Mitzi Dale.
> "Today is an anniversary of sorts. It's a year to the day that I got out of the loony bin. I figured I'd get that in right away in case you're one of those people who's not interested in what someone like me has to say, in which case you can stop reading right now."

Josephine. Kenneth Lillington.
> "Josephine Tugnutt was excusably nervous as she walked up the tree-lined avenue that led to St. Chauvin's College. One girl among 600 boys! She came from a girls' boarding school and was walking into the unknown."
> *(Actually I'm cheating a bit here. This passage occurs on page 4-1/4. See what you might have missed??!!)*

8

Filling in
the Blanks

FILLING IN THE BLANKS

He's been filling in the blanks in workbooks for a whole year in the developmental reading room. Today he's been allowed to accompany his regular English class to the library where we've been having a lively discussion of the business cards. As the class breaks up to get their books signed out, he remains seated beside me, and looks at me wonderingly: "You talk about these characters as though they're real people!" "Yes," I reply, "they seem real to me. Do they sound familiar to you?" After a thoughtful pause, he says, "Yes, that's just like my grandmother. Her favourite is my no-good uncle. He's just a bum, and she keeps giving him money. He'll never pay her back." And he signs out *Teacup Full of Roses.* by Sharon Bell Mathis. I tell him if he's still around the school at 5 o'clock, I'll read the first chapter with him (in the privacy of the then empty library).

Business cards, pp. 106-109.

I hate reading

I could understand Elise's yearning to be shorter, her desire not to be the first person that people noticed in any group.

> "Elise was tall. Very tall. Over [6'2"] in the flattest of heels. Easily the tallest girl in her entire school, probably the tallest girl in town, and quite possibly destined to become the tallest female in the whole country."

It isn't finding a tall boy that is her problem, though.

> "The problem was that no one ever got a chance to find out if Elise was okay or not. Her height got in the way. It was like a wall around her soul, hiding from sight the fact that she was just an ordinary person."

When I read *Shakespeare and Legs* by Nora McClintock I knew I had to connect Elise to someone. I noted pages 12, 13, 125 and 126 on my reading card, and waited...

K seemed intent on spoiling the occasion before I could get started. "So do we have to read? I hate reading. I've never finished reading a book in my life. Once my uncle promised me five dollars if I'd read one book and I couldn't do it." All this was spoken in clarion belligerent tones. Finally she was quiet, puzzled by my patient, silent waiting, and I started the graffiti book talk. Suddenly she blurted out "What's number 9?" (Shakespeare loves Legs) I replied, " Legs is the nickname of 6'2" Elise who wishes people would care what she was really like in her soul, where it counted (K says "Yeah").

Shakespeare is William Shakespeare Jones, friendly, sense of humour, loyal, persistent, 5'7-1/2" He takes Elise to the prom, and insists they dance." (K approves: "Yeah!")

The passage I read starting on page 125 describes their romantic dancing, Shakespeare drawing Elise tightly to him, resting <u>his</u> head on <u>her</u> shoulder, Elise's rigid embarrassment, Shakespeare's gentle coaxing, and then Elise's defiant participation.

"And that's *Shakespeare and Legs*." (Holding up the book).

"I'll take that," said K quickly and determinedly. Later, at the circulation desk, irrepressible as ever she called out, "Hey take a picture, someone. I'm taking out a book!"

...And I left *Avie Loves Ric Forever* in Norma Fox Mazer's *Summer Girls, Love Boys* with a note for K — to be delivered to her via her English teacher:

> "K. The short story *Avie Loves Ric Forever* on pages 7-35 is really
> for Elise. She would know why. I think you will both appreciate it.
>   F.B."

Peer pressure

At the circulation desk:
He holds out *A Long Way From Verona*, by Jane Gardam: Does this girl
    really tell her teacher she's a fool?
Me: Yes, she really does.
He (giggling, covering his mouth): No, No.
She (standing beside him; bracingly): Sure, she does. Come on, take it
    out. It'll be *good* for you. (To me, confidentially) He's just too good
    for his own good.
He takes out the book.

Response Diary

'When Jeff and his father finally found a place, the neglected property on Chesapeake Bay with its honeysuckle vines, wild cherry trees and blue heron, he called it a "safe place." A safe place is one where Jeff can find a sense of space and peace. He can get stronger here, put on some weight, get to understand his father better, and get over the deep hurt inflicted by his mother. A safe place doesn't mean you hide from something; it means you find something.'

Isn't this Grade 12 student writing in her "response diary" to *A Solitary Blue*, the kind of reader who would love to try writing a metaphor for the Professor (page 9) and for Jeff (page 117)?

Metaphors: See p. 170.

My Refuge

I read Constance Beresford-Howe's *The Book of Eve* at a gulp, and thought of Angela, a bright, sometime achieving senior student with whom I'd formed a friendship. I knew when she was depressed (she told me — often). I heard her when she was happy (what a giggler!) She gulped books too. I saved special titles for her, saying little, if at all as I handed them to her. So I gave her *The Book of Eve* "Here's one for you, Angela." She returned it, read, the next day. "Thanks, Miss B., I *loved* it!" and then merrily, cheekily, she nudged me "How *about* that old lady! Not bad for 65, eh?" And she laughed and laughed. We agreed that sex doesn't seem to be confined to those under 30. When she graduated, she sent me a note thanking me, and mentioned six titles, *The Book of Eve* among them, in particular. "The library was my refuge," she wrote.

Protective coating

She is a very young 14, shy, frightened in social situations, and very much under the loving protection of parents from a non-North American culture. I give her "Canadian" *Anne of Green Gables*, by Lucy Maud Montgomery. She tells me how much she loved it, her face alight. All year I provide her with L.M. Montgomery stories. They are, I believe, a breathing space for her.

The haunting

I looked down quite by accident into the eyes of the resident professed Nazi. A Grade 8'er, handsome, clear-eyed, he sported a close-cropped hair style, black shirt, trousers, and knee-high black leather boots. I had been told of his political and racial attitudes, often expressed in class and often rewarded with expulsion from that class. But the expression on his face now! His eyes were filled with tears his face was flushed and contorted with such a look of suffering! I was unnerved and looked quickly away to pull myself together. What had I or his classmates said to elicit such a reaction? I wracked my brain. What comment on a book could have pierced that arrogant armour? He haunts me still. I was a visitor in that school and had no opportunity to further the contact; all I could do was tell my story to the librarian and discuss possible follow-ups. Mindful of my experiences with "the outsiders" the truant girls in the Grade X class who locked me out of our reading room the next time we met after our moving experience with Morris Bird in *The Greatest Thing That Almost Happened*, by Don Robertson (tough girls don't cry and you have to pay if you make them cry). I would not question or pursue the young man about his feelings. Rather I would rejoice that he had had those feelings, and celebrate the human being with lots of eye contact, pleasant greetings and casual recommendations of good reads (no hammering of sad stories). Some day I hope he will read *A Map of Nowhere*, by Gillian Cross which through its compelling plot and characterization can help the reader construct a set of values and an ethical system as a guide to behaviour.

Black leather

"You interested in a book about a kid who's in trouble with the law?" I ask the Grade 12 youth in a black leather jacket with studs. He reads for the rest of the period, oblivious to those around him, *Far from Shore*, by Kevin Major. At the end of the period, he approaches me, slaps the book into my hand, curtly instructs me to "Keep that. I'll be back." And off for a smoke.

Touchy

For prickly, touchy G. who comes into the library each day to test his belligerence on me – *Dodger*, by Libby Gleeson. And I will keep in my memory the words of Dodger's teacher. "If I desert him, I'm saying that I don't believe in the power of people to learn something from their behaviour."

Gifts

You must know of a group of readers who come in often to select books. They have come to look forward to your talks. You have grown to know their tastes; they have come to trust your recommendations. They share their responses to reading readily and gratefully. They have become special. What special treat can you give them?

Make a list of the books these students have taken out after the most recent book-talk. Record the name of the student who took out each book. Can you arrange with the group's teacher to have the group bring their novels with them two weeks later? Now think — and match another book for a character in each novel. Write out a gift card explaining the emotional connection — you offer the book as a healing, a surcease, a reward, a pleasure, a surprise.

To: Minna Pratt (The Facts and Fictions of Minna Pratt) because: you and Mr. Drew will appreciate the carnival spirit of this collection. It is endlessly inventive and a delicious reward for your love of language. I recommend especially the practical gift of a word wizard, the cat who becomes poet and the stories about the Delmonico family. Green marmalade to you!
F.

Minna Pratt of Patricia MacLachlan's *The Facts and Fictions of Minna Pratt* would be given *Non-Stop Nonsense*, by Margaret Mahy with this gift card.

When the group has re-assembled two weeks later, offer each student his/her new book with the gift card tucked into it. Give the students time to read their cards and mull over their messages. They might just want to get on with the new books immediately. Some may want to hear more about your reasons for selection. I hope the accompanying teacher will suggest thank you notes to be written from the first book's character!

Thirteen year old Lyddie who has put her childhood to rest for the sake of family and home (*Lyddie*, by Katherine Paterson) should be given *Waiting Both*, by Thomas Hardy in *Talking to the Sun*, to savour the other poems and art work, too.

Give Celine (*Celine*, by Brock Cole) *Downhill All the Way*, by K.M. Peyton — the spaghetti-eating episode is a match for the hilarity of her non-stop hysterical outburst to the shrink. Give Jake (*Celine*, by Brock Cole) *Maniac Magee*, by Jerry Spinelli, because having had his eccentricities encouraged by Celine, he will appreciate friends such as tough Amanda, bad Mars Bars, pitching has-been Grayson, whistle-blowing Mrs. Pichwell. Give Ellie and Stevie (*My Daniel*, by Pam Conrad) Paulsen's *The Winter Room* because they will enjoy more stories from the elderly about the past. "Uncle" David's and Nels' stories may seem a little exaggerated but Ellie and Stevie will listen not because they are truthful, but because they are the truth.

Why do I have to be here?

They were sullen, determinedly unco-operative. Their body and facial language told me they had been forced to come to the library. I used the teacher's assignment from A.E. Cannon's *Amazing Gracie* (p. 3):

> "If your house was on fire and you had to grab just one thing before getting out, what would it be?"

I let the discussion go on for some time, permitting them a breathing space in which their resentful resistance to being brought into the library, could dissipate.

Then I chose a bizarre item from Lynne Reid Bank's *Melusine*:

> "How about something long, and crisp and empty?
>> (Reading, p. 150)
>>> 'He carried it to the window through which the man had fallen. It was quite perfect in its way. A tube of scales, torn only here and there – a beautiful, transparent thing – a shadow of a snake.'
>
> I'm speaking for Roger, caught between fascination and revulsion with (Holding up) *Melusine*."

I permitted time for their positive, negative, bewildered, appreciative comments, and then suggested that when they finished reading the books they had come in to select, they could imagine what any character in the story might save if his or her house were on fire.

> "If you agree, I'd like to invite you back to hear your choices next time you visit."

Then in a manner assuming their agreement, I started to hand out a few books to get them started.

> "I think Hubbo would save the goat (*Easy Avenue*, by Brian Doyle). Jackson would save a sheepskin (*Eating Between the Lines*, by Kevin Major). Tad would save the elephant. All right, perhaps it would be a barge that was burning. (*The Great Elephant Chase*, by Gillian Cross). Clare would save her mirrored sunglasses (*The Beggar's Ride*, by Theresa Nelson)."

And they stood up, slowly, but agreeably and got their books. The accompanying teacher decided, at the last moment, to hear their "reports" in their own classroom! Never mind, "Better to light a candle, than curse the darkness."

The exasperating reader

He is bright, assured, impatient, self-confident. And has a reading habit that drives me mad:

> "I never finish reading a book. I read about fifty pages and then I make up the rest of the story the way I think it should end."

"And do you check your efforts against the author's later?"

"Nope. Not interested."

"Never?"

"Never."

"And you've never ever finished reading a book?"

"Well, yes, just one and I have read it several times. It..."

(Interrupting) "*The Fountainhead*?"

(Amazed) "How did you know that?!"

> (I can't tell him my yardstick for exasperation is the reader of Ayn Rand – because that is <u>my</u> prejudice.)

He has a total lack of patience, not even looking for instant gratification. As one of my colleagues stated, "he's looking for <u>instant</u>." Have I found a challenge in *The Hillingdon Fox*, by Jan Mark? It's filled with clues, arcane events, political edges, and has a conclusion whose open-endedness should dispute his certainties. Shall I tell him all this?

Your time will come

She wears a highly visible back and neck brace, has a homely nose and very beautiful, sad eyes. I would like to give her, and haven't had the courage, *Where Have All the Tigers Gone?* by Lynn Hall. Jo and Hazel realize at a high school re-union that they could have been the best friends each needed but they "couldn't get past each other's defences... "Yet they turned out just right. They all became... themselves." I think of her when I read Ed Ochester's *In the Library* in *Poetspeak*, edited by Paul Janeczko, p. 205.

> "...white crane
> staring downward
> conscious of her reed neck
> that the smallest stone can break."

"Polkaroo!"

Do you think your older students consider themselves "too mature" to respond to children's interests? Recently at a Fall Fair and Flea Market to raise funds for a local primary school, I watched primary children clustering excitedly about a character from Polka Dot Door, a popular children's television show, when suddenly two teenaged girls burst into the group, shouting "Polkaroo! Polkaroo!" and threw their arms lovingly around the tall green polka-dotted "animal". Should we have the courage to include children's books in our young adult collections?

Andy smiles

Andy is a great lumbering, slow-thinking boy with the sweetest smile I've ever seen. It takes him half an hour to read a page of text. I've never seen him angry. "It's all right," he grins as he skips period 4 to complete an assignment due in period 5. "It's all right," he smiles as the class completes the test before the end of the period, and he's only at question 4 when the bell rings. He usually does his homework in the library at the end of the day, and when he and I are alone then, I 'tell' him a lot of stories, turning pages, reading snippets, looking at illustrations. He asks the odd question. He nods. He smiles.

One step
at a time
we build
the strategies
that can
energize and
invigorate
our programs –
and entertain
ourselves
while we're
at it.

9

Librarians' Meetings

THE GIFT

We were discussing ten assigned reading titles, from the standpoint of Jean Karl's "A book that is alive clings to the reader and gives him a sense of belonging to it." *The Facts and Fictions of Minna Pratt*, by far was our favourite. We all loved Minna and the world Patricia Mac-Lachlan creates for her characters — a space in which we love and are loved. Then we did our 'assignment' — giving a favourite character from our reading list, the gift of a special book. *No one* gave Minna a gift! What, not even *Unclaimed Treasures*? or *Sarah Plan and Tall*? or *Journey*? I think I would offer Minna Margaret Mahy's *The Catalogue of the Universe*. Angela is Minna growing, maturing, realizing the flaws and strengths in those we love. Tycho is a brilliant, sensitive love interest for her, and his love of language a sophisticated extension of the word games she and her brother McGrew loved to indulge in.

To: Minna Pratt

because: beauty also resides in shortness, homeliness, and a prepared mind, intellect reposes in Big Science and the stars, and fun continues in word games – competing platitudes.

(You and Angela are kind enough to share the games with McGrew, and Tycho can teach him about the stars)

THE SHORT AND LONG OF IT...

The consensus at a recent meeting was that short story collections are hard to "sell" as recreational reading. I wonder why that should be, and what a pity if it is true. Thematic collections are, I'm told, an exception. Then why not use them as in the following:

Valentine's Day

Do we ever take the time to read an entire short story to a group?
For example, on Valentine's Day, take 15 to 25 minutes to visit a class to give them your valentine, a reading from an unusual love story, e.g.,

Wearing Glasses, in *Teen Angel and Other Stories of Young Love*.
Marianne Gingher.
or
Three O'Clock Midnight, in *Heartbeats*.
Peter D. Sieruta.
or
Do You Want My Opinion?
M.E. Kerr
in *Sixteen: Short Stories by Outstanding Writers for Young Adults*.
Ed. by Donald R. Gallo.
or
Avie Loves Ric Forever, in *Summer Girls, Love Boys*.
Norma Fox Mazer.
or
A Crush, in *A Couple of Kooks and Other Stories About Love*.
Cynthia Rylant.

More of the same

Do we connect an admired novelist with her/his short stories, e.g., Cynthia Rylant with her *A Couple of Kooks*? Jan Mark with her *Black and White*? Could we connect a short story character with a similar character in a novel? Shall we share a connection for the next meeting, and if we've had the opportunity to test it with a student, share the experience too?

Here are some starts.

From the Clashes section in *Connections,* ed. by Donald Gallo, the angry, disruptive youngster in *White Chocolate* by Robin Brancato. The resentful, tightlipped Mick in *Dodger,* by Libby Gleeson.

The chilling code of *Efflorescence* by Jan Mark. In her *Black and White.* A challenge to 13 year old Michael's brilliant mind in *The Gadget Factor,* by Sandy Landsman.

12 year old Johnny and elderly Jim, the derelicts and buddies of *The Best Side of Heaven,* by Martha Brooks in her *Paradise Cafe.* Homeless Clay and his mentors Calvin and Buddy sleeping on stone in *Monkey Island* by Paula Fox.

Jackie taking all the remedial classes who learns self-respect in *Walking,* by Peter D. Sieruta in his *Heartbeats.* Nick, who has minimal brain disfunction and reaches a kind of acceptance and hope in *Probably Still Nick Swanson,* by Virginia Euwer Wolff.

Tenderhearted Jane whose parents have taught her to be loving and kind in *The Egg-Man* by Janni Howker in her *Badger on the Barge* Peter who realizes after The Preacher betrays him, that while his parents' ideas about the world were different from his, he can always count on them in *A Fine White Dust,* by Cynthia Rylant.

Fat Liv, exploited and unhappy meets an elderly woman by whose example she realizes independence can be hers in *The Blast Furnace,* by Nadia Wheatley in *Landmarks* Jo, now a writer, journeys to her high school re-union and realizes "They turned out just right. They all became ... themselves" in *Where Have All the Tigers Gone?* by Lynn Hall.

Now who can I match up with Seth Slaughters, founder of SPAN (Society for People with Awful Names) and who wants to be a doctor, in the title story of *Misfits* edited by Peggy Woodford?

Can't. Don't. Won't.

"My students/teachers can't, don't, won't read."
"My students/teachers haven't got the time, interest, patience."
How depressingly familiar to our meetings these negatives are.

The solution? Develop action.

We tend to exchange lists of books at our meetings. They are meant to provide short cuts to building collections. But I think they are singularly uninformative, because they don't provide significant content or methodologies. Only we ourselves can do that. The ideas and methods I offer in this book, if worked on co-operatively over a period of time, could keep our librarians' meetings going over a three year period with creativity, energy, practical, inspirational strategies – the key to getting around the excuses mentioned on the previous page.

This habit-forming
procedure
keeps me on my
program toes,
trying to
remain aware,
sensitive,
relevant, active.
And it pays off
in times of stress,
deadlines
and the blah's.

10

Getting Started and Keeping Going

IDEA FILE

This is where I place the articles I clip, the headlines I notice, the brief notes I write to myself about a book, an idea, the nucleus of a conversation, an overheard snatch of comment, etc.

This is also where I place ideas and projects that can fit into a theme, approach, method I have used before.

Often I "talk" to myself in this file, posing "why" or "how" questions. Here they all simmer.

As time passes, I peruse the file, hoping for a spurt of creativity, a spark of energy, that will help me develop a book talk, a bulletin board display, a talking book mark.

This habit-forming procedure keeps me on my program toes, trying to remain aware, sensitive, relevant, active. And it pays off in times of stress, deadlines and the blah's.

Postcards from the edges

What kind of postcard, what sort of message, could be sent from out of the way places — the kind that aren't your typical tourist trap?

> From: Marten, Newfoundland.
> Dad, Here's a few lines from your old outport. Do you miss the sea in Alberta? I try to stay out of trouble. How about you? Well, you never knows.
> Chris.
> (*Far From Shore*. Kevin Major.)

> From: Newfound Creek, Tennessee.
> Dear Me at Berea College: Cement blocks. A river of squirrels. Sharecroppers. The good livers and the sorry. Grandma Smith. Grandpa Smith. Mom. Grandpa Wells. Grandma Wells. Dad. Prickly burrs on chinquapin bushes. Rebecca. Strip min-

ing. Hills toppling their heads to level earth. Forests sliding
out of the sky. Old-fashioned ways and modern ways. Mules
and missiles. I will be Somebody from Somewhere.
(*Newfound.* Jim Wayne Miller.)

From: Hill Road (local route), Reese Point, Tennessee.
    Dear Billy, This week on Wild Kingdom we visited the Conne-
    lys, a reclusive Pennsylvania tribe. Remember, you used to be
    part of us, when we were a family. Your Brother
                    Bobby Connely.
    (*My Brother Stealing Second.* Jim Naughton.)

Find some more isolated, rural communities. Check Paulsen, Rylant,
Branscum, Avi's *A Place Called Ugly.* Or as a variation, an isolated person or family, e.g., *The Solitary,* by Lynn Hall.

Find some places whose settings are arcane or mysterious so that you
can discuss their significance to events, e.g.,
    The Australian hills where the Balyet lures Jo into the mist.
        (*Balyet.* Patricia Wrightson.)
    The island that rises out of the night-gloom leading the broken
        boy and his father to share a Christmas with a family that has
        at long last been united.
        (*Solstice.* Jan Adkins.)
    The remote village of Wilkes Beach, population a few hundred,
        that doesn't pry into the sudden appearance of the strange
        boy and his mother.
        (*The Return.* Barry Faville.)

Now how about finding "a nice place to visit, but I wouldn't want to live
there," e.g.,
    "Monkey Island," the haven in the park for the homeless. "Calvin
        said there were different neighbourhoods among homeless
        people. He said that even in hell there must be different neigh-
        bourhoods." (*Monkey Island.* Paula Fox. p. 33.)
    "Duffy's Rocks", the Irish Catholic ghetto.
        (*Duffy's Rocks.* Edward Fenton.)

Quote of the Day

How long will it take me to build up a cache of these quotes? Can I get some students to volunteer to contribute? Maybe I should begin modestly and plan a month's display initially. Will my reading cards yield 20+ quotes?

> "We live in days, not weeks and months. Each day can be a year. We think... at the end of a day... how we made it. Again. Only because we found an old coat, only because some people don't bother to turn in their cans and bottles, only because somebody gives me change, somebody who doesn't care if I make a few dollars that way because such a somebody knows what a terrible life it is. Other people say, you *like* the pavement — you must be making hundreds of dollars a week! Maybe some of us do, but we have to lick the sidewalks for it."

(*Monkey Island*. Paula Fox. p. 73.)

> "If books could have more, give more, be more, show more, they would still need readers who bring to them sound and smell and light and all the rest that can't be in books. The book needs you."

(*The Winter Room*.
Gary Paulsen. p. 2)

How can I incorporate this ad into or after my t-shirt book talk?

(see page 102)

(This "Ad" is an adaptation of a waterfront festival promoting the city's arts and crafts community)

I want to celebrate the students' writing efforts, their artistic skills, their connecting to people and issues in the books. I want to celebrate the partnering activities of the English teacher, art teacher, and librarian.

Superheroes

There are assertiveness courses called The Effective Woman; advocacy associations, e.g., Action Committees, Status of Women; women running for the office of Vice-President, Prime Minister, Premier, Governor.

T-SHIRT FESTIVAL

Thursday, period 4, 5, 6
and after 3:15

A day devoted to the quintessential symbol of pop culture — the t-shirt!

■

Silk-screening, hand-painting and air-brushing samples

■

Created by members of 10C

■

Worn and displayed by their creators

■

Vote for your favourite.
Prizes awarded at 3:15
FREE ADMISSION   The Library

Are there collectible cards for superheroic, superachieving women?

Supergirl?

"I wish I could think of something to invent so I could be a heroine. But we've all ready got the light bulb and the sewing machine.
   Somebody beat me to the wheel. Do you think I should tie myself to a
   stake so I could be another Joan of Arc?"

(*Sweetly Sings the Donkey*, by Vera Cleaver. p. 11.)

Superwoman?

"'I want to be liked by men, not worshipped. Respected, not
   cherished. There is a madonna with a chipped nose in our front yard,
   and too many people think...' It was an eight-hundred-word essay on
   people's expectations and illusions about women, and the differences
   between deities and role models. Except for the Virgin Mary..., the
   names were changed to protect the innocent. But she wrote about
   Gloria Saccharellia and Rose, and herself and Marge Flynn and
   Lainie and Phyllis Dougherty and the women who watered the
   mayor's trees. It was an essay about disappointment and hope,
   about dreams of perfection and feelings of destruction. And she
   wrote about how this was true not just for East Boston or Catholics,
   but for every town and everyone. If they didn't have a chipped
   madonna, they would find one — metaphorically speaking, that is."

(*Prank*, by Kathryn Lasky. p. 160.)

Is there heroism in small acts too?
"But these were small prices to pay, she thought, for the daily
   growing of an aspect new to her character. She was beginning to admire herself.
The self that she admired was visible in the house, now bright
   and tidy and comfortable; in the neat green row of vegetables that
   were feeding her almost entirely now; in the four rust-red hens that
   she had bought with manure money and learned to care for from library books, and that were giving her scrambled-egg breakfasts, free.
   The admirable self was evident in the growing healthy rabbit herd
   and the growing figures in her checkbook, back up to six hundred
   again, with the jeep retread-shod and legalized and running.
With each solved problem, with each tiny advance in the quality
   of her life, Jane looked her inner self more squarely in the eye and
   smiled in recognition.
'I may not be gorgeous, but by God I can take care of myself.'"

(*The Solitary*, by Lynn Hall. p. 52.)

So – I could gather the accomplishments for each character, e.g.,

12 year old Amanda cradles a baby that gets heavier than a
   house, finishes the wash the boys get behind on, makes the
   meals, leaves school, misses church, "uses it up, wears it out,
   makes it do," and "gets her motherhood early."
   (*Borrowed children*. George Ella Lyon.)

Nancy Antoine lights into English teacher, overwhelms Principal,

convinces Board of Education to provide issues courses at an all-native school.
(*Where the Rivers Meet*. Don Sawyer.)

Rose Olshansky arrived in America at age 10, served as a piece worker for 12 hours a day at the Griffin Cap factory, learned about the possibility of night school, heard stirrings from union organizers, discovered the importance of music, married at 14, made some life and death changes, left for a new life at age 16.
(*One Way to Ansonia*. Judie Angell.)

Shabanu breaks the chains of servitude and emotional bondage, denies traditional obligations, pains her family, frees her spirit.
(*Shabanu: Daughter of the Wind*. Suzanne Fisher Staples.)

Get some cards to put "heroisms" on, e.g., the class could make their own cards for books I've selected for them – or reading of their own choice. Good possibility for a bulletin board for International Women's Day, too.

For starters:

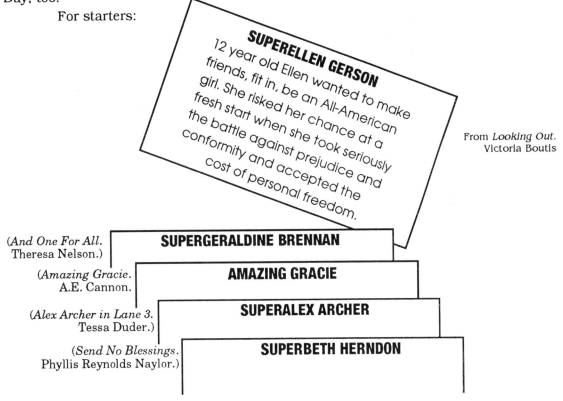

SUPERELLEN GERSON
12 year old Ellen wanted to make friends, fit in, be an All-American girl. She risked her chance at a fresh start when she took seriously the battle against prejudice and conformity and accepted the cost of personal freedom.

From *Looking Out*. Victoria Boutis

SUPERGERALDINE BRENNAN
(*And One For All*. Theresa Nelson.)

AMAZING GRACIE
(*Amazing Gracie*. A.E. Cannon.)

SUPERALEX ARCHER
(*Alex Archer in Lane 3*. Tessa Duder.)

SUPERBETH HERNDON
(*Send No Blessings*. Phyllis Reynolds Naylor.)

Bearing gifts

I am reading Mitzi Dale's *Round the Bend*, and as much as I laugh at Deirdre's ironic wit, I am moved by her hurt and anger. There is an echo here for me. What is it?

It's not another novel.... It's poetry! And I remember *Stories I Ain't Told Nobody Yet*, by Jo Carson. (*Quick, before I forget. Write it down on my Round the Bend reading card.*) Get this down from the shelf ... Check. Yes, on pages 28 and 53*. Add this information to my reading card. If I'm at a comfortable place in the novel, I can write out my "poetry gift" for Deirdre immediately, otherwise I can wait until I'm finished. Then I place my "gift" in my Idea File. Its time will come.

For Deirdre of *Round the Bend: Stories I Ain't Told Nobody Yet.*
>   Because it's maddening to be misunderstood and worse still, "understood", here are two angry people who have the *right* to be.
>   (See pages 28 and 53 and I hope you go on from there.)

* In the section under Observations (page 28) a mountain person objects to stereotypes about her people:
>   "Well, let me tell you:
>   I am from here,
>   I'm not like that
>   and I am damned tired of being told I am."

In the section under Work (page 53) a poor woman bitterly rebuts the accusation about choosing one lifestyle over another:
>   "I get to choose
>   the work I'm goin' to do.
>   Whose john I'm gonna wash which day of the week."

Dedications

When I finish reading a book and don't spend a few moments thinking who else might enjoy it, how I might use it, I know that
>   "To know and not to act is not to know."

So I "dedicate" Michael Bedard's *Redwork* to R., sallow-faced, blank-eyed, listless, who knows a lot about growing up but lives such an emotionally impoverished life she knows nothing about growth. Here is a heart-stopping possibility for her. I will watch and wait for the right moment to give it to her.

I Know That...

Could a book report take the form of a statement(s) telling what, after you have finished reading the book, you know? You can be serious, thankful, funny, appreciative, disagreeable, etc.   Some examples:

>   I KNOW THAT: Somewhere there is a frog whose kiss will turn me
>   green and croaking with happiness.
>   (*Taking the Ferry Home*. Pam Conrad.)
>   I KNOW THAT: pigs might fly
>   there's a unicorn in the garden
>   And it never pigs but it pours.
>   (*Pigs Might Fly*. Emily Rodda.)
>   I KNOW THAT:
>   You can eat spaghetti by rolling the fork vigorously, whirling
>   the spaghetti tightly in place, although it can end up in an
>   enormous wad like a ball of knitting and
>   sucking on it can cause the skeins to flick from side to side
>   splattering red spots in all directions.
>   (*Downhill All the Way*. K.M. Peyton.)

Cliches, stereotypes and plain good sense

Is this a natural theme for that know-it-all class?

>   "What does she see in her/him?"
>   *The Carnival in My Mind*. Barbara Wersba.
>   *Him* *She Loves?* M.E. Kerr.
>   "Such a pretty face"
>   *Fat: a Love Story*. Barbara Wersba.
>   "You're young. You'll get over it"
>   *Say Goodnight, Gracie*. Julie Reece Deaver.
>   *Sex Education*. Jenny Davis.
>   "Your time will come"
>   *Down By The River*. C.S. Adler.

Now what can I find for:

>   "You'll understand when you're older"?
>   "He's not our kind of person"?

3 minute book talk

Remember the hilarious passage near the end when Celine is mistaken for the psychiatrist's patient and pours out her bizarre story? (p. 194-

97) I'll have to practice, so that I can read Celine's outpouring at a rush culminating with "And then the wave breaks and great quantities of salty tears are pouring out of my eyes and nose and down my throat. No, this is too much for simple tears. I think my brain must have dissolved."

(*Celine* . Brock Cole.)

Specialty bookmarks

In the reaction of the moment to your reading, pour out your enthusiasm about the book in a few words on a book mark and place it in a container of other specialty bookmarks at the circulation desk. You could try a display of them as well, e.g., place the bookmark inside the book so that your comment shows and then place the books upright, at various heights in your display area, on a coffee table, in the staff lounge, senior common room if you have one, etc.

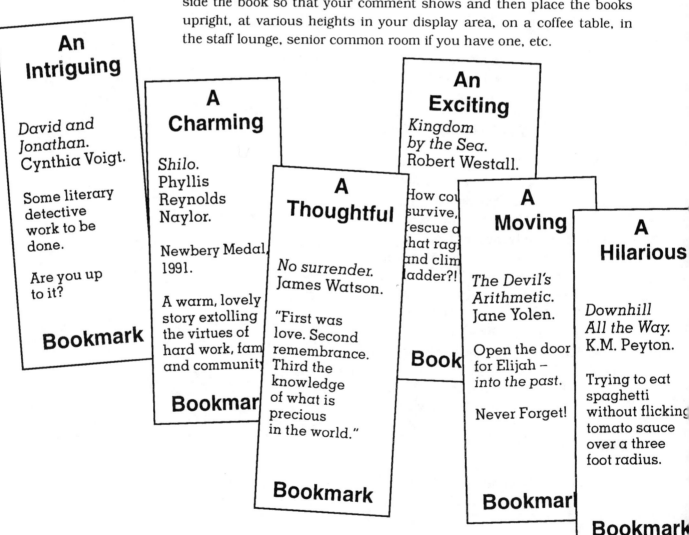

An Intriguing

David and Jonathan. Cynthia Voigt.

Some literary detective work to be done.

Are you up to it?

Bookmark

A Charming

Shilo. Phyllis Reynolds Naylor.

Newbery Medal, 1991.

A warm, lovely story extolling the virtues of hard work, fam and communit

Bookmar

A Thoughtful

No surrender. James Watson.

"First was love. Second remembrance. Third the knowledge of what is precious in the world."

Bookmark

An Exciting

Kingdom by the Sea. Robert Westall.

How cou urvive, escue that rag and clim adder?!

Book

A Moving

The Devil's Arithmetic. Jane Yolen.

Open the door for Elijah – into the past.

Never Forget!

Bookmar

A Hilarious

Downhill All the Way. K.M. Peyton.

Trying to eat spaghetti without flicking tomato sauce over a three foot radius.

Bookmark

Parachuting...

Gilly Hopkins (Katherine Paterson's *The Great Gilly Hopkins)* into Barbara Corcoran's *The Potato Kid.* How would she and Lilac deal with each other?

The fridge door

You can tell a lot about a family from what is on the fridge door: kid's drawings, magnets, messages, notes. So what kind of family do we have here?

A large piece of white cardboard with varying sizes of post-its will suffice in most cases. But other things can be included. Maybe lead in with some examples from family cartoons, e.g., *For Better or For Worse, Family Circus, Sally Forth.* Or a large note:

> Dear Mum,
>   Here's the week's schedule. Mon: football practice,
>   Tues: swimming, cycling, Wed: cycling, f.b. practice,
>   Thurs: f.b. practice, Fri: football game, swimming,
>   Sat: swim meet, cricket match. I'll try to fit in some meals!
>   Love, Lloyd.
> (*Man in Motion.* Jan Mark.)

A slogan done in the shape of a magnet:

Good food equals good grammar

The students should notice the elaborate script and characterize the sentiment as 'picky', 'choosy', 'fussy' which will give me a chance to describe Elliott's fastidiousness, the kitchen complete with blender, copper pans, and a black and white decor. Win was hoping to get a Big Brother like his friend Paul — he and Paul go bowling, see ball games, horror movies, eat enchiladas and tamales, have soda and ice cream and other normal food.

> "But I got matched up with a man who didn't own a TV, made mayonnaise and lived in a museum."

Why would Elliott want to be an Amigo?

> "'Because I believe the future of America is in the hands of its youth. I'm worried about the way this country is going. I want to

have a hand in shaping that future.' I wasn't sure how I felt about being shaped for the future of America. It would have been better, I thought, if Elliott said he just liked kids."

(*Elliott and Win.* Carolyn Meyer. p. 9, 17.)

The past...

"Connecting to the past helps us to survive. This is a very important argument, a "roots" argument, for reading literature from the past." *Read For Your Life.* Joseph Gold p.199.

When I grew up

'When I grow up, I want to be
A grown-up who remembers me.'
From *Fathers, Mothers, Sisters, Brothers: a collection of family poems.* Poems by Mary Ann Hoberman. Illustrations by Marilyn Hafner. p. 27.

Could I, we, imagine what a young person in a book would remember most vividly from her past childhood? when grown to adulthood?

When I was a little boy my grandmother stole my heart completely and utterly with a glass of milk and a piece of apple pie with sugar and 'simmanon' on top and ever since I have wished that all good things could go on forever and ever.

(*The Cookcamp.* Gary Paulsen.)

When I was a little boy, I went to a 2 room school and in the "senior room" we were divided into several classes ages 8 to 13 years. We were supposed to different work so our teacher was very, very busy — but he said he liked the excitement. Perhaps the excitement arose from the pleasure of seeing us grow up unaffected by the demands of our own age group. I think they call this peer pressure now. We talked and behaved not as our friends did, but as our personalities demanded.

(*The Return.* Barry Faville)

When I was a little boy, the worst thing you can imagine happened: my Mama packed her suitcase and left us. Then my grandfather started a new hobby, taking family photographs, and slowly I began to recognize that in his wisdom and love he was giving me a sense of family.

(*Journey.* Patricia MacLachlan)

When I was a little girl, my grandmother was an artist at making quilts but I hated sewing. When she had a stroke, I struggled to complete a

quilt she had been making for the coming baby, "a knowledge passed on." And wrapped in my grandmother's love, that is just what I did.
(*The Canada Geese Quilt.* Natalie Kinsey-Warnock)

What other novels spring to mind as a good source?

> *My Daniel.* Pam Conrad
> *On My Honour.* Mary Dane Bauer
> *One-Eyed Cat.* Paula Fox

More...

Try to tie your new books to popular titles and concerns with the following on a bulletin board, bookmark or even PA announcement:

Athletic Shorts. Chris Crutcher.

> Because you've loved Chris Crutcher's sports novels, you'll welcome these short stories in which familiar characters from *Stotan, The Crazy Horse Electric Game, Running Loose,* etc. make their appearances.

Missing May. Cynthia Rylant.

> If you shed tears over *Bridge to Terabithia*, you'll understand Summer's reconciliation with loss.

Nightjohn. Gary Paulsen.

> Because your heart has remembered *Roots* by Alex Haley, you'll find room for this beautiful, uncompromising story of slavery.

Diana: My Autobiography. Kevin Major.

> If you enjoyed *Eating Between the Lines*' twist on the classics, you'll appreciate this take-off on the other Diana's (Princess, that is) biography.

Thicker Than Water. Penelope Farmer.

Yaxley's Cat. Robert Westall.

> Tired of Pike's formula horror fiction?

The Silver Kiss. Annette Klause.

> Ready for a "different love story? He's a vampire.

Witch Baby. Francesca Lia Block.

Cherokee Bat and the Goat Guys. Francesca Lia Block.

> O joy!! Is it possible that *Weetsie Bat* has <u>two</u> marvellous sequels?

Hero of Lesser Causes. Julie Johnston.

> When was the last time you had a good cry – and laugh?

Notice of meeting

This notice can go up on other bulletin boards in the school, wherever students habitually stop to look at announcements. The source for the answers is the wealth of material in your library about the television programme, *Star Trek: the Next Generation.* Do you have other reading obsessions that could be celebrated in a similar manner?

CHALLENGE TO NEXT GENERATION TREKKIES
In the Library today during the lunch hour(s)
TEST YOUR STAR TREK TRIVIA KNOWLEDGE!
Find out
The name of the ritual suicide Worf asked Riker to help him perform.
Who killed Tasha Yar?
If 'jIQong' is 'I sleep' in Klingon, what is 'you sleep'?
How do you say 'I don't understand' in Klingon?
PRIZES!

(We used *The Klingon Dictionary* and an issue of *Star Trek: the Next Generation* magazine for this notice.)

Games people play

Envisage life as a large gameboard in which Someone or Something manipulates us. As in

    Interstellar Pig, by William Sleator,
    Homeward Bounders, by Diana Wynne Jones,
    The Vandal, by Ann Schlee.

We're Proud...

Readers of the original edition of *Invitations, Celebrations* will realize that I used a variation on the following text in a brochure to promote the library and its value. You could support the brochure with a bulletin board using the principal headings or you could use the individual segments successfully in a series of bookmarks that get added to as time and inspiration permit.

We're PROUD of our library because...

●   *we are not afraid to take on the difficult questions*
    So we have the *Irish Trilogy* by Catherine Sefton who

bravely tries to provide balanced answers to the confusing,
bitter questions of Northern Ireland today:

> *Starry Night*
> *Frankie's Story*
> *The Beat of the Drum*

● *we know a good author when we read one*

So we have the works of Patricia MacLachlan (including
some in our Baby Sitters' Corner*):

> *Arthur For the Very First Time**
> *Cassie Binegar*
> *The Facts and Fictions of Minna Pratt*
> *Mama One, Mama Two**
> *Sarah, Plain and Tall*
> *Journey*
> *Seven Kisses In A Row**
> *Three Names**
> *Unclaimed Treasures*

● *we acknowledge your right to emotion*

"Dear Mum,
I'm going because you've failed me — that's all there is to it. This
pregnancy isn't my fault, it was a hideous accident, and most of
all I needed sympathy, but how quickly you ran out of that!
That's very odd because usually you overflow with it, all the unknown deprived and disadvantaged can count on you. But of
course you're such an intense person, you have all these feelings
and emotions, you overreact, you always have. And somewhere
you feel that I've let you down.

The sad thing is that I've never asked you for anything before —
not anything important. I'm sure if anybody had put my case to
you in theory, you'd have been confident that you'd know what
to do and how to be.

So I'm leaving because I have no alternative. I ought to say, and
this is the truth, that I don't blame you. I don't blame myself either. We are totally and utterly incompatible.

(*This Is Me Speaking*. Josephine Poole.)

● *we recognize your right to be challenged*

So we have *Dance On My Grave,* by Aidan Chambers. *Oranges Are Not the Only Fruit,* by Jeannette Winterson. *The Lives
of the Saints,* by Nino Ricci. *Possession,* by A.S. Byatt.
Progress of Love, by Alice Munro.

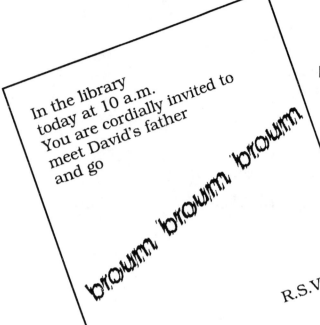

In the library today at 10 a.m. You are cordially invited to meet David's father and go

'broum 'broum 'broum.

R.S.V.P.

From the "Babysitter's Corner"

From the Baby Sitters' Corner collection, send invitations to an ESL group. I'll have fun practicing the reading. I think I'll chose a fairly private corner of the library, and let go. I need to feel comfortable speaking as loudly as David's father.

David's Father, by Robert Munsch.

Or, why not decorate the Princess's paperbag dress, the library providing coloured pencils and felt pens?

Do I need to alert the ESL teacher before hand so that she can help her class "de-code" the invitation? And make sure that they perceive these children's books as something for baby sitters and older siblings to use. I don't want to appear to be patronizing them.

Could I start off a senior class's unit on children's literature introducing them to Kid Lit in this way?

The Paperbag Princess. Robert Munsch.

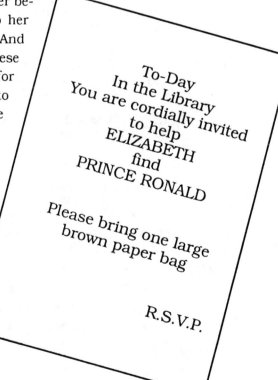

To-Day In the Library You are cordially invited to help ELIZABETH find PRINCE RONALD

Please bring one large brown paper bag

R.S.V.P.

Eating

If life were a [food], how would the character eat it?

> If life were an ice-cream cone, would Arden who desperately
> wants to hold on to the past, lick carefully and evenly,
> shaping it, slowly savouring it until the last bit leaked out the
> bottom of the cone?
> (*A Place Between.* Suzanne Newton.)

> If life were Eggs Benedict, would Lilac know what it was?
> (*The Potato Kid.* Barbara Corcoran.)

> Would Frankie nibble cautiously at an iced cupcake, and would
> he order something different after Pepper gets through with
> him, e.g., Mud Pie or a Dairy Queen Blizzard?
> (*Gleanings.* Lou Willett Stanek.)

> If life were a meringue, would Hoomey attack it so that it shot off
> the plate?
> (*Downhill All the Way*, by K.M. Peyton.)

Color me

In *Monkey Island*, by Paul Fox, Clay's mother, pregnant, deserted, increasingly remote in her misfortune describes the painted chair in
their miserable hotel room as "down-and-out" brown. Would certain
personalities wear or own items of a character-revealing hue? I think...

> Weetsie Bat of Francesca Block's *Weetsie Bat* would wear
> "electric" blue or "shocking" pink.

> Alcoholic teen-ager Buddy in Robert Cormier's *We All Fall Down*
> would drink "inviting" amber scotch.

> Bullet in Cynthia Voigt's *The Runner* would wear "mordant" black.

Would this be a challenging exercise for a confident academic group?

The Assembly Programme

"Young women long to feel more valued by society and crave a greater
role in shaping the world around them, a new national study reveals."
Newspaper article about report on adolescent women: *We're Here, Listen to Us!: A Survey of Young Women* in Canada, published by the Canadian Advisory Council on the Status of Women. The survey probed
issues of self-perception, relationships with family, friends and school,
health, sexuality and politics. 42% of the respondents chose politicians

when asked whom they wanted to have visit their school. 26% chose a person who had a particular social experience or represented a social or political group.

ASSEMBLY PROGRAM
Week of April 23

MONDAY

Pride of the Peacock, by Stephanie Tolan.

    Speaker: **Whitney Whitehurst**, Committee for Nuclear Responsibility.

    Topic: "Better to Light a Candle Then Curse the Darkness."

TUESDAY

I Am the Universe, by Barbara Corcoran.

    Speaker: **Katharine**, daughter, sister, friend.

    Topic: "Women's Role — Baker of Bread/Writer of Stories."

WEDNESDAY

Looking Out, by Victoria Boutis.

    Speaker: **Ellen Gerson**, political activist.

    Topic: "The Legacy of the McCarthy Years."

THURSDAY

Where the Rivers Meet, by Don Sawyer.

    Speaker: **Nancy Antoine**, Sicamous.

    Topic: "Native Education, The Old Ways Today."

FRIDAY

The Visit, by T. Degens.

    Speaker: **Kate**, daughter of history.

    Topic: "The Shadow of Nazism Today."

So can we choose some "speakers" for a week of library assemblies? In the box is a possible selection for a week on women.

Can I reward the inveterate readers I have come to know in the library (some of them may come as a surprise to their teachers) by having them take on the roles of speakers for our library's noon hour program? What an honouring of their accomplishments this could be!

The voice-over

Noise level in lunch hours makes it virtually impossible to do any teaching. Appeals, threats, even an idiosyncratic whistle don't seem to work. How about a voice-over such as in department stores and supermarkets?

Arrange with the main office to pipe announcements into the library only. Guess I'd better test the sound level beforehand. I want to cut through the clamor and/or the steady hum that greets most announcements. Now whose voice shall I use? (Not staff, I think.)

"Good afternoon shoppers. Today's specials are:

    The _____ issue of *Sports Illustrated* with a feature

    article on _____, available on the

    coffee table in the lounge area. *Man in Motion*, by Jan Mark,

which best describes Lloyd's incredible round of athletic after
school activities, and *Stotan*, by Chris Crutcher, a week-long
endurance training for the school swim team, both available
at the Check-Out desk.

Watch for the signs in the 700s too."

An invitation to the staff

TO: Staff
FROM: The librarian

Do you have a "beautiful book" at home? Would you be interested
in putting it in the library display case with your reason for val-
uing it?

— This was my son's first book — it's pretty dog-eared
   because he carried it everywhere and even took it to bed
   with him.
— My wife's first gift to me. Bought it in an old bookshop in
   Paris for 50¢ — it's now out of print.
— Family Bible since 1867.
— Best translation.
— The first book I ever cried over.
— My favourite childhood adventure.
— The first book I ever finished reading.

(This response from the staff was amazing. Over a period of time we
added a display on staff awards and medals (we had an Olympic
bronze medalist), one on crafts (we called it Our Crafty Teachers) and
another on collectibles.

The student response was unbelievable — always a crowd "reading"
the display, always a fascination with this other side of a teacher's life.)

A ghostly book talk

Can you become a ghost, take a tuck in time and prevent a death so that
   another ghostly girl can die an old woman?
   (*Stonewords*. Pam Conrad)
Could you realize you're a ghost, but not know who you're the ghost of?
   (*The Time of the Ghost*. Diana Wynne Jones)
Is is possible for a ghost to leave threatening notes?
   (*The Ghost of Thomas Kempe*. Penelope Lively)

Can a house ghost own *you*?
  (*Ghost Abbey*. Robert Westall)

Reading cards

I continue to keep track of my reading on cards; I should say, meaningful reading intended for use in book talks. Thus, I make no attempt to keep a record of light reads, entertaining though they may be. And on rare occasions, I am so overwhelmed by the emotional impact of a book that I simply – read – and often go back to make notes later (as I did with *Sarah, Plain and Tall*). For the most part, I read, jotting down as I go <u>brief</u> plot developments, significant values, emotions, characterizations, outstanding passages. And always with page numbers, so that at a later time, the illustrative material for the book-talk is at hand. Potential uses for curriculum, themes, activities and related titles are noted as well. You will notice that I file my cards under title. You may consider an activity file or subject or theme file more useful.

The Potato Kid. Barbara Corcoran. Atheneum, 1989.

10 yr old Lilac arrives to spend summer with family of 14 yr old Ellis. From poor potato country of northern Maine. Fearful, angry, suspicious. Tries to run away, p35. But resolved not to return to large, poor family & mother who is to marry for third time. "I'm going to amount to something," p44. The outfit she buys! p49. Doesn't know escalators, credit cards, showers, pizzas, how to ride a bike or swim. Uses credit card to get them all presents – a real con artist, p75. Fear of horses – but loves E.'s grandmother's farm. E. realizes she is jealous of L. & L. of her. Writes L. apologetic letter, p154. Breaks leg jumping horse. L. shares her coveted suitcase at last, p165, mementos of past, most of her dead father whom she'd lost at 6. And grandparents will keep L.
  Loving supportive family
  Lilac is distant cousin of Gilly Hopkins
  Gr 5 - 8

Use for:
Summons or This child,
Ann Landers,
Invitation for rebels

Teachers are open
to the unique
perspectives that fiction
can bring to
their subjects.
What is needed
is the *opportunity*
to discuss
that perspective
and the *expertise*
to present
that perspective
in a meaningful and
stimulating manner.

11

Getting Together. Getting It All Together.

PARTNERING WITH TEACHERS

The past ten years since *Invitations, Celebrations* first appeared have made me more convinced than ever that teachers are open to the unique perspectives that fiction can bring to their subjects. What is needed is the *opportunity* to discuss that perspective and the *expertise* to present that perspective in a meaningful and stimulating manner.

I have discovered that contrary to popular misconception, *all* subjects have fictional possibilities, and if I *share* my conviction with the subject teacher, by reading a brief illustrative paragraph, showing an illustration, examining a postscript, a footnote, posing a "what-if" possibility, initiating a book-talk, I will be partnering the subject teacher in a significant educational enterprise.

Furthermore, I will have done my share of the homework — I will be familiar with the fiction, trying not to offer a load of books or a booklist in lieu of an enthusiastic familiarity with the material and a methodology for presenting it.

I hope some of the experiences that follow will make clear some possibilities.

GETTING IT ALL TOGETHER.

MATHEMATICS:
A Grade 9 Language Arts activity.

Paperback title:
Forever Friends.

I was reading *Breadsticks and Blessing Places* by Candy Dawson Boyd and came upon the following passage (p. 165 ff.):

"Mrs. Swallow was absent the next morning. When she returned in the afternoon, she called the bottom math group together.

"This morning I attended the last in a series of five special math workshops. I have something wonderful to teach you!' she said, laying out blank sheets of paper and crayons.

Toni rolled her eyes to the ceiling. *Another one of Mrs. Swallow's baby games! I'm not going to play this time.*

Despite her lack of enthusiasm, Toni went along with the lesson. Mrs. Swallow had learned a new way to teach them how to understand math word problems. Toni reread the steps on the ditto sheet before her. Read the problem three times and underline the math words. Circle the numbers and draw a box around what the problem asks you to do. Then state the problem in your own words. Ask yourself, what do they want to know?

Toni laughed at the next step. Draw a picture of the problem. Then set up the problem and estimate the answer. Check the answers on the test to see if one is close to your estimate. Finally solve the problem and ask yourself, "Does this answer make sense?" If your answer makes sense, compare it to your estimate. Pick the response on the test that is closest.

Toni shook her head. Wow! *By the time I'm through doing all this, the test will be over!*

"Okay, what's the answer to number one? Write your answer on your personal chalkboard right under your estimate."

The six children in the group did that. Unconvinced, Toni followed their lead. She looked around the group. Her answer agreed with that of two others.

"Toni, Joseph, and Latwanda, you are correct! Now, the rest of you, that was a good try. This is a hard problem. Let's see where you got off the track."

Startled, Toni reexamined her answer. She was right! And she understood the problem. She listened as the teacher went over the responses of the kids who had failed to get the correct answer. Best of all, she understood where they had gotten confused."

My memory went back to my own miserable days in the bottom math group, when I could have responded to such an explanation, I'm sure. I sought out a friend in the math department.

"Don, can I just show you this page and a half and ask you your opinion of the methodology?"

GETTING IT ALL TOGETHER.

He looked at the source, bemused, but read the passage and responded, "I start by telling the student to read what the problem asks you to do. That will clarify the task."

"Then I'm reading sentences first and foremost??!!"

"Yes," he answered, "it's a language arts activity." I was stunned as he went on to say. "A math problem is more like a poem than a math fact, 8 x 7. It's really a language arts activity. As a matter of fact, I'm giving a workshop in a few days, entitled Math as a Second Language."

"Does this apply to high school math as well?"

"Oh yes" he answered, "In grade nine we do word problems."

Word problems — Why did I suddenly think of Cynthia Voigt's *Homecoming?* "You know", I said, "there's a story about four kids, ages 6 to 13 who are abandoned in a parking lot in Provincetown, Massachusetts with $11.50 to their names. The eldest, Dicey, decides to gather her siblings and make their way to their grandmother's home on the shores of Chesapeake Bay.

Is there a math problem in there somewhere?" And we talked about an assignment in which the librarian would gather books with "mathematical possibilities," the student would read the novel and write up a math problem for it.

It occurred to me while we were talking that an English teacher could see the possibility of accepting the math problem as a book report and the student would get a double credit. (What if I found more novels about journeys and the geography teacher gave credit for a mapping of the journey and the math teacher gave credit for working out a problem of logistics for that journey, and the English teacher gave a book report credit. What if the art teacher...) But for now... Here are some of the titles I gathered:

> *Morelli's Game.* Patricia Gauch.
> > The English teacher sends two teams on a 200 mile bicycle trip with just a map and $5.00 — and tells them to look out for dragons.

> *One Proud Summer.* Marsha Hewitt and Claire Mackay.
> > Would you see the need for a union if you were a thirteen year

GETTING IT ALL TOGETHER.

old millworker, had your pay docked for mistakes, making washroom visits and taking half-hour lunches?

Singin' Somebody Else's Song. Mary Blount Christian.

"It's a heartbreak away from Texas to Nashville, Tennessee; It's a short way if you are travelin' by car. But it's a long way if you are travelin' by guitar"

Secret City, U.S.A. Felice Holman.

Wandering the wasteland of the city streets Benno comes upon a space that he is sure he can turn into a haven for the homeless.

Pickle and Price. Pieter Van Raven.

They are unlikely companions for a cross country adventure that begins the day Price is released from prison and Pickle decides to run away from home.

Flight of the White Wolf. Mel Ellis.

Russ knew the wolf was not a killer, but if he couldn't get Gray north into the wilderness, the wolf would be shot. Together boy and wolf meet the test of courage and trust.

POETRY:
A response to my 'rebels'.

I always enjoy my "rebel book talks" (see Still Inviting p. 4) and like to follow up at least one of them with a poetry book talk, especially when the teacher is willing to give a further credit for an appropriate poem or portion thereof. Here is what happened on one such occasion when the class accompanied by their teacher returned to the library three weeks after first meeting the rebels.

Librarian: I've just found something to give your rebels. It's also called "The Rebel":

> When I
> die
> I'm sure
> I will have a
> Big Funeral
>
> Curiosity
> seekers
>
> coming to see
> if I
> am really
> Dead
> or just
> trying to make
> Trouble

by Mari E. Evans.
Reproduced from
*Sounds and Silences:
Poetry for Now*,
edited by Richard Peck.

Does this seem appropriate for your book's hero or heroine?

Students: (Some discussion, reasons were given. Students also seemed to enjoy the selection for itself: two people argued hotly as to their characters' "rights" to the poem.)

Teacher (summing up):   Most of you consider the poem a good match for the book's main character, and you've given reasons – "in character", a release, a validation, an acknowledgement, an unexpressed (till now) feeling, etc. Let's see if you can find some more "matching poetry."

Choose any character from your book, major or minor,

GETTING IT ALL TOGETHER.

young or old. Then give that person a poem that seems just right for him or her. Ms. Librarian has started us off with a few anthologies here on the cart, and is ready to point out some more poetry on the shelves. We will spend two more days in here, browsing and selecting. When you have your poem, write it out, and then add a few sentences explaining your choice. This is due on Friday when we will start to read each others choices. Any questions?

Students: Does it have to be a whole poem? (no)
Does it have to be from this library? (no)
Can we bring some from home? (you bet!)
Can we select more than one? (why not!!)
Can we write our own? (!!!)
Then we're almost ready to begin. Ms. L.?

Librarian: I'd like to invite you back on Friday, to read your choices in this corner of the library — and — can I select a poem too?
(I'll be ready with *Charlie Wallinsky* in Mel Glenn's *Class Dismissed.*)

I watched the students browsing through the poetry sections, scanning the pages, mesmerized as they read standing at the shelves, strolling to the circulation desk, hunkering at the lowest shelves, perching on window ledges. They were intense, absorbed, private. They realized the emotional connections poetry makes to themselves and to others.

The quality of the poems selected amazed me. Much thought had gone into the selections. Most students chose more than one poem, and were willing to read entire pages and expound at length about their reason for selecting their favourites. There is always at least one poet-in-the-making, too. How well I remember the girl who wrote eleven poems!

I noticed the students' fascination with the Mel Glenn collections. (*Class Dismissed! Class Dismissed II; Back to Class and My Friend's Got This Problem, Mr. Candler.*) The photo-illustrations, page layouts and large print are all inviting, a perfect support for the poems about

GETTING IT ALL TOGETHER.

the lives and feelings of these present-day high school students. The teacher and I agreed that the staff must read these poems too.

And I like the poem-kids so much I wanted to give each of them a gift of a book. Do you think the real kids would too? Would someone give Penny Arkanian (page 85, *My Friend's Got This Problem, Mr. Candler) My Name is Sus5an Smith. The 5 Is Silent?* Penny needs to be reassured: trusting and loving inappropriately happens. It hurts. It'll get better before too long.

I'm delighted that the teacher usually gathered a batch of her own favourites (as did I, I confess) and told her colleagues in the English department about "our assignment". The idea usually spread to other teachers.

GETTING IT ALL TOGETHER.

GUIDANCE:
Sexual awareness. Why should we care?

"Dear C,

I came upon my clipping of Robert Unsworth's article "Holden Caulfield, Where Are You?" (*School Library Journal,* January 1977) in which he noted major omissions in male adolescent literature. Attached to the clipping was my old annotated male and female book list (*Invitations, Celebrations,* p. 136). I mused over developments in adolescent issues since that year: children having children, AIDS, cuts to social services, and that curse of the 90's — instant gratification. Where is the perspective of respect — self and others — and responsibility? I believe it is there — in young people. I couldn't help starting a new list, and as I worked on it, a theme suggested itself.

WHY SHOULD I CARE?

NIK. Aidan Chambers.

> "She makes me think. And she likes a good argument. And she doesn't deny that sex is something to be enjoyed. But for her... having sex was such an important part of *her,* of her self, that she couldn't treat it as if she was just having an enjoyable meal with a friend." (p. 154)

Up in Seth's Room. Norma Fox Mazer.

> "You humored me. You pretended to believe me. 'Sure, Finn, sure, if that's the way you feel, that's okay with me. We won't do anything you don't want to do.' Then you went ahead anyway and tried to do everything you wanted!"
> "Well, I thought you were just saying that." He dug his hands into his pockets.
> "No, I don't understand you. Why would I just say it?"
> "Girls do —"
> "No, " she said. "No. Why do you say such a terrible thing? I never faked you out. Whatever I felt, I told you. If you loved me, you wouldn't think I was a liar."
> "I don't!" he said. "I don't think you're a liar. Where'd you get that idea?"
> She stared at him. It seemed so obvious to her. "From you," she said. (p. 182)

After the Rain. Norma Fox Mazer.

> Helena wanted Rachel to wear makeup, smile more, not to show her brains quite so obviously.
> "I don't like makeup. I smile enough. What can I do about my brains?" Rachel said. She was stubborn.
> "You could flirt a little, it won't kill you."
> "You mean, act dumb for a boy? Helena, that's depressing."

GETTING IT ALL TOGETHER.

"Why? You know you're smart, that's what matters. Flirting just
   makes boys feel better."
"What's the matter with them? Why do they have to feel better by
   my pretending I'm dumber than they are?"
"It's just one of those things, Rachel."
"No. Forget it."
"Do you have to get that look on your face?"
"What look?"
"That look. The Look!" (p. 21)

Rabbit Back and Doubled. Allan Frewin Jones.

Increasingly less inclined to run with the pack, suspecting their
attitude to girls is immature and sexist, Tony is attracted to
Rachel, aware that in this relationship tact and maturity are
required.

Ghosts. Ursula Perrin.

He was decidedly the wrong sort of person for her. But what he
gave her was the realization that having once loved, even selfishly,
she might ultimately love generously.

*(At this point, I realized the list was getting too long for inclusion in one
letter. So although I continued to work at the list, these titles were as
much as I sent at this point.)*

I have over a dozen titles in addition to these ready and can show
you the rest of the list if you decide you're interested.

It's taken me a few days of checking my reading cards, the shelves,
my memory, and writing. But it's been a feel-good experience as I realized how much I liked the decent kids in these stories and how readily faces of students who would respond with gratitude, relief, surprise,
pride, joy rose before me. A lot happened to me as I read and re-read
— a lot will happen to our students too.

Please pardon the length of this letter, (I hope you've read this far!)
but I've been wondering how to get these books to the kids. Do I trust
to a serendipitous occasion? Do I give a book talk? to whom? and in
what context? Do you and your colleagues in the Guidance Department have any thoughts? Some years ago the guidance, physical
education, English Department and I got together to develop a reading
programme for a group of "problem" kids. Is it time for another programme?

Your patience and consideration please.

F.

P.S.: I just realized I haven't made separate female and male lists as I'd
   done before. So I've learned something!

GETTING IT ALL TOGETHER.

The list continues:

Cloudy Bright. John Rowe Townsend.

They started as friendly adversaries, arguing about money, class, and the equality or otherwise of the sexes, and their sometime differing views on photography — that told a lot about them as people — and as a couple.

Marcia. John Steptoe.

She's only fourteen, and so is Danny — but that doesn't mean they aren't aware of their sexuality and their needs. Listen to Marcia stake claim on her womanhood.

Running Loose. Chris Crutcher.

"I guess I'm sort of a wussy....I spend about half my life worrying about hurting other people's feelings and wondering if they like me.... Like one of the reasons I never made it with a girl was I was afraid she'd cry and feel crappy when it was over. I've heard that happens sometimes. And I knew that would make me feel crappy." (p. 14)

Roadside Valentine. C.S. Adler.

"I just figured out that the reason I was trying to squeeze myself into the tight little mold Vince wanted me to fit was that I didn't have confidence anyone — any guy — would love me as I am, " she said. "I know I'm a big, bossy, hard-headed female, and most boys are scared stiff of women like me. I was so busy trying to make myself over that I didn't even see that you liked me as I am." (p. 184)

The Mole and Beverley Miller. Allan Frewin Jones.

Michael and Beverley tell each other what they love about the other.

He: "You're so strong and independent, and so clever and so...so...so sure of yourself."
She: "You're gentle, and you're thoughtful and kind and selfless."
He: "What about sexy.. you forgot sexy."
She: "Oh yes, very sexy." Oh yes — sex — which they discuss — responsible sex. (p. 152)

Chinese Handcuffs. Chris Crutcher.

Dillon understands what the psychiatrist is getting at. Hoping to have as a girlfriend someone who has been sexually abused means you can't have a real relationship without help. "You can't repair that kind of damage without a lot of therapy."

A Very Touchy Subject. Todd Strasser.

Scott knows that Paula is "easy". Even at 15. But there is something in him, and about her, that prevents him from using her despite his strong sexual urges.

The Girl of his Dreams. Harry Mazer.

Willis thinks of the girl of his dreams — an idealized phantom. Sophie isn't at all like that fantasy so he overlooks her kindness and decency until it's almost too late.

GETTING IT ALL TOGETHER.

Me and Luke. Audrey O'Hearn.

"I believe it to be in the best interests of the child Luke, to be raised by his father, a young man who demonstrated strong emotional ties to his son from the day the baby was born, " the judge ruled. (p. 143)

Thus Matt, an unmarried father, takes on the responsibility that goes with sexual freedom.

Permanent Connections. Sue Ellen Bridgers.

"You have to know I care about you," Rob said. "I didn't plan what happened any more than you did ...."
"I know that, Rob, it was spontaneous, but this isn't like that."
"So it's OK if it's spontaneous but not OK if I've been thinking about it?"
"That's not what I mean. It's just that you expect something now." (p.138)

Daniel and Esther. Patrick Raymond.

"It's not a question of what you'll be, young man. It's a question of what you are. Now." (p. 45)

Dying for Love, from *Paradise Café, and other stories.* Martha Brooks.

"My mother's going through early menopause and I'm going through late puberty", Rachel is in palliative care. "We aren't any age, yet all ages. There is no death. Only us, each somebody's daughter, three conspirators on the battlefield of love." (p. 72)

The Language of Goldfish. Zibby Oneal.

Eighth grader Carrie remembers her older sister and her lying beside the fish pond, leaning over the edge and calling the fish. "I wish we could just lie there forever, calling fish." Perhaps this longing for nothing to change has something to do with Carrie's breakdown?

The Leaving. Lynn Hall.

Her mother had told her to find out what she really wanted and not settle for less. Marrying Randy, or someone like him, would be settling for less than the life that, from the deepest part of her, Roxanne knew to be the existence she was meant for.

Summer Girls, Love Boys. Norma Fox Mazer.

Six-foot Richie tires of the crushes her best friend forever (and 5'6") Stephen has on sweet little girls — "I declare it as an eternal truth that girls should never be sweet, and boys always ought to be! Then the world might shake itself into shape."

Sex Education. Jenny Davis.

As part of the sex education curriculum Mrs Fulton assigned them a "caring project". Livvie thought that the purpose of it was to understand that you don't have sex because he says he loves you, you don't have sex because you don't know what else to do to show him that you love him, that you care. The caring project was about finding other ways to show love beside sex.

LITERATURE:
A Grade 8 newspaper-based activity.

I watched the Grade 8 class browsing aimlessly, unfocused, a small group idling through a stack of newspapers. They had arrived in the library, unannounced, with their teacher who assured me they wouldn't "bother" me, and just to go ahead with what I was doing; they were here to "find something to read". "This, " I thought to myself, "needs 'doing'."

Librarian (indicating):   Do they usually read newspapers?

Teacher: I wouldn't have thought so, but they do seem interested.

Librarian: Oh, I thought perhaps you had done a unit on newspapers.

Teacher (thoughtfully):   Actually, no.
(I show the teacher some samples of headline-inspired writing created for a librarian's workshop. See the first edition of *Invitations, Celebrations,* p. 181)

Librarian: I could select some titles and show some samples to get your group started, if you're interested.

Teacher: Not a bad idea. Let me get back to you.

Librarian (two lunch hours later): I've been thinking about that newspaper unit, and I've got something to show you, if you have a minute this afternoon.

Teacher (trapped): How about I come down to the library at 1:05?
(The lunch hour ends at 1:15.)

Librarian: Great. I'll be ready.

Teacher (rueful): I'll bet.

GETTING IT ALL TOGETHER.

Later, I showed the teacher the kind of helpful hand-out I could give her class. At first hesitantly and then more enthusiastically the teacher considered a newspaper unit. From our discussions, two about 10 minutes in length, and a third about 40 minutes, we agreed on goals, procedures and the assignment.

A CO-OPERATIVE NEWSPAPER UNIT

Goals: Students will become familiar with newspaper format and style (T).
Students will be capable of writing a newspaper report (T, L).
Students will read one fiction title, appropriate for a newspaper report (T, L).

Procedure: After 4 periods in the English classroom studying newspapers, students will visit the library for a motivational book talk by the librarian.
The class will receive their assignment (T).
Assignment due: In 3 weeks.

Here is the book talk:

Librarian: Have you found your favourite section of the newspaper by now?

Students: (Various replies, from sports to comics to front pages.)

Librarian: Do you go directly to your favourite section? What makes you stop on your way?

Students: Pictures.
Headlines.

Librarian (unfolding sheet of headings): You mentioned the Sport Section
(Pointing, continuing with *Bad Boy* by Diane Wieler in hand)
A.J. and his best friend Tully have it made — they're on the high school hockey team.
(Reading from p. 55)

GETTING IT ALL TOGETHER.

"A.J. slammed down on top of him, all 176 pounds. Elbows first. And while Number Five turned white and gasped for breath, A.J. pushed himself up on the centre's stomach, hard.

'You trip me again and you'll be chewing this [bleep] stick,' he hissed into the boy's face. And he got the message. "

So A.J. becomes an "enforcer" working through his anger and confusion about personal relationships — with his best friend, his best friend's sister, his father, his father's girlfriend, until he becomes a winner on all counts.

Have you become familiar with the Life section?
(Pointing to heading)

Student: It's about issues in our daily lives.

Librarian: Right — such as teen-age suicide as in *Singin' Somebody Else's Song* by Mary Blount Christian, sexual abuse as in *Mac* by John Maclean, and educating the uneducable as in Sheila Solomon Klass' *Kool Ada* :
(Reading)

"I had only been in her class for a couple of weeks, transferred there for my bad attitude: I was a fighter. I didn't speak. I cut school."

The vice-principal is at her wit's end. (continue reading)
"Your stubbornness beats all. We know you used to talk. Now I shall personally escort you to Ms. Walker's special class for girls..."

where she learns to read and substitute cunning for fighting.

What have you found in the medicine or science sections?

Student: Oh, they discovered something about cystic fibrosis — a Canadian doctor discovered why some kids who are cured of cancer will develop a second, different cancer later.

And lots about transplants.

Librarian: Anything about human neuron memory transferred to chimpanzees (holding up *Eva*, by Peter Dickinson)?

Student: You're kidding??!! (Hand her the book.)

GETTING IT ALL TOGETHER.

Librarian: So many headlines, so many stories.

Teacher: (Handing out assignment) And here is what we're going to do
             with these headlines and stories. Here are some helpful
             hints. (Reading and explaining further where necessary).
             On the reverse side of the assignment are some possible
             headings and titles to go with them. The librarian has
             many more book recommendations to make. So if you
             need that kind of help, ask her; if you need clarification on
             the assignment itself, ask me.

The calibre of writing depends very much on the amount of instruction
and practice given the students by the English teacher. As a teacher-
librarian I was pleased that the students were connecting headlines to
the flesh and blood of the books' characters. Here is the assignment:

1. Choose a headline, or feature heading, or section from the daily
   newspaper or make up your own.
2. Choose a book you have read that seems to fit that headline.
3. Write up the newspaper account that fits your book and headline.
   Will readers read past the first few sentences?
   Does your write-up merit a "by-line"?
   Would your editor reward you with a regular column?
4. Exchange the "newspaper accounts" with your classmates.
5. Help your classmates set up your "newspaper" in the library.
   (This became a bulletin board promotion: 'In the News'.)

On the back of the assignment, examples of headlines and supportive
titles were provided as a working example:

A WORKING MOTHER'S CHALLENGE
Silver. Norma Fox Mazer.
Harriet's Daughter. Marlene Nourbese Philip.
Pick-Up Sticks. Sarah Ellis.

APARTHEID FIGHT NEEDS HELP
Waiting For the Rain. Sheila Gordon.
Beyond Safe Boundaries. Margaret Sachs.
Chain of Fire. Beverley Maidoo.

DON'T PUT ME IN HOME, ELDERLY PLEAD
After the Rain. Norma Fox Mazer.
Sweet Bells Jangled Out of Tune. Robin Brancato.
Memory. Margaret Mahy.

GETTING IT ALL TOGETHER.

FAMILY
The Keeper. Phyllis Reynolds Naylor.
Angel Dust Blues. Todd Strasser.
Dixie Storms. Barbara Hall.

LIFE
Singin' Somebody Else's Song. Mary Blount Christian.
Mac. John Maclean.
Kool Ada. Sheila Solomon Klass.

PARENTS OF MENTALLY ILL DREAD FUTURE
Seems Like This Road Goes on Forever. Jean Van Leeuwen.
About David. Susan Beth Pfeffer.
So Much to Tell You. John Marsden.

PEOPLE
Just One Friend. Lynn Hall.
Me and Luke. Audrey O'Hearn.
The Great Elephant Chase. Gillian Cross.

TRAVEL
Crabbe. William Bell.
Tracker. Gary Paulsen.
Hatchet. Gary Paulsen.
The Island. Gary Paulsen.

SCIENCE/MEDICINE
Goodbye Tomorrow. Gloria Miklowitz.
Downwind. Louise Moeri.
Singularity. William Sleator.
Eva. Peter Dickinson.

SEARCH ABANDONED FOR MISSING TEENS
The Elephant Tree. Harriett Luger.
Taking Terri Mueller. Norma Fox Mazer.
The Year Without Michael. Susan Beth Pfeffer.

SHOP GUTTED BY BOMB, TWO KILLED, ONE INJURED
Across the Barricades. Joan Lingard.
Zed. Rosemary Harris.
The Seventh Raven. Peter Dickinson.

SPORT
The Outside Shot. Walter Dean Myers.
Hoops. Walter Dean Myers.
American Sports Poems. R.R. Knudson.
Bad Boy. Diane Wieler.
Stotan! Chris Crutcher.

THE PREJUDICES OF DAILY WORDS
Rainbows of the Gutter. Rukshana Smith.
The Murderer. Felice Holman.
The Prank. Kathryn Lasky.

LITERATURE:
A Grade 8 activity using metaphors

> "He saw the world as a great big bland glass of niceness and he was an acid tablet, dropped in to start things fizzing."

I laughed out loud when I read this metaphor from Betsy Byar's *The Animal, the Vegetable and John D. Jones,* and realized how often I jot down on my reading cards memorable figures of speech. I read this quote to a teacher of Grade 8 Literature, and asked whether we "still teach figures of speech". The answer, in the affirmative, prompted me to ask how N taught this, and we had a lovely talk about methodology, goals, etc. We agreed that for their next book report, N's students would select a strongly delineated character from a novel, and write a metaphor for her/him in John D's style:

> "He/she saw the world as ....and he/she was................."

I got them started with these recommendations:

Dicey in *The Homecoming* and *Dicey's Song,* by Cynthia Voigt.
Gloria in *A Summer's Lease,* by Marilyn Sachs.
Warren in *The Two Thousand Pound Goldfish,* by Betsy Byars.
Mark in *Switching Tracks,* by Dean Hughes.
Ada in *Kool Ada,* by Sheila Solomon Klass.
Belle in *Belle Pruitt,* by Vera Cleaver.

N and I now exchange our favourites quotes. Here are some I quite like:

> "Sometimes it feels like my head's a cheap hotel with everybody yellin' at everybody else and I'm the night clerk." (p. 91)
> *The Arizona Kid.* Ron Koertge.

> "Sienna, her 15 year old sister fitted into Charlie's life like a splinter, the kind that pushed in deeper and deeper with each attempt to pull it out."
> *Charlie Pippin.* Candy Dawson Boyd.

> "Crazier than a bag of hammers" (p. 38)
> *Easy Avenue.* Brian Doyle.

> "Dinner at our house is like picnicking on the freeway." (p. 18)
> *Joshua Fortune.* Cynthia D. Grant.

GETTING IT ALL TOGETHER.

"The prairie was like a giant plate stretching all the way to the
   sky at the edges. And we were like two tiny peas left over from din-
   ner, Lester and me." (p. 1)
Prairie Songs. Pam Conrad.

"He hated the way she spoke in that false soothing voice, as if she owned
   the country of calm and he was some kind of fool who'd stumbled
   across its borders." (p. 151)
One-Eyed Cat. Paula Fox.

"I ran towards humiliation as if it were male and in love with me."
   The Girl Who Invented Romance. Caroline B. Cooney.

[About Henry's freckles]
   "He looked as if he'd been sunbathing through a tea strainer." (p. 17)
   Henry's Leg. Ann Pilling.

"... curiosity burns in her like a pilot light." (p. 53)
   M.V. Sexton Speaking. Suzanne Newton.

"Vlad was less a walking encyclopaedia than a quiz book from which
   someone had torn the pages where the answers were printed." (p. 38)
   Man in Motion. Jan Mark.

"But really she couldn't live in New York, where the subways made her
   nerves feel like a charm bracelet of plastic skeletons jangling on a
   chain." (p. 20)
Weetsie Bat. Francesca Lia Block.

"He was a man who, ever since his boyhood, had eagerly awaited the
   time when his body would catch up with the middle-aged spread in
   his mind." (p. 9)
Josephine. Kenneth Lillington.

[About Bella the nubile, untidy temptress]
   "She looked like a burst parcel." (p. 56)
   Daniel and Esther. Patrick Raymond.

"... the ants that crawled down from the blooms, crisscrossing the house
   like sightseers." (p. 27)
   Journey. Patricia MacLachlan.

"... naturally curly hair is as attractive as a brillo pad." (p. 9)
   Two Moons in August. Martha Brooks.

"Phil just sits there smiling as if he's a huge buried treasure and
   Roberta's the one with the map." (p. 140)
   Two Moons in August. Martha Brooks.

"A quick shot of grief each morning leaves me free for the rest of the day.
   As though it's an antiperspirant or something." (p. 3)
   My Brother Stealing Second. Jim Naughton.

"My parents and I are on a boat no harbor will have." (p. 8)
   My Brother Stealing Second. Jim Naughton.

CULTURAL DIVERSITY:
Dictionaries for understanding

R. was intrigued by *Gaffer Samson's Luck*. She had not heard of Jill Paton Walsh. I was able to wax enthusiastic about the language in the novel, told her that 'gaffer' referred to an elderly rustic, an old fellow, that the 'luck' was a good luck piece, that there were lots of other rich local allusions (East Anglian).

Of course I rushed off that same day to find the book, consulted my reading card to find the page references and therefore quickly informed her that a 'mauther' was a young girl, a 'bor' was a neighbor, a 'fen nightingale' was a frog. What an opportunity for a language arts project: compiling a dictionary of localisms. And what other subjects could we pull into a multi-disciplinary study? For *Gaffer Samson's Luck* is a geographic mystery, a social history, an adventure story about gangs and peer pressure.

Then I remembered Kevin Major's *Thirty-Six Exposures*, a rebellious coming of age story, in which Lorne attempts in pictures and poetry to capture the essence of his Newfoundland fishing village, and finds himself in the history and people that have nourished him. My reading card provided the page numbers for dialect (p. 37 "hes": i.e. his pronounced as hees) localism (p. 77 "make no wonder": i.e. it's no wonder) figurative language (p. 33 "my son": among males, a friendly form of address regardless of relationship or age) social customs (p. 100 "mummering": the practice of visiting houses elaborately costumed and disguised at Christmas. The mummers would knock on doors, shout out "Mummers allowed in?" and then once inside begin a jogging half-dance, called the "mummer's walk." An early newspaper reference to mummers is dated 1812.)

Inevitably I moved on from small local communities to other lands.

Elizabeth Laird's compelling story of one Kurdish family's travails fleeing persecution in Iraq and encountering hostility and deprivation in Iran is a good source of cultural, social and political issues. *(Kiss the Dust)* A dictionary of terms seems a logical exercise for this book, since

GETTING IT ALL TOGETHER.

most of the terms can be defined from context, from conversation with students from those lands, and from newspaper files. For younger readers, try *Pig* by Paul Geraghty, winner of the MML Young Africa Award.

In these culturally diverse times I'm sure all of us keep track of titles to match up with the cultural heritages of our students. We are always looking for ways to sensitize ourselves and our students to the many cultures represented by young people in the schools today. We believe that the more we know about others, the more we value and respect them.

Join your class in reading a novel about other peoples, creating as you read, cultural dictionaries of terms, customs, beliefs, language, etc. culled from the book. Illustrations could be a welcome addition. Most of the entries in your dictionary will be defined from their contexts in the novel, others will be contributed by class members and staff where applicable, as well as family members particularly the elderly who are the repositories and guardians of memory and values. (the latter a way of forming bridges to the community) You and your students will be amazed to discover how much you will learn. How will you advertise your efforts? By adding the "dictionaries" to your collection? By displays? By informing your Board's consultant for multiculturalism? By contacting your local synagogue, mosque, temple, church? By alerting your local tv station? Spread your good news! Here's a start:

Among the Volcanoes. Omar S. Castaneda.
> When her mother falls ill, Isabel, a Mayan girl living in present-day Guatemala, must care for her and the family, searching for her identity in a world of old expectations resisting change. (Contains reference to a medical picture dictionary of symptoms).

Shabanu: Daughter of the Wind. Suzanne Fisher Staples.
> An eleven year old Pakistani pledged in marriage to an older man must accept the custom or risk the consequences of defying her father's wishes.

Dog Runner. Don H. Meredith
> 16 years old Jim Redcrow, a Metis, enters his dog team in the 3-day Trappers Trek in the process of which he identifies and becomes one with the spirits of his people who haunt his dreams.

GETTING IT ALL TOGETHER.

The Roller Birds of Rampur. Indi Rana.

Returning from England to her grandparents' home in Rampur, 17 year old Sheila Mehta rages.

"I had to be either British or Indian. Either-or. Either-or. Why couldn't it be 'and' I thought suddenly. Why can't I be both British and Indian? But something inside me wouldn't agree."

Poona Company. Farrukh Dhondy

From Poona, on the western coast of India, south of Bombay, a rich collection of stories about adolescence, teeming with humour and pathos.

Taking Root: a multicultural anthology. Ed. by Anthony Masters

"Apathy and lack of interest are the roots of hatred: curiosity can be the root of love." (From the Foreword)

These stories celebrate the joyful power of multiracial society.

Chain of Fire. Beverley Maidoo

When the villagers learn they are to be forcibly evicted from their homes and sent to a barren piece of land designated by the apartheid government of South Africa as their "homeland" they decide to rebel.

A Handful of Stars. Rafik Schami

Helping out in his father's bakery, experiencing the inequities of the educational system, listening to Uncle's folk tales, writing in his diary, a 14 year old Syrian youth shapes his life.

Waiting for the Rain. Sheila Gordon.

Nine years in the lives of two South African youths — one black, one white — as their friendship ends in a violent confrontation as adults — one student, one soldier.

Harriet's Daughter. Marlene Nourbese Philip.

14 year old Margaret resists the cultural memories and values of her parents. What use are they in Toronto? She'd rather be Harriet Tubman's daughter.

Rice Without Rain. Minfong Ho.

After rebels convince the headman of a small village in northern Thailand not to pay the land rent, his seventeen year old daughter joins the student uprising in Bangkok.

GETTING IT ALL TOGETHER.

Salt on the Snow. Rukshana Smith.

17 year old Julie's tutoring of 47 year old Rashmi puts their cultural assumptions and biases to the test and Julie discovers she must take sides with the family that despite everything she loved, or with a stranger, thin and ill with no one to turn to.

Against the Storm. Gaye Hicyilmaz.

Mehmet's family's move to the Turkish capital Ankara places stress on values both familial and cultural.

Children of the River. Linda Crew.

Fleeing Cambodia to safety in the U.S., Sundara struggles to be both "a good Cambodian girl" at home and an accepted student at an American high school.

A Thief in the Village, and Other Stories. James Berry.

A magical collection of stories about young people which make you hear, see, feel and smell Jamaica.

My Name is Seepeetza. Shirley Sterling.

Now that she is studying at an Indian residential school, her name is Martha Stone and all the rules, regulations, teachers' attitudes amount to a denial of all that being an Indian means to her.

Silent Words. Ruby Slipperjack.

Abused by the mindless attacks of white youths, and the vindictiveness of his stepmother, Danny runs away, making his way through a series of of native communities by which he learns their values of nonjudgement, openness, acceptance, sharing, and respecting elders.

Under the Bridge. F.G. Paci.

Marco Trecochi grows up in Northern Ontario stifled by his Italian immigrant family and their way of life.

Would an art teacher be interested in having a class illustrate cultural maps for a book, e.g., for *Silent Words*, a student would have to illustrate the topography of the Northern Ontario communities, draw principal buildings, figures putting up tents, skinning rabbits, drinking from canoe paddles, conceptualize the Memregivesiwag who live in nature, decorate the map borders in some appropriate manner, etc.

GETTING IT ALL TOGETHER.

HISTORY:
Grade 12 / The invention of childhood.

> "They've got this notion about the past, about history — they forget that folks lived in it."
>
> *Isaac Campion.* Janni Howker

Isaac Campion was a moving experience for me. Twelve year old Isaac's life in England in 1901, is one of punishing work under the direction of a brutalizing father, harshly superstitious, bitterly against education and who forces him to leave school to help him at his horse dealing.

> "To be fair, I would say he didn't know how hard he treated us. I would say he treated me the way his father... had treated him ... And I'll tell you what I think it was, why those men were like that. They'd got it from religion. And I'm not talking about the religion of love. I'm talking about the Old Testament. The Bible of masters and work. 'Spare the rod and spoil the child', and pleasure was a sin. My great-grandfather had beaten that into my grandfather, and my father had it beaten into him."

       p. 37

Mutely suffering, Isaac batters at the bars of his prison

> "Ever since I was born, I'd seen all the indifferent cruelty that was inflicted on horses to make them work... And how patiently they bowed their heads to their lot, those working horses, I just knew that even if I tried all the days of my life I'll not stop feeling this awful pity for the lives and deaths of animals and men... I was rising thirteen... I was thinking, *I know I can endure it. I was put on the earth to endure it. But there must be more to living a life than this.*"

       p. 63

Can any reader fail to be moved by these words?

I showed these passages to a history teacher who wasn't a great user of the library, but I knew his students liked his classes, and I liked his friendly face, so I took a chance and initiated a conversation about how he taught social history. After all I like to talk about my field, so why wouldn't he? It turned out he was not a text explicator, but believed in teaching from a variety of sources (I guess he used other libraries!) And when I drew his attention to Isaac's comment when an old man, "I have a notion in my head that children weren't invented until after the Great War" he decided then and there to use that quota-

       p. 85

GETTING IT ALL TOGETHER.

tion as the statement which students would explore as their major essay for the term. Did I have many more books like that?

Librarian: Yes — about any particular country or time?

Teacher: I think I won't apply any restrictions. Let them examine the past and the present. Maybe we can nurture a more thoughtful, socially aware and responsible generation. I still believe that young people have a capacity for compassion and idealism.

Librarian: It's going to be a labour of love finding materials for you. Would you like to bring the class to the library to start them off?

Teacher (warily): Are you going to instruct them on how to do re search?

Librarian: No, no. I'm certain they know that already.

Teacher (relieved): Then how would you like to introduce them to some novels, the way you did me, as a kind of emotional and mind set?

Librarian: I'd love to, and I promise not to take up the whole period. The class will have time to select and begin reading.

We set the time and place. Interesting isn't it that if I hadn't taken the initiative, the teacher's perception of the librarian's role as researcher only would have remained unchanged and his students would have missed an opportunity to exercise their intellectual and emotional muscles in a fresh way.

Here is the hand-out I prepared for the students to accompany the talk. About another 30 books were on the cart.

The Poacher's Son. Rachel Anderson.
    Arthur was poor, couldn't read, was sent to Reform School for truancy, forced to take a probationary job as a cowherd getting up at 4 in the morning and receiving half salary. His sister Alice, forced to leave school to be a maid can aspire to be a butcher's wife. Arthur can aspire to be cannon fodder in the Great War.

GETTING IT ALL TOGETHER.

Children of the House. Brian Fairfax-Lucy and Philippa Pearce
> To uphold the tradition of the family, its name, the house, horses, great parties, the lives of the four children are sacrificed.

Children of the Wolf. Jane Yolen.
> In India in 1920, two children raised by wolves are discovered and brought to missionaries to be taught human behavior again. How? Treat them as animals to make them biddable.

A Strong and Willing Girl. Dorothy Edwards.
> "When I look back on me young days, I don't remember a time when I wasn't working. I can't remember playing with dollies... the year I went into service I was just past my tenth birthday." (p. 9)

Lyddie. Katherine Paterson.
> When Lyddie was 13 her mother hired her out at the local tavern where she put on the clothes of servitude, was ordered to bed late and obliged to rise early; then worked a 10 hour day in a mill where her reward was still another loom to tend, and less food to eat. "Oh, I cannot be a slave, I will not be a slave."

So Far from the Bamboo Grove. Yoko Kawashima Watkins.
> Nineteen forty-five was a bad time for a Japanese girl to be living in northern Korea.

The Devil's Arithmetic. Jane Yolen.
> "Still the camp seemed curiously lightened because of it, as if everyone knew that as long as others were processed, they would not be. A simple bit of mathematics, like subtraction where one taken away form the top line becomes one added on to the bottom. The Devil's arithmetic." (p. 145)

Shadow of the Wall. Christa Laird.
> 14-year-old Misha, one of the orphans imprisoned within the ghetto, is forced to make a decision whether to escape and become a liaison worker with other ghettos or stay with his little sister. Thus he must weigh a public against a private need.
> "I suppose I was a Jew before I was Rachel's brother." (p. 107)

Borrowed Children. George Ella Lyon.
> Twelve year old Mandy is told the only way the family can survive the crisis:
> "...school is the one thing I've got. I don't want to give that up. Willie's not my baby. I don't know how to take care of him and I don't want to either." (p. 41)

Looking Out. Victoria Boutis.
> It is 1953. Reds, Paul Robeson, the Rosenbergs are bad words, and Ellen knows she'll never be an ordinary American girl. Did it

GETTING IT ALL TOGETHER.

really matter all that much? She wished she could answer no and mean it. It did matter. Not enough, though. Not enough to make her bend her knees.

The Girl. Robbie Branscum.

Abandoned with her four brothers and sisters, an eleven year old girl struggles for survival in a world of blinding poverty, back-breaking work, ignorance, and deprivation of schooling, elementary health care and even food.

throwaways. Ian Strachan.

When 11 year old Sky and 6 year old Chip are abandoned by their parents, they become part of that growing army of homeless children on our city streets. Look into their eyes and not away when you see them.

Kiss the Dust. Elizabeth Laird.

We come to know Tara and her family intimately so that when the cruelties of politics and nationalism shatter their lives, we recognize *fellow* human beings in Iran and Iraq today.

Isaac Campion. Janni Howker.

"They've got this notion about the past, about history — they forget that folks lived in it... the young ones they think they are going to live forever. And good luck to them, I say! Good luck to the young ones... let them live to a hundred!" (p. 1)

As the due date for the assignment drew near, I shared my observations of the students at their work in the library with their teacher, the slow conversion of the doubters to believers in power of fiction, the seriousness with which all the students treated the topic, the increasing confidence they had in the librarian's recommendations (and memory). When I mentioned an article I had kept from *Social Education,* April/ May, 1986 entitled "Teaching the History of Childhood", that his students might respond to after their reading, he expressed a pleased surprise that I read his professional materials. Of course I consider *Social Education* (among others) *my* professional reading too!

What I learned from co-operating with this teacher —

- His students view the history programme as dealing with real and personally meaningful issues, problems and content.
- His students see their moral lives in his classroom, hence the school, hence the world.

GETTING IT ALL TOGETHER.

HISTORY:
Workers, bosses, union-busting, unions and strikes

Librarian: Have you been following the *Star* series on the 100th
birthday of the newspaper?

Teacher: You mean the replication of pages from the first years of the
paper. Indeed I have; we've been discussing them in class
and putting them up on the bulletin board.

Librarian: Reporting language was so different then. Did you notice
this?   (Reading from the paper)
> 'Police Escorting Non-Union Men Were Mobbed
> and Plied Great Whips on the Rioters.'

Teacher: What was the date of that one?

Librarian: 1902 (noticing the English teacher listening). Oh, E, you'll
appreciate this loaded language too. The strikers are never
referred to as that, or workers but rather, 'a mob' 'a
crowd', and when the strikers try to break through the
lines of mounted police guarding some incoming non-
union men,
> 'The promptitude of the policemen alone saved
> them. Out came their blacksnake whips, and they
> rode into the crowds, slashing as fast as their arms would
> move. The effect was instantaneous. The
> crowd swept back like the turning of the tide.'

We then carried on a discussion that ranged over subjective and ob-
jective writing, language as a tool or weapon, union history, the right
to strike, etc.

Librarian: All this is still alive in some books...

Teachers (interrupting, laughing): Oh yes, and it's mostly good fiction,
isn't it? O.K. when are you going to show us some? We get
the idea — we'll probably have kids do their own newspaper reports. Shall we talk later?

Librarian (with smiles of appreciation, enthusiasm — and love): Let's

GETTING IT ALL TOGETHER.

fix a time in the library so you can have coffee and cookies
while we look at the material.

Later, amid the crumbs and coffee stains (never mind), I showed them:

The Bonnie Pit Laddie. Frederick Grice.
> A mining strike in the '20's in England where the owner has the
> power to put the strikers and those who shelter them out of their
> homes, and when the strike is broken, has them all black-listed. I
> marked pages 103-05 and 148-50, moving testaments to the coal
> miner's solidarity and belief in a loving and compassionate God.
> Also I noted the judge's citation in the granting to this novel of the
> Other Award for "one of the first books to portray working people
> in a sympathetic and totally realistic way."

To the Bright and Shining Sun. James Lee Burke.
> Just 30 some years ago in the Cumberland Mountain range of
> eastern Kentucky when the pay was $1.20 an hour and the coal
> operators were locked in grim battle with the United Mine Work-
> ers. I mark page 22
>> "...right or wrong, we ain't got no chance against the operator with-
>> out the union. They got our land for hardly nothing. They ruined the
>> ground for growing anything. They give us shacks to live in, and they
>> paid us in script so we couldn't buy from nobody excepting them.
>> They taken all they could get and they never give nothing back. I put
>> 27 years in the hole, and I didn't get out with nothing except a
>> cheque for part of the doctor's bill."
>
> When I read this to a class last year, a student fervently agreed
> and told us of a relative who had worked all his adult life in the
> mine in Sudbury and used to say all he got out of it was a bad
> back. I must look for a 'mining book' from the woman's stand-
> point, something to equal the power of the documentary, *Harlan
> County U.S.A.*, for which Director Barbara Kopple won an Oscar.

Lyddie. Katherine Paterson.
> The efforts to organize mill workers, all female, for a ten hour
> work day demand in Vermont in 1843. I marked pages 62-65 and
> 75-76 in which are described the incredible dehumanizing sound
> and movements of the weaving room in the factory. After her first
> full day of work 13 year old Lyddie can barely eat and escapes her
> supper to take off her boots, massage her abused feet, and lay
> down her aching head. Gentle Betsy reads her Dickens' *Oliver
> Twist* and Lyddie experiences another hunger — for knowledge. I

mark page 92 where Lyddie listens to her fellow workers discuss wages and working hours and one sings,

> "Oh isn't it a pity such a pretty girl as I
> Should be sent to the factory to pine away and die?
> Oh! I cannot be a slave,
> I will not be a slave
> For I'm so fond of liberty
> That I cannot be a slave."

One Proud Summer. Marsha Hewitt and Claire Mackay.

Based on the Valleyfield, Quebec mill workers' strike in 1946. I marked the Author's note about what is historical fact and what is fiction, pages 22-23 and 34-35 for strike issues, pages 60-61 for the police attack on the strikers, and page 40 for the impassioned speech of one of the organizers,

> "This union you now trust, brothers and sisters, isn't the old one, without plans or strength or courage. This union won't be frightened by a black cassock, by a policeman's club, by an English curse, not even by Premier Duplessis himself. This union is new. It is founded on your struggle, your hope. This union will fight!" He stopped for breath, then said softly, "And this union will win!"

On Fire. Ouida Sebestyen.

Takes place around 1911, a story of brotherly love and moral responsibility, the core of which is a murder (of the saintly Papa in *Words by Heart*) and the scabbing activities of the boy responsible. I marked page 56:

> "Being a scab's a dangerous way to make a living,' she said carefully...
> "So how come it's dangerous? Do the miners try to scare the scabs off?" He said the word deliberately, tasting it. Tater was a scab.
> "Wouldn't you? If they came pushing in, willing to work for the low pay and bad conditions?... But the scabs say, look, you quit doing what you were hired to do, so let us — we got kids to feed. And suddenly it's like a war."
> A chill went down his back. A war. People got killed in wars. Her brother had."

For the history teacher I marked these pages in which social and political issues are expressed most effectively, quite often in direct speech: pp. 28, 42, 44, 67. For the English teacher I marked pages 71, 75 as examples of how language can be used in the newspaper report to give the colour and feeling of the times. I also dropped a suggestion to an art teacher about possibilities of her students doing illustrations for the novels. In anticipation I am marking pages 79 (a big-wheeled water wagon), 80 (the main street with the boot and shoe store, chili parlor, hotels, with their curlicued signs), 30 (the pathetic funeral procession for Nellie, one of "the girls.")

GETTING IT ALL TOGETHER.

A Strong and Willing Girl. Dorothy Edwards.

I marked page 20.

> "I shall always remember the year 1887 for it was the year of the Old Queen's Golden Jubilee — the year I went out into service. I was just past my tenth birthday by then... Of course I cried when I left home. My mom and my dad and the eight younger children cried too, but I was the eldest and there wasn't room for me anymore and Dad's wages went nowhere. I was the eldest, the first to go, the others would follow when their times came."

Robert Micklewright's illustrations of pre-union Victorian life as experienced by Nan and others are wonderful. Students could research some of the domestic items for newspaper advertisements, e.g., carpet beaters (p. 20) oil lamps (32) cameras (65), could try to identify the items on pages 77, 78, and 80, and elaborate on the incident which led to the use of the ambulance of that day — a stretcher with a buggy-like canvas cover on wheels (84) operated by one or two men on foot. And to go with another heading on the newspaper I had originally shown, DEATH LIST HEAVY AMONG CHILDREN, I noted page 103,

> "...his name was Mason...[he slept] in the stable. He wasn't sure how old he was, and he thought his other name was Dick."

Poor and unwanted, without nourishment in him to fight off pneumonia, the boy dies.

> "He'll be all right," I [say] "three hot meals a day and a nice white outfit and wings to get around with and no one to hustle him about."

Other titles:

The Baitchopper. Silver Donald Cameron (fisherman's union).

Dinah Blow Your Horn. Jack Bickham (railroad strike).

Twopence a Tub. Susan Price (mining).

The Nine Days Wonder. Frederick Grice (general strike).

The Barefoot Man. Davis Grubb (mining-Virginia-1930).

> "Pray for the dead. And fight like hell for the living!" .

The Winchesters. James Lincoln Collier (mining strike; split family loyalties).

The teachers' discussion that followed the presentation led to

▲ a confirmation of the purpose of utilizing these novels, that is, reinforcing the connections between issues in history and the everyday lives of human beings in other times and today; reaffirming the power of literature to make us see, feel and understand.

▲ an agreement that the assignment would be a newspaper

report based on events in a novel about labour unions, and of a character in keeping with the tenor of the times.

▲ an agreement that a student would receive a separate grading from each of the history, English, (and art if she joined us) teachers for work on a single book.

I believe that students learned from this assignment that *human beings* struggled and died for social justice, that *ordinary people* unacknowledged by historians, were capable of acts of heroism, and that they themselves will look upon historic and current events with fresher and more compassionate insights.

"Connecting to the past", Joseph Gold avers, "helps us to survive."
(*Read For Your Life*)

GETTING IT ALL TOGETHER.

HISTORY:
Grade 9 / More than just details.

Teacher: What is this book about?

I suppose I could have summarized the story, keeping in mind how annoyed I become at overly detailed, lengthy summaries of books, movies, anecdotes. Historical fiction is more than a type of fiction. It is fiction personalizing and vitalizing the facts. History occurred; fiction *happens.* So I answered.

by James Lincoln Collier and Christopher Collier.

Librarian: *My Brother Sam is Dead* is about the death of a sixteen-year old "traitor" and the impact of that death on his family. It isn't about death in the abstract — but about a pain in the heart, a gap in the human family.
              (That's good. An encouraging interested look.)
              Here at the beginning of the story is a map of the town and another one tracing the troop and rebel movements in this corner of the American Revolutionary War. Here is an example of the divided loyalties and political views within one family (page 131):

> "Of course I still hadn't figured out what [Sam] was fighting for. It seemed to me we'd been free all along. What had the English government ever done against me?'"

              And here at the end of the novel is the author's note:
> "How much of this book is true?" (page 212)

Teacher: Oh so it's based on historical research.

Librarian: Yes, that combination of sound research and the *human* aspects of Revolutionary War life is what makes this such compelling historical fiction.

Teacher: Well, I certainly wish every historical novel did that.

Librarian: Why not?...

Teacher: Aha...

Librarian: I promise you that the historical fiction I can collect will be

GETTING IT ALL TOGETHER.

well-written, and will present the human impact of historical events.

Teacher: Sounds interesting — but a lot of work.

Librarian: I agree — but the background preparation is already complete in that I've done all the reading. Look, I'll collect three more books, clip one or two outstanding and brief passages in each, and bring them to you on ...??

Teacher: Would Thursday be o.k.? And then we can talk further.

Librarian: Fine. I'm so pleased you're interested. Will you tell me about *your* teaching methods then? I think that your teaching style must be based on using a variety of resources — films, video, audio tapes and in print, magazines, social sciences, biography etc. as well as history.

Teacher: How do you know that?

Librarian: I hear your students' requests, and I'd love to hear more about your aims and objectives. (Laughing) If you show me yours, I'll show you mine.

Teacher: Seems fair — I'm looking forward to our next meeting too. I have an idea I've overlooked a perspective on history — fiction.

Here is what I chose for our meeting:

The Poacher's Son, by Rachel Anderson is about the class system in England in the 1900's. An excellent author afterward (p. 138):

> "In the Victorian Church Schools, a lot of the instruction was based on a straightforward system of fear and intimidation, and village children were taught a sense of their own inferior status in the social order. They learned that, in God's order of things as well, they were lesser beings than the gentry."

On pages 5 & 6 our students will be shocked and incensed when the rector refuses to let a girl plan to be a teacher because of her "stupidity and insolence" in turning down a job as a maid of all work.

A Chance Child, by Jill Paton Walsh. I marked the Author's Note:

> "The landscape of this book is fantasy, and yet for every place

GETTING IT ALL TOGETHER.

> described in it, some such place somewhere exists.... the work described in this book was really carried out by young children in mines and cotton mills, both in Great Britain before the Factories Act controlled working conditions, and in industrialized areas of the United States."

Students will be appalled and moved to outraged pity at the dedication;

> "To: Robert Blencoe, poorhouse apprentice; Thomas Moorhouse, aged nine, a collier; Margaret Leveston, aged six, a coal bearer; Witness No. 96, aged sixteen as far as he could guess, a nailer; Jacob Ball, aged twelve, a dish mold runner; Joseph Badder, spinner who was sorry to beat little children; Joseph Hebergam, a worsted spinner from seven years old, whose mother wept to see him grow crooked; William Kershaw, aged eight, a 'piecner' whose mother beat his master over the head with a billy roller; Emmanuel Lovekin, mining butty, who learned to read and write while lying injured; and many others whose names and stories I have made use of in this book..., and to innumerable others like them."

Beyond the Divide, by Kathryn Lasky is about the emotional and physical travails a 14 year old Amish girl suffers as she crosses the continent by wagon train from Pennsylvania to California. Certainly the "adventure" is like nothing I have ever seen in the movies or TV. I learned about curing the wooden wheels, double hitching up perilous mountains, the dangers of disease, the deaths en route, the social tensions among the members of the train, the brutalization, the ever-present danger of rape. There is a fascinating section on Mill Creek Indians, p. 234 ff, and an excellent author note, p. 253.

And I was ready with a few more titles just in case:

> *The Fighting Ground.* Avi.
> *Prairie Songs.* Pam Conrad.
> *The Bone Wars.* Kathryn Lasky.
> *Brothers of the Heart.* Joan Blos.

I know that my efforts were appropriate and functional, but getting at the emotional, intellectual and literary *values* of the books helped convince the teacher (and her students) that the learning applications of fiction can be *significant*.

My challenge was to present fiction in a manner that would provoke reaction and involvement.

HEALTH AND PHYSICAL EDUCATION:
Grade 12 / Summons to an issue.

The student-created summons and trial worked out very well for health issues in the Health and Physical Education course, and at a later date for social issues in a Sociology course. This approach developed as a result of my reading the guidelines for Health and Physical Education for intermediate and senior classes, noting the many issues of an emotional, individual, familial and societal nature, and the stress on role-playing as a teaching method.

Dear V:

Thank you for talking to me about the observations I made from reading your course guideline. I would like to suggest some fiction titles that will support the issues you are studying and a format in which role-playing will be natural: the court summons and subsequent hearing. Attached are some specific books for which summons could be readily developed. Each indicates the charge and who the witnesses might be. For your interest, I have included brief descriptions of the books.

Some questions that we would need to iron out if you think the idea is good include:
   Who sends the summons?
   Where should the court be held? (I suggest the library.)
   How many students read each book? (Will groups be assigned
       different titles? What role is played by the Health teacher?
       Judge? Jury?
   What role is played by the librarian? (I have read all the
   books.)
   Over what period of time will the cases be heard?
   Are there more titles available? (You bet!)
   Are reading levels appropriate? (I can comment.)

   I will drop in to your office some time in the morning.
                    Fay.

There is no lack of "cases" that can be developed. Here are a few:

GETTING IT ALL TOGETHER.

Sex Education. Jenny Davis.

Charge: Failure to exercise professional responsibilities of the classroom.

Witnesses: Olivia Sinclair, 16

Mr. and Mrs. Sinclair, parents

Dr. Hirsch, psychiatrist, University Psychiatric Institute

Marie Kindler, mother of the deceased, David Kindler

Mrs. Fulton, Health teacher, defendant

Mrs. Fulton is "different". Her first term Biology class would be devoted to sex-education. "For homework tonight think about sex." Later she assigned Livvie and David to share a "caring project"; they took on Mrs. Parker, who they suspected was being abused by her husband. Preoccupied by their growing love and need to be together, they told no one of the increasing danger of the situation.

Dixie Storms. Barbara Hall.

Charge: Application for foster family. Norma Peyton, 15 years of age, in need of temporary home while parents sort out their differences.

For the application:

Mr. Peyton, uncle

Macy Peyton, spinster, aunt

Robert Dean "Bodean" Peyton, 9, second cousin

Against the application:

Margaret "Dutch" Peyton, 14, cousin

Flood Peyton, 35, cousin

Norma was the kind of girl "who could trip on the sidewalk, laugh all the way down, and make you look stupid for standing up," the kind of girl who had learned to mask her feelings so much that at 15 it was hard to tell what was the mask and what was real.

The True Story of Spit MacPhee. James Aldridge.

Charge: Application for adoption.

Witnesses: Spit MacPhee, 11 years of age, without legal and humane protection under the law.

Jack and Grace Tree, applicants

Sadie Tree, age 11 — co-applicant

Betty and Frank Arbuckle, applicants

Ben Arbuckle, age 11 — co-applicant

One small gutsy boy pitted against well-meaning townsfolk, religious convictions and the law.

GETTING IT ALL TOGETHER.

Here are some observations I made as the students worked their way through their presentations:

▲ The students within a designated cluster became aware of their peers' strengths, and rather than assigning a popular student to be one of the stars, e.g., a lawyer, as would have been the case in other circumstances, chose instead on the basis of intellectual or verbal powers.

▲ Weaker academic students were given supportive but not inferior roles, e.g., court stenographer, bailiff, etc.

▲ Winning the case was viewed as a *triumph for the book's characters.*

▲ Group dynamics unfolded in a democratic manner. Students focused their tensions by capturing the conflicts and tensions of a courtroom drama, the ups and downs of personal relationships, the emotional complexities of characters, the intricacies of bureaucracy, the disinterestedness of the law.

Try a variation on this format for senior law and sociology courses by appealing a case to an ombudsman or arbitrator. This would make for a smaller grouping, but a less rigid format than a court hearing. Here are some "issues" and stories where they are handled:

Teen-age alcoholism:
We All Fall Down. Robert Cormier.
Addie's moving attempt to control Buddy's drinking, p. 77 ff.
The family problems, p. 26.

Teen-age vandalism:
We All Fall Down. Robert Cormier.
Harry's explanation of how he got out of the charge, p. 105 ff.

Violence:
So Much To Tell You. John Marsden.
Social workers, teachers, fellow students could testify as to impact on Marina's personality. Marina could speak on behalf of her father (see p. 66, 72, 82).

Child Custody:
Somewhere In the Darkness. Walter Dean Myers.
Mama Jean and Crab were such contrasting people to care for Jimmy. The character of the feckless Crab is superbly drawn., e.g., p. 53, 99.

HISTORY:
Grade 12 / The reasons people fight.

Would T. be repeating his "Would you die for your country?" assignment this year? Sadly he answered he would, but he would be handling it a little differently. The assignment would read, "Would you die for your cause?" What he wanted from me was an annotated list of books with no headings or groupings. Rather the students would read a minimum of three novels and then create their own headings and/or groupings according to the circumstance in the novels. Could I find some "good complex stories?" Here were some of my selections:

And One For All. Theresa Nelson.

> Geraldine's close relationships with her older brother Wing and his best friend Sam change when Wing volunteers for Vietnam and Sam leaves for Washington to join a peace march.

Fallen Angels. Walter Dean Myers.

> "I thought about what Peewee had said. That I had better think about killing the Congs before they killed me. That had better be my reason, he had said, until I got back to the world. Maybe it was right. But it meant being some other person than I was when I got to Nam. Maybe that was what I had to be. Somebody else." (p. 200)

After the Dancing Days. Margaret Rostkowski.

> A forbidden friendship with the badly scarred, bitter soldier forces 13 year old Annie to redefine the word "hero" and to question conventional ideas of patriotism.

Shades of Gray. Carolyn Reeder.

> "I guess you didn't love Virginia enough to fight for her," Will said smugly.
> "That's the Virginia I love," [his uncle] said, swinging his arm in a wide arc that took in the woods and hills and the mountains in the distance. Then he scooped up a handful of small clods. "And this is the Virginia I love." He crumbled the dirt and watched it trickle between his fingers. "And I didn't want any part of bloodying Virginia's soil." (p. 70)

The Fighting Ground. Avi.

> "Young friend, this Corporal [a mercenary soldier] is a man that is known as — well, how to say, a man who — fights. Bravely. When the fighting happens, yes, of course, he is what one wants. To be sure. But when the fighting stops, well, no perhaps that is something that is different. Then, perhaps, you hope that he ... that he is not there. Do you understand me?" (p. 128)

GETTING IT ALL TOGETHER.

Echoes of War. Robert Westall.

Five unusual stories that bring to life the conflicts and traumas that war creates in those who lived through it.

We Were Not Like Other People. Ephraim Sevela. Translated from the Russian.

"My generation considers our childhood to have ended in 1941 when the war began. My childhood ended when I was only nine years old."

No Hero for the Kaiser. Rudolf Frank.

The author who was forced to serve the German artillery in August 1914, described this novel as "an anti-war novel to warn young people." It was banned and publicly burned by Hitler in 1933.

Bury the Dead. Peter Carter.

Into the unclouded life of Erika Nordern, a gifted high jumper, comes Uncle Karl, from the horrors of Germany's past. Nothing will be the same for the family.

Starry Night. Catherine Sefton.
Frankie's Story. Catherine Sefton.
Beat of the Drum. Catherine Sefton.

In northern Ireland just over the border separating it from Eire, in an Estate "fair down the road to proclaiming itself a Catholic Republic," in a Loyalist area of Northern Ireland, three young people struggle against a future ordained by years of hatred, bloodshed and unyielding memory.

The Visit. T. Degens.

At a family gathering in Berlin years after World War II, Kate relives some of the events described in the diary of an aunt who was once a member of the Hitler Youth.

The Last Enemy. Rhoda Kaellis.

Because of her indoctrination at the orphanage where she was sheltered, Holocaust survivor Lilly has come to believe that "the only way to be safe is not to be a Jew." "How will we ever heal these wounds?" "We're all of us Holocaust victims."

Forbidden City. William Bell.

17-year-old Alex Jackson, accompanying his CBC news cameraman father to China becomes involved in the student demonstra-

GETTING IT ALL TOGETHER.

tion at Tian An Man Square. Returning home he destroys his collection of lead soldiers: none of his heroes had worn a uniform.

No Surrender. James Watson.

Between two momentous events – free elections in Nambia in 1989 and the release from 27 years imprisonment of Nelson Mandela in 1990 — a white soldier who refuses to serve and a black political prisoner become pawns in the ongoing brutal racial wars of Southern Africa.

Wolf. Gillian Cross.

Would he die for The Cause? Certainly. Would he kill? If necessary. Would he kill his mother and child?

December Stillness. Mary Downing Hahn.

Thirteen year old Kelly wants to add the name of the disturbed homeless Vietnam War veteran to the memorial wall in Washington: the war isn't over yet while people like him are still suffering. (good selections of war poetry).

The Man From the Other Side. Uri Orlev.

Liquidating the Warsaw Ghetto was the Nazi's birthday present to Hitler. During these desperate days, 14 year old Marek discovers what is both noble and vicious in his fellow citizens, and where his own loyalties lie.

Harpoon Island. Pieter Van Raven.

The village turns against Brady's father at the outbreak of the war because of the teacher's pacifism and German background.

The Boy From Over There. Tamar Bergman. Translated from the Hebrew.

Avramik, a young Holocaust survivor has difficulties adjusting to life on a Kibbutz in the days preceding the first Arab-Israeli War.

The War Orphan. Rachel Anderson.

Simon's middle-class family adopts Vietnamese war orphan Ha, and discovers its calm, confident life disrupted by Ha's violent flashbacks.

Forever Nineteen. Grigory Baklanov. Translated from the Russian.

Of the nineteen year old Soviet lieutenant and others like him on the front during World War II as they defend their Russian homeland from the Nazis, the author writes "...they have remained for-

GETTING IT ALL TOGETHER.

ever young. This book is about them, about their youth, their love, their sacred faith."

On Foreign Ground. Edwards Quiroga.

A young Argentinian conscript in the Falklands living under Galtieri's dictatorship fights his war, not his own.

The Hideout. Sigrid Heuck. Translated from the German.

Rebecca remembers only her first name. Sami knows much beyond his years. The two survivors cling to each other as the bombers roar overhead, sustained by Sami's magic-making and dreams of a peaceable kingdom.

The Foothold. Grigory Baklanov. Translated from the Russian.

"When the war is over, I told myself, I want to have a son, so that I can sit him on my knee, my own flesh and blood, and with my hand on his head tell him about everything."

Voices of Danger. Alick Rowe.

"Do you know what a war is? Old Men Killing Young Men. That's what war is."

Number the Stars. Lois Lowry.

It is 1943 in occupied Denmark, and 10 year old Annemarie becomes part of the heroic Danish Resistance as they manage to smuggle almost the entire Jewish population, nearly 7000 people, across the sea to Sweden.

Why There Is No Heaven on Earth. Ephraim Sevela. Translated from the Russian.

Berele did not demand gratitude from mankind. He just could not live any other way ...

"It takes my breath away even to think what he might have done for people. And what our sinful planet might look like now.

But Berele Mats left us early.

And that is why there is no heaven on earth." (p. 21)

A Handful of Stars. Rafik Schami.

In modern Damascus, a teenager records in a daily diary his adventures, feelings and thoughts, increasingly exploring his frustration with government injustices until he finds his political voice in a subversive underground newspaper.

SCIENCE:
Grade 10 / Hazardous wastes.

Dear P:

When we talked the other day about your assignment on hazardous wastes and I gave you some sources for the case-study folders you were preparing for your students, I neglected two excellent titles:

When the Stars Begin to Fall. James Lincoln Collier.

A boy discovers that the local carpet factory is dumping chemicals in the river. There are several good names to put in the 'Task 4: Roles' section of the folder, e.g., The factory owner, the mayor, the police, the boy's father.

Spud Sweetgrass. Brian Doyle.

Spud discovers that used grease from the chip wagon where he works is being dumped into the Ottawa River. This will fit especially well into the 'Task 3: Errors' section of the folder because there are errors of omission, too. Doyle's use of humour emphasizes the issues we face today.

I'll continue to look for some more fiction which can validate your assignment.

Fay.

SCIENCE:
Grade 9 / Organ transplant

Dear M:

Just a note to tell you how much I admire your Grade 9 Organ Trans-
plant Project. Your succinct description of the "case" intrigued me immediately. What a great way to get the whole class participating (di-
viding them into interest groups such as politicians and lawmakers,
doctors, family, religious leaders). I look forward to helping your
groups in the library on Thursday. – and do you think I could come
into your class to hear the outcome of the debate?

Cheers,
Fay.

P.S.: Have you ever read *Eva* by Peter Dickinson. It's a story about human and animal medical experimentation. The issue is: Who owns
your memory and brain patterns? And I must dig up a copy of *Joshua,
Son of None* by Nancy Freedman – about the cloning of JFK! It's out of
print, alas.

ENGLISH:
Grade 9 enrichment.

... I showed the opening paragraph of *A Chance Child* by Jill Paton Walsh to an English teacher who admired it, took it away to read and told me later she would be using it with a small group of very bright Grade 9's who needed to be challenged. And did I have some others, equally well-written, provocative and evocative?

> "Oh yes. Please consider Alan Garner's *Stone Book* quartet. Such wonderful use of language — simple, subtle, supple. And narratives that haunt me still. Enough, you'll see.
>
> I think I'll bring you Bruce Brook's *Everywhere* which someone described as being in the literary tradition of Capote and McCullers.
>
> I've just thought of a picture book for older readers, *Rose Blanche*, by Roberto Innocenti. I can't trust myself to talk about it, only show it to you. And it makes me think of Gary Paulsen's *Nightjohn*. And have you considered writing by William Mayne or Diana Wynne Jones?
>
> Enough. I'll stop — but I'll be back. Oh, would you like me to pack up some holiday reading? O.K. O.K. I'm leaving."

Down the corridor, murmuring to myself —
> "*I Am David*...Mollie Hunter... the three books of *The Justice Cycle* (by Virginia Hamilton)... *On the Edge* (by Gillian Cross)..."

I'm in the library now and checking the opening lines of *Inside My Feet.*
> "When I was a child we lived on a lonely road near the edge of a forest where the darkness went in forever like a bottomless lake. Our nearest neighbour was out of sight and sound, and I remember always one night when both my father and mother were carried off down that road in that deep forest."

And yes, the final line still fills me with tears.

The curriculum
potential,
reactions
and ideas
that spring
from my reading.
More occasions for
co-operative building
of curriculum with
fiction perspectives,
waiting for the
opportune moment.

12

Musings

Newfound, by Jim Wayne Miller

Where does this gem fit into the curriculum? Literature? Social studies? Family studies? Such a strong sense of place and belonging. Do we teach in neighborhoods as rooted and culturally rich as this one? In the fractured, anonymous world so many of our students come from, where could this fit? Would students respond longingly? hopefully? or angrily? (Also: *The Winter Room.* Gary Paulsen; *Windward Island.* Karleen Bradford; *Hold Fast.* Kevin Major; *Jacob Have I Loved.* Katherine Paterson; *Shiloh.* Phyllis Reynolds Naylor.)

In *Newfound,* Robert gives the graduation address entitled "Citizens of Somewhere". (page 205) Using this as a model could our students write their own "Citizens of Somewhere"?

Would students be interested in Miller's poem, *A Kinsman* on p. 81 of *The Music of What Happens: Poems That Tell Stories,* selected by Paul Janeczko?

Progress of Love. Alice Munro

In her title story *The Progress of Love,* Alice Munro writes of family divisions and resentments, misunderstandings:

> "... love and grudges could be growing underground, so confused
> and stubborn, it must have seemed they had forever." "It was
> just as well," she writes, "to make up right away. Moments of
> kindness and reconciliation are worth having, even if the
> parting has to come sooner or later."

As a possible follow-up to the study of *The Progress of Love,* could students respond to one of the following books by describing such a "moment" — and why it made an impression on them or by inserting the kindness and reconciliation where they think it might have occurred — and what difference it might have made?

Good Bye and Keep Cold. Jenny Davis.

Teen Angel. Marianne Gingher.

No Kidding. Bruce Brooks.

Bad Blood. Bernard Ashley.

Journey. Patricia MacLachlan.

Babyface. Norma Fox Mazer.

Julie's Daughter. Colby Rodowski.

Title poem (p. 81) from Jo Carson's *Stories I Ain't Told Nobody Yet.*

Social education

I discover an old cache of articles from *Social Education*. I'll collect a couple of titles for each article, put them aside for now, and send copies of the articles to a few teachers of geography, history, health and physical education, literature.

"Grow Old Along With Me... Teaching Adolescents About Age" (Nov./Dec. 1980):

> *Memory.* Margaret Mahy.
>
> *Julie's Daughter.* Colby Rodowski.
>
> *Shadow and Light.* Katharine Joy Bacon.

"Literary Geography and Mapping" (January, 1985):

> *Going For the Big One.* P.J. Peterson.
>
> *Pickle and Price.* Pieter Van Raven.
>
> *The Freedom Machine.* Joan Lingard.

"Teaching History, Mathematics, and Morality: An Integrated Approach" (January, 1980):

> *Twopence a Tub.* Susan Price.
>
> *Lyddie.* Katherine Paterson.
>
> *Sunrising.* David Cook.

"Slow Learners and the Study of Contemporary Problems" (April, 1980):

> *Kool Ada,* by Sheila Solomon Klass.
>
> *It Ain't All For Nothin'.* Walter Dean Myers.
>
> *Thunderbird.* Marilyn Sachs.

A woman's perspective on history

You are the granddaughter/grandson/ancestor of the young person in any one of the stories in the list. Unpack the trunk left to you in a woman's will (or handed down to you through the generations). In a ten-minute oral presentation (you may use drawings and real items if you wish or are able to) tell us what you have learned of a woman's perspective on history.

> *Lyddie.* Katherine Paterson.
>
> *My Daniel.* Pam Conrad.
>
> *Borrowed Children.* George Ella Lyon.
>
> *Harbour Thieves.* Bill Freeman.
>
> *Granny Was A Buffer Girl.* Berlie Doherty.
>
> *Prairie Songs.* Pam Conrad.

A Circle Unbroken. Sollace Hotze.

Scarecrow. Vladimir Zheleznikov.

Sarah Plain And Tall. Patricia MacLachlan.

The Gift Of Sarah Barker. Jane Yolen.

The Borning Room. Paul Fleischman.

Could this be preceded by? followed by? students' contributions from their own grandparents' or family's memories? Is this a way of developing student sensitivity to women's lot through time? a way of honouring different ways and cultures?

Drama Department: Do you have a late night talk show in your future?

Can we bear yet another talk-show? Would the drama teacher be interested in using this format? Themes? How about – Street People: Victims or Alternate Lifestyle (*The Beggars' Ride* by Theresa Nelson, *Monkey Island* by Paula Fox, *Street Family* by Adrienne Jones, *throwaways* by Ian Strachan).

Guidance counsellors or health teachers

"People don't have to be the way they worry they might turn out to be."
Two Moons in August. Martha Brooks (p. 128).

Appropriate for a group counselling session? Consult staff counsellor or social worker on possibilities for comfort, contemplation and growth as students discuss the idea of repeating family history, and how to break out of it with any or all of these titles as a case study source.

Violence — Kieran in Brooks' *Two Moons in August.*

Alcoholism — Buddy in Robert Cormier's *We All Fall Down.*

Emotional coldness — Josh in Irene Hunt's *No Promises in the Wind.*

Dishonesty — Fergy in James Lincoln Collier's *Outside Looking In.*

Hereditary disease — Bent in Liza Fosburgh's *The Wrong Way Home.*

Infidelity — Tod in Harry and Norma Fox Mazer's *Heartbeat.*

Sexuality — Jack in A.M. Homes' *Jack.*

Guidance: While there is death there is also love

Is Joel's overwhelming sense of guilt at his friend Tony's death too harsh for young readers? Will they recognize that profound sense of pain we experience when we cry, "If only..." at life's unfairness? Thank goodness Marion Dane Bauer consoles Joel (and the reader) with the security of Joel's father's enveloping and steadfast love in *On My Honor*. Yes, while there is death there is also love.

Who else addresses these issues so beautifully? Katherine Paterson in *Bridge to Terabithia*; Virginia Hamilton in *Cousins*; Rose Blue in *Grandma Didn't Wave Back*; Will Hobbs in *Changes in Latitude*.

Now I'm not suggesting that we unload a burden of tears on our students by presenting these titles in a single book-talk. But I *would* like to take the theme, "While There Is Death There Is Also Love", these books, Joseph Gold's *Read for Your Life*, and make an appointment with the Guidance Department and/or the school psychologist.

I think I will begin by saying that "Joseph Gold believes that 'fiction is a human survival strategy'. These four novels I've brought along deal with grief, guilt, loss — and love. I think the experience of reading them has healing powers. Can you suggest how they might be used?"

For backup be prepared with Gold's chapter, *Everyone Loses Some of the Time* (pages 233-248). Its examples of coping with loss range from Doris Buchanan Smith's *A Taste of Blackberries* to Henry James.

I can't remember...

Newspaper headline:
'Amnesia victims can't remember why they can't remember things.'

> I have one pin I wear that says: ' I have a mind like a Teflon pan. Nothing sticks.' And another that says: 'I've got everything together but I can't remember where I put it.' I used to wear a T-shirt that said 'Beyond repair.' Then I got one: 'Repairs in progress.' Now I have a new one: 'It's working.'

The article describes how many victims rely on memory books.

For the imaginative English teacher: Will kids create memory books for themselves? for an aged person? Possibly a memory book of an aged person in a book they're reading?

For the creative Health teacher: Will kids create a memory book for an
aged "forgetful" person? Can I suggest titles to students who do
not know personally someone like this? (*Memory*, by Margaret
Mahy. *Grandma Didn't Wave Back*, by Rose Blue. *Sweet Bells Jangled Out of Tune*, by Robin Brancato. *Going Backwards* by Norma
Klein). How about a children's picture book? (For instance, Mem
Fox's *Wilfrid Gordon McDonald Partridge*.)?

"Be an active learner, not a passive pupil!"

At a conference I see a stimulating independent study unit on Statistics by a mathematics teacher. Topics covered, among others, are
sampling and surveying, predicting from samples, frequency dis-
tributions, empirical data, etc. Objectives include studying an environ-
mental concern of today or a social concern of today. Suggested topics
for these statistical objectives reminded me of some titles.

Environmental concerns
Diminishing resources:
The Wolfman of Beacon Hill. Kathleen Kilgore.
Changes In Latitude. Will Hobbs.

Social concerns
Child abuse:
Afternoon of the Elves. Janet Taylor Lisle.
Gillyflower. Ellen Howard.
Mac. John Maclean.
Dating violence:
Everything is Not Enough. Sandy Asher.
Hunger / poverty:
Send No Blessings. Phyllis Reynolds Naylor.
The Girl. Robbie Branscum.
The breakdown of the family:
I Will Call It Georgie's Blues. Suzanne Newton.
The Keeper. Phyllis Reynolds Naylor.

I believe that some of the experience and data that the teacher ex-
pected the students to find in their readings could be found in these
novels. Could I take my list and a few marked passages in some of the
titles to the math teacher and ask whether her students might include
fiction as another resource? Surely a teacher who exhorted her students to "Be an active learner not a passive pupil" would agree!

Problem-solving team

This headline, "Problem Solving Team," in a newspaper suggests to me a book report format. Could the class construct a problem-solving team(s) from their recent reading?

> A good friend: Rufus in *A Fine White Dust*, by Cynthia Rylant.
> Psychiatrist: Dr. Metcalf in *Celine*, by Brock Cole.
> Speech therapist: Roberta Clemm in *The Boy Who Could Make Himself Disappear*, by Kin Platt.
> Lawyer: Corelli in *Necessary Parties*, by Barbara Dana.
> Grandfather: Grandfather in *Journey*, by Patricia MacLachlan.
> Minister: Mr. Wallis in *One-Eyed Cat*, by Paula Fox.
> Parent: The comforting father in *On My Honour* by Marion Dane Bauer.
> Teacher: Mr. Lindell, the English teacher in *So Much To Tell You* by John Marsden or Miss Etting in *The Keeper*, by Phyllis Reynolds Naylor.
> Psychotherapist: Stan in *Round the Bend*, by Mitzi Dale.

Calendars

Keeping track of significant events of an adventure, quest, journey story in one of those engagement diary books or on a calendar could make a lively substitute for those plot summaries demanded by some teachers.

'Image in the mind'

William Bell says "a novel begins with an image in the mind." For him *Absolutely Invincible* began when he and a student stood waiting at the side of the road for Terry Fox to appear. And over the edge of a hill, a curly head appeared bobbing above that heartbreaking familiar step-and-skip. Then his face, then the body of the young man who ran for a cure for cancer.

Did Theresa Nelson begin *And One For All* with a memory of a candlelight vigil at the Washington Memorial?

Did Francesca Lia Block see a carload of eccentrics, out of which came "Weetsie and My Secret Agent Lover Man and Dirk and Duck and

Cherokee and Witch Body and Slinkster Dog and Go-Go Girl and the puppies Pee Wee, Wee Wee, Teenie Wee, Tiki Wee, and Tee Pee were driving down Hollywood Boulevard on their way to the Tea Room for turkey platters." (*Weetsie Bat.*)

Could students be encouraged to wonder with what image a favourite book might have begun its creative existence? They could share a passage that illustrates it.

Geography and English Departments (copy to Science Department)

"A reading guide to survival in a hostile environment"
(*Invitations, Celebrations*, p. 131ff).

Additional titles:

The North: *Black Diamonds*. James Houston; *The Hour of the Wolf*. Patricia Calvert.

The Wilds: The Book of Wirrun series: *The Ice is Coming. The Dark Bright Water. Behind the Wind*. Patricia Wrightson; *The Sign of the Beaver*. Elizabeth George Speare; *Hatchet*. Gary Paulsen; *The Boundary Riders*. Joan Phipson.

Mountains: *Coming Back Alive*. Dennis Reader; *Walk Out a Brother*. Thomas Baird. *Pursuit*. M. French.

New headings:

Voyages and Travels: *The Sea Runners*. Ivan Doig; *Morelli's Game*. Patricia Lee Gauch; *The Great Elephant Chase*. Gillian Cross; *The Way to Sattin Shore*. Philippa Pearce.

Islands: *The Island Keeper*. Harry Mazer; *Jacob Have I Loved*. Katherine Paterson;*The Island*. Gary Paulsen.

On the Streets: *Monkey Island*. Paula Fox; *The Beggar's Ride*. Theresa Nelson; *throwaways*. Ian Strachan; *Streetsmarts*. Bruce Reeves.

Ecosystems – *The Talking Earth*. Jean Craighead George; *The Wolfman of Beacon Hill*. Kathleen Kilgore.

Whenever the teachers get together

A fellow librarian told me that his principal assigned him 5 minutes to address the staff on library issues at each monthly staff meeting. It had become a chore. Alas, I learned that M. had been talking about library overdues, discipline, notices of assignments, etc. Of course these "housekeeping" concerns are important to *us*; they sap our energy, shorten our tempers, sour relationships. Better to keep them to one on one discussions; that way only the guilty need suffer.

I suggested M give 5 minute book talks. He looked wary.

L: It's no big deal, M. Tell them:
        'The library is as au courant as the daily headlines. To prove
        my point I've clipped some headlines from the last few weeks
        and gathered a few books that provide a fictional perspective
        on them on the back.
                (As I pass out the hand-out opposite.)
        I hope there is some way we can bring them to the attention of
        our students. The last three titles could be useful for your Na-
        tive Studies courses and for the study of fragile communities
        units in Economics and Sociology. And Lois Lowry's *Number
        the Stars* is a Newbery Medal winner. I hope you can find time
        to read some yourselves."

M: So that's all you'd say?

L: Is my 5 minutes up?

M: Hm. Got any more ideas?

L: Sure: "Wheniwasalittleboy" to introduce the Baby Sitters' Corner.

M: ???

L: I'd just start right in reading Rachna Gilmore' *Wheniwasalittlegirl*.
        It'll take about 3-4 minutes. Then tell them,
        "This is from our Baby Sitters' Corner which includes
                (Hold up each book in turn at its most
                intriguing page or cover)
        Alexandra Day's *Frank and Ernest Play Ball* which includes a
        set of baseball cards I've laminated so kids can actually use
        them after they finish reading the book; *The Very Best of
        Friends* (by Margaret Wild and Julie Vivas) which is about
        death, grief and the redemptive power of love; and *The True
        Story of The Three Little Pigs* and *The Frog Prince Continued* by
        Jon Scieszka, two modern hilarious re-tellings of the three lit-
        tle pigs and the big bad wolf and the princess and the frog (if
        you can, read one cheeky line from each). You don't have to be
        a baby sitter to sign these out — you can be an aunt, uncle,
        grandparent, parent – or a big kid."

M: O.K. O.K. Let's do more.

L: Let's do more at our next librarians' meeting, and start by creat-

Titles to be connected
with the headlines
opposite:
1. *Tug of War.* Joan
   Lingard.
2. *Forever Nineteen.*
   Grigory Baklanov.
   *We Were Not Like
   Other People.*
   Ephraim Sevela.
3. *Number the Stars.*
   Lois Lowry.
   Shadow of the Wall.
   Christa Laird.
   *The Man from the
   Other Side.* Uri
   Orlev.
4. *Beyond Safe
   Boundaries.*
   Margaret Sachs.
   Chain of Fire.
   Beverley Maidoo.
   Paper Bird. Maretha
   Maartens.
5. *The Boy from Over
   There.* Tamar
   Bergman.
6. *Where the Rivers
   Meet.* Don Sawyer.
   Dog Runner. Don H.
   Meredith.
7. *Windward Island.*
   Karleen Bradford.

Summit of three Baltic presidents
seeks to re-establish 1934 alliance

1. Demand to suspend declaration
rejected by Lithuanian legislators

2. The Great Patriotic War is losing its power to unify Soviets
Shedding a tear at the last parade

France searches soul after Jewish graves defiled

3. Rally
decries grave
desecration

4. South African police
open fire on blacks
on eve of peace pact

5. 3 are killed
as new riots
hit Gaza

6. The Akwesasne war:
why can't the Mohawks
settle it themselves?
Reserve quiet, police say

7. Digby shuns idea of working outside fishery
Digby fish workers clinging to home
despite plant closings, huge layoffs
These jobs what we know,
all we want, residents say

ing intriguing themes, e.g., "Nag. Nag. Nag" for books about rebellious kids...

M: ...or "Time Warps" for science fiction or fantasy
     or "Acts of Love"

L: for romance, heroism, sacrifice?

M: Let's tell the librarians how this all came about. You do it.

L: No, you do it.

M: O.K. — and as much as I hate Pollyannas, I'll call my talk. "Silver
     Linings"!

Documentary

Intriguing style in Avi's *Nothing But the Truth*, a "documentary novel"
constructed with memos, diary entries, portions of letters, phone conversations, exam questions, discussions in drama form, etc. This ex-
perimenting with form reminds me of Aidan Chambers' *NIK*, which in-
cludes camera shots, (stock shots, undercuts) poetry, notebook
entries, letters, demonstration signs, cartoons, etc.   These "documents" give depth, texture, levels to a story. Could our readers provide
the "documents" for a novel they've read?

A Bibliography of
Works Cited

WORKS CITED

Adams, Douglas. The Hitchhiker's Guide to the Galaxy. Crown, 1989. 48, 105

Adams, Douglas. Life, The Universe and Everything. Pan, 1982. 48, 105

Adams, Douglas. Mostly Harmless. Crown, 1992. 48, 105

Adams, Douglas. The Restaurant at the End of the Universe. Crown, 1982. 48, 105

Adams, Douglas. So Long and Thanks for All the Fish. Pan, 1985. 48, 105

Adkins, Jan. Solstice: A Mystery of the Season. Walker, 1990. 19, 48, 80, 132

Adler, C.S. Down by the River. Simon & Schuster, 1981. 137

Adler, C.S. If You Need Me. Macmillan, 1988. 67

Adler, C.S. Roadside Valentine. Macmillan, 1983. 160

Albert, Louise. But I'm Ready to Go. Bradbury, 1976. 77

Aldridge, James. The True Story of Lilli Stubeck. Hyland, 1984. 5

Aldridge, James. The True Story of Spit MacPhee. Viking, 1986. 186

Allen, R.E. Ozzy on the Outside. Delacorte, 1989. 80

Anderson, Rachel. The Poacher's Son. Oxford University Press, 1982. 174, 183

Anderson, Rachel. The War Orphan. Oxford University Press, 1988. 190

Angell, Judie. In Summertime It's Tuffy. Dell, 1979. 29

Angell, Judie. One Way to Ansonia. Macmillan, 1985. 135

Angell, Judie. Suds. Dell, 1983. 37

Anno, Mitsumasa. Anno's Flea Market. Bodley Head, 1984. 12

Asher, Sandy. Everything Is Not Enough. Delacorte, 1987. 57, 201

Asher, Sandy. Missing Pieces. Delacorte, 1984. 68

Ashley, Bernard. Bad Blood. Walker Books, 1988. 197

Avi. The Fighting Ground. Lippincott, 1984. 184, 189

Avi. Nothing But the Truth: A Documentary Novel. Orchard, 1991. 5, 47, 48, 206

Avi. A Place Called Ugly. Pantheon, 1981. 54, 132

Avi. The True Confessions of Charlotte Doyle. Orchard, 1990. 110

Bacon, Katharine Joy. Shadow and Light. Macmillan, 1987. 58, 198

Baird, Thomas. Walk Out a Brother. Harper, 1983. 203

Baklanov, Grigory. The Foothold. Chapman & Hall, 1962. 191

Baklanov, Grigory. Forever Nineteen. Lippincott, 1989. 92, 190, 204

Banks, Lynne Reid. Melusine: A Mystery. Hamish Hamilton, 1988. 49, 120

Bannerji, Himani. Coloured Pictures. Black Women and Women of Colour Press, 1991. 43, 45, 57

Bauer, Marion Dane. On My Honour. Clarion, 1986. 141, 200, 202

Bauer, Marion Dane. Rain of Fire. Houghton, 1983. 92

Bedard, Michael. Redwork. Macmillan, 1990. 47, 48, 136

Bell, William. Absolutely Invincible. General, 1991. Original Title: The Cripples' Club. Irwin, 1988. 11, 59, 86, 97, 202

Bell, William. Crabbe. Irwin, 1986. 166

Bell, William. Forbidden City. Doubleday, 1990. 49, 189

Beresford-Howe, Constance. The Book of Eve. McClelland, 1989. 117

Bergman, Tamar. The Boy From Over There. Houghton, 1988. 190, 204

Berry, James. A Thief In the Village and Other Stories. Orchard, 1988. 172

Bickham, Jack. Dinah Blow Your Horn. Tempo, 1983. 180

Block, Francesca Lia. Cherokee Bat and the Goat Guys. Harper, 1992. 141

Block, Francesca Lia. Weetsie Bat. Harper, 1989. 5, 141, 145, 168, 203

Block, Francesca Lia. Witch Baby. Harper, 1991. 141

Blos, Joan W. Brothers of the Heart: A Story of the Old Northwest 1837-1838. Scribner, 1985. 184

Blos, Joan W. A Gathering of Days: A New England Girl's Journal 1830-1832. Macmillan, 1979. 48

Blue, Rose. Grandma Didn't Wave Back. Watts, 1972. 200, 201

Booth, David, Ed. Voices on the Wind: Poems for All Seasons. Morrow, 1990. 49

Bosse, Malcolm J. The 79 Squares. Harper, 1979. 38

Boutis, Victoria. Looking Out. Four Winds Press, 1988. 135, 146, 175

Boyd, Candy Dawson. Breadsticks and Blessing Places. Macmillan, 1985. Paperback Title: Forever Friends. 152

Boyd, Candy Dawson. Charlie Pippin. Macmillan, 1987. 167

Bradford, Karleen. Windward Island. Kids Can Press, 1989. 197, 204

Brancato, Robin. Sweet Bells Jangled Out of Tune. Knopf, 1982. 38, 165, 201

Branscum, Robbie. The Girl. Harper, 1986. 176, 201

Bridgers, Sue Ellen. Permanent Connections. Harper, 1987. 69, 161

Brin, David. The Postman. Bantam, 1985. 22

Brooks, Bruce. Everywhere. Harper, 1990. 194

Brooks, Bruce. Midnight Hour Encores. Harper, 1986. 6

Brooks, Bruce. The Moves Make the Man. Harper, 1984. 93

Brooks, Bruce. No Kidding. Harper, 1989. 20, 22, 197

Brooks, Martha. Paradise Café and Other Stories. Little, 1990. Thistledown, 1988. 127, 161

Brooks, Martha. Two Moons In August. Little, 1992. Groundwood, 1991. 101, 110, 168, 199

Bunting, Eve. Such Nice Kids. Clarion, 1990. 111

Burke, James Lee. To the Bright and Shining Sun. Scribner, 1970. 178

Burns, Olive Ann. Cold Sassy Tree. Ticknor & Fields, 1984. Dell, 1986. 48

Buselle, Rebecca. Bathing Ugly. Orchard, 1989. 67

Byars, Betsy. The Animal, the Vegetable, & John T. Jones. Delacorte, 1982. 167

Byars, Betsy. Bingo Brown and the Language of Love. Viking Kestrel, 1989. 43, 49

Byars, Betsy. Bingo Brown, Gypsy Lover. Viking, 1990. 43, 49

Byars, Betsy. Bingo Brown's Guide to Romance. Viking Penguin, 1992. 43, 49

Byars, Betsy. A Blossom Promise. Delacorte, 1987. 49

Byars, Betsy. The Blossoms and the Green Phantom. Delacorte, 1987. 49

Byars, Betsy. The Blossoms Meet the Vulture Lady. Dell, 1987. 49

Byars, Betsy. The Burning Questions of Bingo Brown. Viking Kestrel, 1988. 44, 102

Byars, Betsy. Computer Nut. Viking, 1984. 37, 38

Byars, Betsy. Cracker Jackson. Viking, 1985. 38, 39, 41

Byars, Betsy. The Not-Just-Anybody Family. Delacorte, 1986. 49

Byars, Betsy. The Two-Thousand-Pound Goldfish. Harper, 1982. 83, 167

Byars, Betsy. Wanted...Mud Blossom. Delacorte, 1991. 49

Byatt, A.S. Possession: A Romance. Random, 1990. 143

Callan, Jamie. Over the Hill at Fourteen. NAL. 38

Callan, Jamie. The Young and the Soapy. NAL, 1984. 37

Calvert, Patricia. The Hour of the Wolf. Scribner, 1983. 203

Cameron, Silver Donald. The Baitchopper. Lorimer, 1982. 180

Cannon, A.E. Amazing Gracie. Delacorte, 1991. 77, 120, 135

Carris, Joan Davenport. The Revolt of 10-X. Harcourt Brace Jovanovich, 1980. 48

Carson, Jo. Stories I Ain't told Nobody Yet: Selections From the People Pieces. Orchard, 1989. 98, 136, 197

Carter, Alden R. Sheila's Dying. Putnam, 1987. 58

Carter, Peter. Bury the Dead. Farrar, 1987. 189

Castaneda, Omar S. Among the Volcanoes. Dutton, 1991. 170

Cave, Hugh B. The Voyage. Macmillan, 1988. 77

Chambers, Aidan. Booktalk: Occasional Writing on Literature and Children. Bodley Head, 1985.

Chambers, Aidan. Breaktime. Bodley Head, 1986. 49

Chambers, Aidan. Dance on My Grave. Harper, 1983. 143

Chambers, Aidan. NIK: Now I Know. Harper, 1987. 5, 87, 101, 158

Christian, Mary Blount. Singin' Somebody Else's Song. Macmillan, 1988. 80, 154, 164, 166

Cleaver, Vera. Belle Pruitt. Harper, 1988. 167

Cleaver, Vera. Sweetly Sings the Donkey. Harper, 1985. 134

Cohen, Barbara. People Like Us. Bantam, 1987. 68

Cole, Brock. Celine. Farrar, 1989. 4, 94, 97, 101, 119, 138, 202

Cole, Brock. The Goats. Farrar, 1987. 45

Collier, James Lincoln and Christopher. My Brother Sam Is Dead. Four Winds, 1984. 182

Collier, James Lincoln. Outside Looking In. Macmillan, 1987. 199

Collier, James Lincoln. When the Stars Began to Fall. Delacorte, 1986. 192

Collier, James Lincoln. The Winchesters. Macmillan, 1988. 180

Conrad, Pam. My Daniel. Harper, 1989. 119, 141, 198

Conrad, Pam. Prairie Songs. Harper, 1985. 168, 184, 199

Conrad, Pam. Stonewords: A Ghost Story. Harper, 1990. 147
Conrad, Pam. Taking the Ferry Home. Harper, 1988. 77, 137
Cook, David. Sunrising. Allison Press, 1984. 198
Cooney, Carolyn B. The Girl Who Invented Romance. Bantam, 1988. 101, 168
Corcoran, Barbara. Face the Music. Atheneum, 1985. 79
Corcoran, Barbara. I Am the Universe. Atheneum, 1986. 146
Corcoran, Barbara. The Potato Kid. Macmillan, 1989. 74, 139, 145, 148
Cormier, Robert. Beyond the Chocolate War. Knopf, 1985. 101, 104
Cormier, Robert. The Bumble Bee Flies Anyway. Dell, 1991. 58
Cormier, Robert. 8 Plus 1. Pantheon, 1980. 97
Cormier, Robert. Fade. Delacorte, 1988. 21, 22, 98
Cormier, Robert. Other Bells for Us to Ring. Delacorte, 1990. 48
Cormier, Robert. We All Fall Down. Delacorte, 1991. 145, 187, 199
Cresswell, Helen. Time Out. Macmillan, 1990. 22, 84
Crew, Linda. Children of the River. Delacorte, 1989. 172
Cross, Gillian. The Great Elephant Chase. Oxford University Press, 1992. 120, 166, 203
Cross, Gillian. A Map of Nowhere. Holiday, 1989. 118
Cross, Gillian. On the Edge. Holiday, 1985. 194
Cross, Gillian. Wolf. Holiday, 1991. 190
Crutcher, Chris. Athletic Shorts. Greenwillow, 1991. 141
Crutcher, Chris. Chinese Handcuffs. Greenwillow, 1989. 5, 160
Crutcher, Chris. The Crazy Horse Electric Game. Greenwillow, 1987. 141
Crutcher, Chris. Running Loose. Dell, 1986. 87, 141, 160
Crutcher, Chris. Stotan! Greenwillow, 1986. 79, 141, 147, 166
Dale, Mitzi. Round the Bend. Doubleday, 1991. Groundwood Bks., 1988. 111, 136, 202
Dalton, Annie. Night Maze. Methuen, 1989. 18
Dana, Barbara. Necessary Parties. Harper, 1986. 93, 101, 103, 202
Davis, Hunter. Saturday Night. Viking Kestrel, 1989. 5
Davis, Jenny. Good-Bye and Keep Cold. Orchard Books, 1987. 93, 197
Davis, Jenny. Sex Education. Orchard, 1988. 87, 101, 137, 161, 186
Davis, Terry. Vision Quest. Viking, 1979. 79
Day, Alexandra. Frank and Ernest Play Ball. Scholastic, 1990. 204
De Paola, Tomie. Strega Nona: An Old Tale Retold. Prentice-Hall, 1975. 23
De Saint Pierre, Michel. The New Aristocrats. Gollancz, 1962. 80
Deaver, Julia Reece. Say Goodnight, Gracie. Harper, 1989. 137
Degens, T. The Visit. Viking, 1982. 146, 189
Dhondy, Farrukh. Poona Company. Gollancz, 1980. 1985. 171
Dickinson, Peter. Eva. Delacorte, 1988. 85, 164, 166, 193
Dickinson, Peter. The Seventh Raven. Dell, 1991. 166
Dillon, Leo and Diane. Aida. J.T.G. Nashville, 1992. 49
Doherty, Berlie. Grannie Was a Buffer Girl. Orchard, 1986. 198
Doig, Ivan. The Sea Runners. Penguin, 1983. 203
Doyle, Brian. Covered Bridge. Groundwood, 1990. 49, 77
Doyle, Brian. Easy Avenue. Groundwood, 1988. 49, 77, 120, 167
Doyle, Brian. Spud Sweetgrass. Groundwood, 1992. 48, 192
Dragonwagon, Crescent. The Year It Rained. Macmillan, 1985. 94, 110
Duder, Tessa. Alex Archer In Lane 3. Houghton, 1989. 49, 135
Duder, Tessa. Alex In Winter. Houghton, 1989. 49, 70
Edmonds, Walter. The South African Quirt. Little, 1985. 80
Edwards, Dorothy. A Strong and Willing Girl. Methuen, 1980. 175, 180
Ehrlich, Amy. Where It Stops Nobody Knows. Dial, 1988. 84
Ellis, Mel. Flight of the White Wolf. Scholastic, 1970. 154
Ellis, Sarah. Pick-Up Sticks. Macmillan, 1992. Groundwood, 1991. 30, 38, 39, 54, 56, 83, 93, 165
Ellis, Sarah. Next-Door Neighbours. Macmillan, 1990. 46
Elmer, Martin. Mondays Will Never Be the Same. Groundwood, 1988. 94, 101
Emecheta, Buchi. The Wrestling Match. Brazillier, 1983. 85

Ende, Michael. Momo. Penguin, 1985. 22

Fairfax-Lucy, Brian and Pearce, Philippa. The Children of the House. Longmans, 1968. 97, 175

Farmer, Penelope. Thicker Than Water. Walker Bks., 1989. 141

Faville, Barry. The Return. Oxford, 1989. 18, 94, 132, 140

Fenton, Edward. Duffy's Rocks. Dell, 1989. 77, 101, 132

Fine, Anne. Goggle-Eyes. Hamish Hamilton, 1989. American Title: My War With Goggle Eyes. Joy
    St./Little, 1989. 92

Fine, Anne. A Pack of Liars. Hamish Hamilton, 1988. 46

Fleischman, Paul. The Borning Room. Harper, 1991. 199

Fleischman, Paul. Rear-View Mirrors. Harper, 1986. 84

Fosburgh, Liza. The Wrong Way Home. Bantam, 1990. 101, 199

Foster, Aisling. The First Time. Walker, 1988. 80

Fox, Mem. Wilfrid Gordon McDonald Partridge. Illus. by Julie Vivas. Kane Miller, 1984. 201

Fox, Paula. Monkey Island. Orchard, 1991. 57, 83, 127, 132, 133, 145, 199   203

Fox, Paula. One-Eyed Cat. Macmillan, 1984. 15, 141, 168, 202

Frank, Rudolf. No Hero for the Kaiser. Lothrop, 1986. 189

Freedman, Nancy. Joshua, Son of None. Delacorte, 1973. 193

Freeman, Bill. Harbour Thieves. Lorimer, 1984. 198

French, Michael. Pursuit. Delacorte, 1982. 203

Gallo, Donald R., Ed. Connections: Short Stories by Outstanding Writers for Young Adults.
    Doubleday, 1989. 127

Gallo, Donald A., Ed. Sixteen: Short Stories by Outstanding Writers for Young Adults. Delacorte,
    1984. 126

Gardam, Jane. A Long Way From Verona. Abacus, 1982. 116

Garner, Alan. Red Shift. Collins, 1973. 49

Garner, Alan. Stone Book. Collins, 1983. 194

Garrigue, Sheila. The Eternal Spring of Mr. Ito. Bradbury, 1985. 58

Gauch, Patricia Lee Morelli's Game. Putnam, 1981. 153, 203

George, Jean Craighead. The Talking Earth. Harper, 1983. 203

Geraghty, Paul. Pig. Masken Miller Longman, 1988. 170

Gilmore, Rackna. Whenlwasalittlegirl. Second Story Press, 1989. 204

Gingher, Marianne. Teen Angel and Other Stories of Young Love. Macmillan, 1988. 49, 126, 197

Gleeson, Libby. Dodger. Turton & Chambers, 1990. 85, 118, 127

Glenn, Mel. Back to Class: Poems by Mel Glenn. Clarion, 1988. 156

Glenn, Mel. Class Dismissed! High School Poems by Mel Glenn. Clarion, 1982. 57, 59, 156

Glenn, Mel. Class Dismissed Two: More High School Poems. Clarion, 1986. 156

Glenn, Mel. My Friend's Got This Problem, Mr. Candler: High School Poems. Clarion, 1992. 156, 157

Gold, Joseph. Read for Your Life: Literature As a Life Support System. Fitzhenry & Whiteside, 1990.
    140, 181, 200

Goodman, Linda. Linda Goodman's Sun Signs. Taplinger, 1968. 78, 79, 80

Gordon, Sheila. Waiting for the Rain: A Novel of South Africa. Orchard, 1987. 165, 171

Grant, Cynthia D. Joshua Fortune. Atheneum, 1980. 167

Gravel, Francois. Le Zamboni. English edition: Mr. Zamboni's Dream Machine. Lorimer, 1992. 49

Greene, Constance C. Other Plans. St Martin's Press, 1985. 79, 101

Grice, Frederick. The Bonnie Pit Laddie. Oxford University Press, 1960. 178

Grice, Frederick. The Nine Days' Wonder. Oxford University Press, 1976. 180

Grubb, Davis the Barefoot Man. Zebra, 1992. 180

Hahn, Mary Downing. Daphne's Book. Clarion, 1983. 38, 39

Hahn, Mary Downing. December Stillness. Houghton, 1988. 190

Hall, Barbara. Dixie Storms. Harcourt, 1990. 166, 186

Hall, Lynn. The Giver. Scribner, 1985. 69

Hall, Lynn. Just One Friend. Macmillan, 1985. 68, 166

Hall, Lynn. The Leaving. Scribner, 1980. 161

Hall, Lynn. Letting Go. Scribner, 1987. 93

Hall, Lynn. The Secret Life of Dagmar Schulz. Macmillan, 1988. 1991.

Hall, Lynn. The Solitary. Macmillan, 1986. 5, 83, 85, 132, 134

Hall, Lynn. Where Have All the Tigers Gone? Macmillan, 1989. 120, 127

Hamilton, Virginia. Cousins. Philomel, 1990. 46, 200

Hamilton, Virginia. In the Beginning: Creation Stories from Around the World. Harcourt Brace Jovanovich, 1988. 23

Hamilton, Virginia. The Justice Cycle. (Justice and Her Brothers; Dustland; The Gathering.) 194

Harris, Lavinia. Soaps In the Afternoon. Scholastic, 1985. 37, 38

Harris, Rosemary. Zed. Faber, 1990. Magnet, 1985. 166

Hegarty, John. The Haunted House Joke Book. Red Fox Books, 1990. 49

Heuck, Sigrid. The Hideout. Dutton, 1988. 191

Hewitt, Marsha and Mackay, Claire. One Proud Summer. Women's Press, 1981. 153, 179

Hicyilmaz, Gaye. Against the Storm. Viking, 1990. 172

Hinton, Nigel. Collision Course. Oxford University Press, 1983. 35

Hinton, S.E. Taming the Star Runner. Doubleday, 1988. 92

Ho, Minfong. Rice Without Rain. Lothrop, 1990. 171

Hobbs, Will. Changes In Latitudes. Atheneum, 1988. 200, 201

Hoberman, Mary Ann. Fathers, Mothers, Sisters, Brothers: A Collection of Family Poems. Little, Brown, 1991. 140

Hogrogian, Nonny. The Contest. Greenwillow, 1976. 23

Holm, Anne. I Am David. Mammoth, 1989. 194

Holman, Felice. The Murderer. Scribner, 1978. 57, 166

Holman, Felice. Secret City, U.S.A. Macmillan, 1990. 56, 154

Holman, Felice. The Wild Children. Scribner, 1983. 85

Homes, A.M. Jack. Macmillan, 1989. 92, 199

Horvath, Polly. No More Cornflakes. Farrar, 1990. 94

Horwitz, Joshua. Only Birds and Angels Fly. Harper, 1985. 84

Hotze, Sollace. A Circle Unbroken. Clarion, 1988. 199

Houston, James. Black Diamonds: A Search for Arctic Treasure. Penguin, 1983. 203

Howard, Ellen. Gillyflower. Atheneum, 1986. 57, 201

Howker, Janni. Badger on the Barge and Other Stories. Puffin, 1987. 127

Howker, Janni. Isaac Campion. Greenwillow, 1986. 173, 176

Hughes, Dean. Family Pose. Atheneum, 1989. 75

Hughes, Dean. Switching Tracks. Macmillan, 1982. 37, 38, 68, 167

Hughes, Monica. Hunter In the Dark. Macmillan, 1982. 44

Hunt, Irene. No Promises In the Wind. Berkley, 1987. 54, 199

Hutchinson, R.C. A Child Possessed. Michael Joseph, 1977. 15

Innocenti, Roberto and Gallaz, Christophe. Rose Blanche. Stewart, Tabori & Chang, 1991. 194

Jackson, Shirley. We Have Always Lived In the Castle. Viking, 1962. 111

Jaffe, Rona. Mazes and Monsters. Dell, 1982. 19

Janeczka, Paul B. The Music of What Happens: Poems That Tell Stories. Orchard, 1988. 197

Janeczko, Paul B. Poetspeak: In their Work, About their Work. Budbury, 1983. 121

Johnston, Jill. Hero of Lesser Causes. Lester Publishing, 1992. 141

Jones, Adrienne. Street Family. Harper, 1987. 199

Jones, Allan Frewin. Rabbit Back and Doubled. Hodder, 1989. 159

Jones, Allan Frewin. The Mole and Beverley Miller. Hodder, 1989. 47, 48, 160

Jones, Diana Wynne. Archer's Goon. Greenwillow, 1984. 17

Jones, Diana Wynne. Cart and Cwidder. Macmillan, 1990. 17

Jones, Diana Wynne. Castle In the Air. Greenwillow, 1991. 17

Jones, Diana Wynne. Charmed Life. Knopf, 1989. 17

Jones, Diana Wynne. Dogsbody. Greenwillow, 1988. 17

Jones, Diana Wynne. Eight Days of Luke. Greenwillow, 1988. 17

Jones, Diana Wynne. Fireside and Hemlock. Greenwillow, 1984. 17

Jones, Diana Wynne. Hidden Turnings: A Collection of Stories Through Time and Space. Greenwillow, 1989. 18

Jones, Diana Wynne. The Homeward Bounders. Greenwillow, 1981. 17, 142

Jones, Diana Wynne. The Lives of Christopher. Chant, Greenwillow, 1988. 17

Jones, Diana Wynne. The Time of the Ghost. Macmillan, 1981. 20, 22, 147

Jones, Diana Wynne. Wild Robert. Methuen, 1989. 17
Jones, Diana Wynne. Wilkin's Tooth. Puffin, 1975. 17
Jones, Diana Wynne. Witch Week. Knopf, 1988. 17
Kaellis, Rhoda. The Last Enemy. Pulp Press, 1989. 189
Kennedy, Richard. Inside My Feet: The Story of a Giant. Harper, 1979. 194
Kerr, M.E. Dinky Hocker Shoots Smack. Harper, 1972. 27
Kerr, M.E. Him She Loves? Harper, 1984. 137
Kerr, M.E. I Stay Near You: 1 Story In 3. Harper, 1985. 78
Kerr, M.E. Mememememe: A Not a Novel. Harper, 1983. 98
Kilgore, Kathleen. The Wolfman of Beacon Hill. Little, 1982. 201, 203
Kincaid, Jamaica. Annie John. Farrar, 1985. 48
King, Clive. The Sound of Propellers. Viking, 1986. 49
Kingman, Lee. Head Over Wheels. Dell, 1981. 86
Kinsey-Warnock, Natalie. The Canada Geese Quilt. Dutton, 1989. 141
Klass, Sheila Solomon. Kool Ada. Scholastic, 1991. 74, 164, 167, 198
Klass, Sheila Solomon. Page Four. Scribner, 1986. 80
Klause, Annette Curtis. The Silver Kiss. Delacorte, 1990. 141
Klein, Norma. Going Backwards. Scholastic, 1986. 201
Klein, Robin. Laurie Loved Me Best. Viking, 1988. 83
Knudson, R.R., Comp. American Sports Poems. Orchard, 1988. 166
Koch, Kenneth and Farrell, Kate. Talking to the Sun: An Illustrated Anthology of Poems for Young People. Holt/Metropolitan Museum of Art, 1985. 119
Koertge, Ron. The Arizona Kid. Little, 1988. 167
Kropp, Paul. Moonkid and Liberty. Little, 1990. Stoddart, 1988. 81
Laird, Christa. Shadow of the Wall. Greenwillow, 1990. 175, 204
Laird, Elizabeth. Kiss the Dust. Dutton, 1992. 169, 176
Landsman, Sandy. The Gadget Factor. Atheneum, 1984. 37, 38, 104, 127
Lasky, Kathryn. Beyond the Divide. Macmillan, 1983. 184
Lasky, Kathryn. The Bone Wars. Morrow, 1988. 184
Lasky, Kathryn. Home Free. Four Winds Press, 1985. 55
Lasky, Kathryn. Pageant. Macmillan, 1986. 5, 85
Lasky, Kethryn. Prank. Macmillan, 1984. 57, 134, 166
L'Engle, Madeleine. Camilla. Dell, 1982. 93
Leviton, Sonia. Incident at Loring Groves. Dial, 1988. 49
Leviton, Sonia. A Season for Unicorns. Macmillan, 1986. 54
Lillington, Kenneth. Josephine. Faber, 1991. 111, 168
Lingard, Joan. Across the Barricades. Heinemann, 1975. 166
Lingard, Joan. The Freedom Machine. Hamish Hamilton, 1986. 54, 198
Lingard, Joan. Glad Rags. Hamish Hamilton, 1990. 77
Lingard, Joan. The Guilty Party. Hamish Hamilton, 1987. 56
Lingard, Joan. Rags and Riches. Hamish Hamilton, 1988. 77
Lingard, Joan. Tug of War. Dutton, 1990. 204
Lisle, Janet Taylor. Afternoon of the Elves. Orchard, 1989. 67, 79, 201
Lively, Penelope. The Ghost of Thomas Kempe. Dutton, 1973. 147
Lloyd, Carole. The Charlie Barber Treatment. MacRae, 1989. 78
Lowry, Lois. Anastasia Again! Houghton, 1981. 49
Lowry, Lois. Anastasia and Her Chosen Career. Houghton, 1987. 49
Lowry, Lois. Anastasia, Ask Your Analyst. Houghton, 1984. 49
Lowry, Lois. Anastasia at This Address. Houghton, 1991. 49
Lowry, Lois. Anastasia at Your Service. Houghton, 1982. 49
Lowry, Lois. Anastasia Has the Answers. Houghton, 1986. 49
Lowry, Lois. Anastasia Krupnik. Houghton, 1979. 49
Lowry, Lois. Anastasia on Her Own. Houghton, 1985. 49, 58, 77
Lowry, Lois. Number the Stars. Houghton, 1989. 191, 204
Lowry, Lois. Switcharound. Houghton, 1985. 77
Lowry, Lois. Taking Care of Terrific. Houghton, 1983. 42, 68

Luger, Harriett. The Elephant Tree. Viking, 1978. 166

Lyon, George Ella. Borrowed Children. Orchard, 1988. 59, 101, 134, 175, 198

Maartens, Maretha. Paper Bird: A Novel of South Africa. Clarion, 1991. 204

Macaulay, David. Black and White. Houghton Mifflin, 1990. 21, 49

MacEvoy, R.A. The Book of Kells. Bantam, 1989. 19

Mackay, Claire. The Toronto Story. Illus. by Johnny Wales. Firefly, 1991. Annick, 1990. 12

MacLachlan, Patricia. Arthur for the Very First Time. Harper, 1980. 143

MacLachlan, Patricia. Cassie Binegar. Harper, 1982. 143

MacLachlan, Patricia. The Facts and Fictions of Minna Pratt. Harper, 1988. 84, 119, 125, 143

MacLachlan, Patricia. Journey. Doubleday, 1991. 110, 125, 140, 143, 168, 197, 202

MacLachlan, Patricia. Mama One, Mama Two. Harper, 1982. 143

MacLachlan, Patricia. Sarah Plain and Tall. Harper, 1985. 125, 143, 199

MacLachlan, Patricia. Seven Kisses In a Row. Harper, 1983. 143

MacLachlan, Patricia. Three Names. Harper, 1991. 143

MacLachlan, Patricia. Unclaimed Treasures. Harper, 1984. 1987. 125, 143

Maclean, John. Mac. Houghton, 1987. 57, 164, 166, 201

Magorian, Michelle. Back Home. Harper, 1984. 54

Mahy, Margaret. The Catalogue of the Universe. Macmillan, 1986. 101, 125

Mahy, Margaret. The Door In the Air and Other Stories. Delacorte, 1991. 21, 22

Mahy, Margaret. Memory. Macmillan, 1987. 41, 165, 198, 201

Mahy, Margaret. Non-Stop Nonsense. Macmillan, 1989. 119

Maidoo, Beverley. Chain of Fire. Lippincott, 1990. 165, 171, 204

Major, Kevin. Blood Red Ochre. Delacorte, 1989. 16

Major, Kevin. Dear Bruce Springsteen. Delacorte, 1987. 16

Major, Kevin. Diana: My Autobiography. Doubleday, 1993. 141

Major, Kevin. Doryloads: Newfoundland Writings and Art Selected and Edited for Young People. Breakwater Books, 1974. 16

Major, Kevin. Eating Between the Lines. Doubleday, 1991. 16, 42, 84, 120

Major, Kevin. Far From Shore. Delacorte, 1981. 16, 118, 131

Major, Kevin. Hold Fast. Delacorte, 1980. 7, 16, 197

Major, Kevin. Thirty-Six Exposures. Delacorte, 1984. 4, 16, 169

Marek, Margot. Matt's Crusade. Four Winds Press, 1988. 56

Mark, Jan. Black and White and Other Stories. Viking, 1991. 19, 126, 127

Mark, Jan. Man In Motion. Viking, 1989. 77, 139, 146, 168

Marsden, John. So Much to Tell You. Little, 1989. 166, 187, 202

Martin, Katherine. Night Riding. Knopf, 1989. 54, 75

Martz, Sandra, Ed. When I Am An Old Woman I Shall Wear Purple. Papier-Mache, 1987. 15

Mason, Bobbie Ann. In Country. Harper, 1985. 48

Masters, Anthony, Ed. Taking Root: A Multicultural Anthology. Methuen, 1988. 171

Mathis, Sharon Bell. Teacup Full of Roses. Puffin, 1987. 115

Mayne, William. A Game of Dark. Dutton, 1971. 49

Mayne, William. Gideon Ahoy! Delacorte, 1989. 41

Mazer, Harry. Cave Under the City. Crowell, 1986. 44, 53

Mazer, Harry. City Light. Scholastic, 1988. 92

Mazer, Harry. The Girl of His Dreams. Harper, 1987. 87, 94, 96, 160

Mazer, Harry. Hey Kid! Does She Love Me? Crowell, 1984. 78

Mazer, Harry. The Island Keeper. Delacorte, 1981. 43, 44, 203

Mazer, Harry. Someone's Mother Is Missing. Delacorte, 1990. 77

Mazer, Norma Fox. After the Rain. Morrow, 1987. 158, 165

Mazer, Norma Fox. Babyface. Morrow, 1990. 84, 197

Mazer, Norma Fox. Silver. Morrow, 1988. 93, 165

Mazer, Norma Fox. Summer Girls, Love Boys and Other Short Stories. Delacorte, 1982. 97, 116, 126, 161

Mazer, Norma Fox. Taking Terri Mueller. Avon Flare, 1981. 166

Mazer, Norma Fox. Up In Seth's Room. Delacorte, 1979. 7, 87, 158

Mazer, Norma Fox. When We First Met. Scholastic, 1983. 66

WORKS CITED

Mazer, Norma Fox and Harry. Heartbeat. Bantam, 1989. 199

Mazer, Norma Fox and Lewis, Marjorie, Ed. Waltzing on Water: Poetry by Nomen. Dell, 1989. 40

McCaughrean, Geraldine. A Pack of Lies. Oxford University Press, 1988. 83

McLintock, Norah. Shakespeare and Legs. Scholastic, 1988. 101, 115

McKissek, Patricia and Frederick. A Long Hard Journey: The Story of the Pullman Porter. Walker, 1990. 49

McRae, Russell. Going to the Dogs. Penguin, 1987. 3, 4, 94

Meredith, Don H. Dog Runner. Western Producer Prairie Books, 1989. 170, 204

Meyer, Carolyn. Elliott and Win. Atheneum, 1986. 140

Miklowitz, Gloria D. Good-Bye Tomorrow. Delacorte, 1987. 85, 166

Miller, Jim Wayne. Newfound. Orchard, 1989. 132, 197

Moeri, Louise. Downwind. Dell, 1987. 166

Mohr, Nicholas. Going Home. Dial, 1986. 77

Montgomery, L.M. Anne of Green Gables. Godine, 1989. McClelland, 1989. 117

Morck, Irene. A Question of Courage. Western Producer Prairie Books, 1988. 11

Morpurgo, Michael. Mr. Nobody's Eyes. Heinemann, 1989. 54

Mosel, Arlene. The Funny Little Woman. Dutton, 1972. 23

Mulford, Philippa Greene. If It's Not Funny, Why Am I Laughing? Delacorte, 1982. 94

Munro, Alice. Progress of Love. Knopf, 1986. 143, 197

Munsch, Robert. David's Father. Annick, 1983. 144

Munsch, Robert. The Paperbag Princess. Annick, 1980. 144

Myers, Walter Dean. Fallen Angels. Scholastic, 1988. 97, 188

Myers, Walter Dean. Hoops. Delacorte, 1981. 166

Myers, Walter Dean. It Ain't All for Nothin'. Viking, 1978. 198

Myers, Walter Dean. The Mouse Rap. Harper, 1990. 1992.

Myers, Walter Dean. The Outside Shot. Dell, 1987. 166

Myers, Walter Dean. Somewhere In the Darkness. Scholastic, 1992. 187

Naughton, Jim. My Brother Stealing Second. Harper, 1989. 132, 168

Naylor, Phyllis Reynolds. The Agony of Alice. Atheneum, 1985. 37, 38

Naylor, Phyllis Reynolds. The Keeper. Macmillan, 1986. 166, 201, 202

Naylor, Phyllis Reynolds. Send No Blessings. Macmillan, 1990. 135, 201

Naylor, Phyllis Reynolds. Shiloh. Macmillan. 48, 49, 138, 197

Naylor, Phyllis Reynolds. The Year of the Gopher. Macmillan, 1987. 101

Nelson, Theresa. And One for All. Orchard, 1989. 135, 188, 202

Nelson, Theresa. The Beggars' Ride. Orchard, 1992. 120, 199, 203

Neufeld, John. Lisa, Bright and Dark. S.G. Philips, 1969. 64

Newton, Suzanne. An End to Perfect. Viking Kestrel, 1984. 49

Newton, Suzanne. I Will Call It Georgie's Blues. Viking, 1983. 78, 93, 201

Newton, Suzanne. M.V. Sexton Speaking. Viking, 1981. 42, 68, 168

Newton, Suzanne. A Place Between. Viking Kestrel, 1986. 49, 145

O'Hearn, Audrey. Me and Luke. Groundwood, 1987. 161, 166

O'Hearn, Audrey. Rob Loves Stell. Groundwood, 1989.

Okrand, Marc. The Klingon Dictionary. English/Klingon, Klingon/English. Pocket Books, 1992. 142

Oneal, Zibby. In Summer Light. Viking, 1985. 79

Oneal, Zibby. The Language of Goldfish. Viking, 1980. 161

Orlev, Uri. The Man From the Other Side. Houghton, 1991. 190, 204

Owen, Gareth. Never Walk Alone. W. Collins, 1989. 55

Paci, F.G. Under the Bridge. Oberon Press, 1992. 172

Paretsky, Sara. Burn Marks. Delacorte, 1990. 48

Park, Ruth. Playing Beatie Bow. Macmillan, 1982. 19, 21 22

Parker, Jackie. Love Letters to My Fans. Bantam, 1986. 37, 38

Paterson, Katherine. Bridge to Terabithia. Crowell, 1977. 15, 141, 200

Paterson, Katherine. Come Sing, Jimmy Jo. Dutton, 1985. 77

Paterson, Katherine. The Great Gilly Hopkins. Crowell, 1978. 139

Paterson, Katherine. Jacob Have I Loved. Harper, 1980. 197, 203

Paterson, Katherine. Lyddie. Dutton, 1991. P6, 119, 175, 178, 198

Paulsen, Gary. Canyons. Delacorte, 1990. 80

Paulsen, Gary. The Cookcamp. Orchard, 1991. 48, 140

Paulsen, Gary. The Foxman. Puffin, 1990. 45

Paulsen, Gary. Hatchet. Macmillan, 1987. 44, 166, 203

Paulsen, Gary. The Island. Orchard Books, 1988. 166, 203

Paulsen, Gary. The Monument. Delacorte, 1991. 83, 97

Paulsen, Gary. Nightjohn. Delacorte, 1993. 141, 194

Paulsen, Gary. Popcorn Days & Buttermilk Nights. Dutton, 1983. 48

Paulsen, Gary. The River. Doubleday, 1991. 44, 96

Paulsen, Gary. Sentries. Macmillan, 1986. 56

Paulsen, Gary. Tracker. Macmillan, 1984. 166

Paulsen, Gary. The Voyage of the Frog. Orchard, 1989. 79

Paulsen, Gary. The Winter Room. Orchard, 1989. 119, 133, 197

Pearce, Philippa. Tom's Midnight Garden. Harper, 1992. 22

Pearce, Philippa. The Way to Sattin Shore. Penguin, 1985. 203

Pearson, Gayle. Fish Friday. Macmillan, 1986. 49

Peck, Richard. Remembering the Good Times. Delacorte, 1985. 69

Peck, Richard, ed. Sounds and Silences: Poetry for Now. Dell Laurel, 1970. 155

Perl, Lila. The Secret Diary of Katie Dinkerhoff. Scholastic, 1987. 111

Perrin, Ursula. Ghosts. Knopf, 1972. 159

Peterson, P.J. The Boll Weevil Express. 54

Peterson, P.J. Going for the Big One. Delacorte, 1986. 198

Peterson, P.J. Would You Settle for Improbable? Delacorte, 1981. 101

Peyton, K.M. ""Who, Sir? Me, Sir?"" Oxford University Press, 1983. 11, 104

Peyton, K.M. Downhill All the Way. Oxford University Press, 1988. 77, 119, 137, 138, 145

Peyton, K.M. Fly-By-Night. Oxford University Press, 1968. 77

Pfeffer, Susan Beth. About David. Delacorte, 1980. 166

Pfeffer, Susan Beth. The Year Without Michael. Bantam, 1987. 65, 166

Philip, Marlene Nourbese. Harriet's Daughter. Heinemann, 1988. Women's Press, 1988. 4, 165, 171

Phipson, Joan. The Boundary Riders. Penguin, 1983. 203

Pilling, Ann. The Big Pink. Viking Kestrel, 1987. 77

Pilling, Ann. Henry's Leg. Viking, 1985. 83, 93, 168

Pinsker, Judith. A Lot Like You. Bantam, 1988. 79, 94

Platt, Kin. The Boy Who Could Make Himself Disappear. Dell, 1971. 202

Plummer, Louise. My Name Is Sus5an Smith. The 5 Is Silent. Delacorte, 1991. 6, 157

Poole, Josephine. This Is Me Speaking. Hutchinson, 1990. 143

Price, Susan. Twopence a Tub. Faber, 1975. 49, 180, 198

Prince, Alison. Nick's October. Methuen, 1986. 78

Pringle, Terry. The Preacher's Boy. Algonquin Books, 1988. 5

Quiroga, Eduardo. On Foreign Ground. Norton, 1987. 191

Rana, Indi. The Roller Birds of Rampur. Bodley Head, 1991. 171

Raymond, Patrick. Daniel and Esther. Macmillan, 1990. 4, 85, 92, 161, 168

Reader, Dennis J. Coming Back Alive. Random, 1981. 54, 203

Reaver, Chap. Mote. Dell, 1992. 49

Reeder, Carolyn. Shades of Gray. Macmillan, 1989. 188

Reeves, Bruce. Street Smarts. Ace, 1982. 203

Ricci, Nino. The Lives of the Saints. Cormorant, 1990. 143

Richards, Adrienne. Into the Road. Dell, 1978. 35

Richmond, Sandra. Wheels for Walking. Little, 1985. 86

Robbins, Ruth. Baboushka and the Three Kings. Parnassus, 1960. 23

Robertson, Don. The Greatest Thing That Almost Happened. 1970. 118

Robertson, Wendy. French Leave. Hodder & Stoughton, 1988. 80

Rodda, Emily. Pigs Are Flying! Original Title: Pigs Might Fly. Greenwillow, 1986. 77, 137

Rodowsky, Colby. Julie's Daughter. Farrar, 1985. 81, 197, 198

Rodowsky, Colby. Sydney, Herself. Farrar, 1989. 77

Rostkowski, Margaret I. After the Dancing Days. Harper, 1986. 188

Roth, Arthur. The Secret Lover of Elmtree. Fawcett, 1981. 77
Rowe, Alick. Voices of Danger. Methuen, 1990. 191
Rushforth, P.S. Kindergarten. Godine, 1989. 14
Rylant, Cynthia. A Couple of Kooks and Other Stories About Love. Orchard Books, 1990. 126
Rylant, Cynthia. A Fine White Dust. Bradbury, 1986. 53, 77, 127, 202
Rylant, Cynthia. A Kindness. Orchard, 1988. 78
Rylant, Cynthia. Missing May. Orchard, 1992. 141
Sachs, Margaret. Beyond Safe Boundaries. Dutton, 1989. 165, 204
Sachs, Marilyn. Circles. Dutton, 1991. 87
Sachs, Marilyn. The Fat Girl. Dutton, 1984. 87
Sachs, Marilyn. Fourteen. Dutton, 1983. 38, 39
Sachs, Marilyn. A Summer's Lease. Dutton, 1979. 167
Sachs, Marilyn. Thunderbird. Dutton, 1985. 198
Sanders, Scott R. Bad Man Ballad. Bradbury, 1986.
Santiago, Danny. Famous All Over Town. Simon and Schuster, 1983. 78
Savitz, Harriet May. Come Back Mr. Magic. NAL, 1983. 86
Sawyer, Don. Where the Rivers Meet. Pemmican, 1988. 135, 146, 204
Schami, Rafik. A Handful of Stars. Dutton, 1990. 171, 191
Schlee, Ann. The Vandal. Crown, 1981. 43, 44, 142
Scieszka, Jon. The Frog Prince Continued. Viking, 1991. 22, 204
Scieszka, Jon. The True Story of the Three Little Pigs. Viking, 1989. 22, 204
Sebestyen, Ouida. I.O.U's. Little, 1982. 29, 83
Sebestyen, Ouida. On Fire. Little, 1985. 179
Sefton, Catherine. The Beat of the Drum. Hamish Hamilton, 1989. 49, 143, 189
Sefton, Catherine. Frankie's Story. Hamish Hamilton, 1988. 49, 143,189
Sefton, Catherine. Starry Night. Hamish Hamilton, 1986. 49, 143, 189
Senn, Steve. In the Castle of the Bear. Macmillan, 1985. 54
Sevela, Ephraim. We Were Not Like Other People. Translated by Antonia Boris. Harper, 1989. 188
Sevela, Ephraim. Why There Is No Heaven on Earth. Harper, 1982. 191
Shanks, Anne Zane. Old Is What You Get: Dialogues on Aging by the Old and the Young. Viking Press, 1976. 13
Sieruta, Peter D. Heartbeats and Other Stories. Harper, 1989. 1991. 126, 127
Silberkleit, Tom., Ed. The Do-It-Yourself Bestseller: A Workbook. Dolphin, 1982. 14
Skorpen, Liesel M. Grace. Harper, 1984. 38, 39
Sleator, William. Interstellar Pig. Dutton, 1984. 142
Sleator, William. Singularity. Dutton, 1985. 166
Slepian, Jan. The Alfred Summer. Macmillan, 1980. 11   65, 86
Slepian, Jan. Getting on With It. Four Winds Press, 1985.
Slepian, Jan. Lester's Turn. Collier Macmillan, 1981. 11
Slepian, Jan. Night of the Bozos. Dutton, 1983. 84, 92
Slipperjack, Ruby. Silent Words. Fifth House Publishers, 1992. 172
Smith, Dodie. I Capture the Castle. Little, Brown, 1948. 111
Smith, Doris Buchanan. Laura Upside-Down. Viking Kestrel, 1984. 67
Smith, Doris Buchanan. A Taste of Blackberries. Harper, 1973. 1988. 200
Smith, Robert Kimmel. Bobby Baseball. Delacorte, 1989. 54
Smith, Robert Kimmel. The Squeaky Wheel. Delacorte, 1990. 94
Smith, Rukshana. Salt on the Snow. Bodley Head, 1988. 172
Smith, Rukshana. Rainbows of the Gutter. Bodley Head, 1983. 79, 166
Snyder, Carol. Leave Me Alone, Ma. Bantam, 1989. 38, 39
Snyder, Carol. Memo: To Myself When I Have a Teen-Aged Kid. Pacer, 1984. 38, 39
Snyder, Zelpha Keatley. Libby on Wednesday. Doubleday, 1990. 97
Soto, Gary. Taking Sides. Harcourt Brace Jovanovich, 1991. 67
Speare, Elizabeth George. The Sign of the Beaver. Houghton, 1983. 203
Spinelli, Jerry. Jason and Marcelline. Dell, 1988. 87
Spinelli, Jerry. Maniac Magee. Little, 1990. 48, 49, 83, 119
Spinelli, Jerry. Space Station Seventh Grade. Little, 1982. 84, 85

Spinelli, Jerry. There's a Girl In My Hammerlock. Simon and Schuster, 1991. 38, 39, 67
Spinelli, Jerry. Who Put That Hair In My Toothbrush? Little, 1984. 84
Stafford, Ellen. Was That You at the Guggenheim? Macmillan, 1990. 60
Stanek, Lou Willett. Gleanings. Harper & Row, 1985. 185
Staples, Suzanne Fisher. Shabanu: Daughter of the Wind. Knopf, 1989. 135, 170
Steptoe, John. Marcia. Viking, 1976. 160
Sterling, Shirley. My Name Is Seepeetza. Groundwood, 1992. 172
Stolz, Mary. Ivy Larkin. Harcourt Brace, Jovanovich, 1986. 78
Strachan, Ian. The Flawed Glass. Little, 1990. 80, 83
Strachan, Ian. Throwaways. Methuen, 1992. 98, 176, 199, 203
Strasser, Todd. Angel Dust Blues. Dell, 1981. 166
Strasser, Todd. A Very touchy Subject. Delacorte, 1985. 56, 87, 94, 160
Sweeney, Joyce. Face the Dragon. Delacorte, 1990. 43, 45
Swindells, Robert. Follow a Shadow. Holiday, 1989. 18, 77
Tamar, Erika. It Happened at Cecelia's. Macmillan, 1989. 30
Tanner, Louise. Dr. I.R.T. Coward, 1976. 79
Taylor, Andrew. The Coal House. Collins, 1986. 84
Taylor, Mildred D. Let the Circle Be Unbroken. Dial, 1981. 48
Taylor, Mildred D. The Road to Memphis. Dial, 1990. 48, 49
Taylor, Mildred D. Roll of Thunder, Hear My Cry. Dial, 1976. 49
Taylor, Theodore. Walking Up a Rainbow. Delacorte, 1986. 31
Thomas, Ruth. The Runaways. Hutchinson, 1987. 45, 46, 54, 74
Thomas, Ruth. The Secret. Hutchinson, 1990. 44, 54, 75
Thompson, Julian F. The Taking of Mariasburg. Scholastic, 1988. 101
Tolan, Stephanie S. Pride of the Peacock. Scribner, 1986. 146
Tolan, Stephanie. The Great Skinner Strike. NAL, 1985.
Towne, Mary. Supercouple. Delacorte, 1985. 69
Townsend, John Rowe. Cloudy Bright. Harper, 1984. 160
Townsend, John Rowe. Noah's Castle. Penguin, 1984.
Treat, Lawrence. The Clue Armchair Detective. Ballantine Books, 1983. 13
Truss, Jan. A Very Small Rebellion. General, 1990. 56
Ure, Jean. One Green Leaf. Delacorte, 1989. 58
Ure, Jean. After Thursday. Delacorte, 1987. 78
Usher, Frances. Maybreak. Methuen, 1990. 54
Van Leeuwen, Jean. Seems Like This Road Goes on Forever. Dell, 1981. 166
Van Raven, Pieter. Harpoon Island. Macmillan, 1989. 190
Van Raven, Pieter. Pickle and Price. Scribner, 1990. 154, 198
Voigt, Cynthia. Come a Stranger. Atheneum, 1986. 80
Voigt, Cynthia. David and Jonathan. Scholastic, 1992. 47, 48, 138
Voigt, Cynthia. Dicey's Song. Atheneum, 1982. 167
Voigt, Cynthia. Homecoming. Macmillan, 1981. 153, 167
Voigt, Cynthia. Izzy Willy-Nilly. Macmillan, 1986. 59, 78, 86
Voigt, Cynthia. The Runner. Macmillan, 1985. 4, 53, 93, 145
Voigt, Cynthia. Seventeen Against the Dealer. Macmillan, 1989. 78
Voigt, Cynthia. A Solitary Blue. Macmillan, 1983. 92, 117
Wallace, Ian. Mr. Kneebone's New Digs. Groundwood, 1991. 56
Walsh, Ann. Your Time, My Time. Beach Holme, 1984.
Walsh, Jill Paton. A Chance Child. Farrar, 1978. 7, 16, 183, 194
Walsh, Jill Paton. The Dolphin Crossing. Dell, 1990. 16
Walsh, Jill Paton. The Emperor's Winding Sheet. 1974. 16
Walsh, Jill Paton. Fireweed. Farrar, 1970. 16
Walsh, Jill Paton. Gaffer Samson's Luck. Farrar, 1984. 16, 169
Walsh, Jill Paton. Goldengrove. Farrar, 1985. 16
Walsh, Jill Paton. A Parcel of Patterns. Penguin, 1985. 16
Walsh, Jill Paton. Unleaving. Macmillan, 1976. 16
Watkins, Yoko Kawashima. So Far From the Bamboo Grove. Lothrop, 1986. 175

WORKS CITED

Watson, James. No Surrender. Gollancz, 1991. 138, 19

Wersba, Barbara. The Carnival In My Mind. Harper, 1982. 54, 137

Wersba, Barbara. Fat: A Love Story. Harper, 1987. 85, 137

Wersba, Barbara. Love Is the Crooked Thing. Harper, 1987. 79

Westall, Robert. Break of Dark. Chatto & Windus, 1982. 19

Westall, Robert. The Cats of Seroster. Macmillan, 1984. 49

Westall, Robert. Echoes of War. Farrar, 1991. 188

Westall, Robert. Ghost Abbey. Scholastic, 1989. 1990. 147

Westall, Robert. The Kingdom by the Sea. Farrar, 1991. 138

Westall, Robert. A Walk on the Wild Side. Methuen, 1989. 49

Westall, Robert. Yaxley's Cat. Scholastic, 1992. 49, 141

Wheatley, Nadia. Landmarks. Turnton & Chambers, 1991. 15, 127

White, Ellen Emerson. Life Without Friends. Scholastic, 1987. 1988. 79

Wieler, Diana. Bad Boy. Groundwood, 1989. 87, 96, 163, 166

Wieler, Diana. Last Chance Summer. Delacorte, 1991. 77

Wiesner, David. Tuesday. Clarion, 1991. 49

Wild, Margaret and Vivas, Julie. The Very Best of Friends. Harbrace, 1990. Kids Can Press, 1990. 204

Wilson, Budge. The Leaving. Putnam, 1992. Anansi, 1990. 93

Wilson, Gina. All Ends Up. Faber and Faber, 1984. 80

Wilson, Jacqueline. Amber. Oxford University Press, 1988. 69

Windsor, Patricia. The Sandman's Eyes. Delacorte, 1988. 49

Winn, Dilys. Murderess Ink: The Better Half of Mystery. Workman Publishing, 1979. 12

Winterson, Jeanette. Oranges Are Not the Only Fruit. Atlantic Monthly, 1987. 143

Wolff, Virginia Euwer. Probably Still Nick Swanson. Holt, 1988. 11, 59, 127

Wolitzer, Hilma. Toby Lived Here. Farrar, 1978. 101

Woodford, Peggy, Ed. The Misfits: An Anthology of Short Stories. Bodley Head, 1984. 78, 127

Wrightson, Patricia. Balyet. Macmillan, 1989. 17, 132

Wrightson, Patricia. Behind the Wind. Book III, the Book of Wirren Series. Penguin, 1983. 17, 203

Wrightson, Patricia. The Dark Bright Water. Book II, the Book of Wirren Series. Penguin, 1983. 17, 203

Wrightson, Patricia. The Ice Is Coming. Book I, the Book of Wirren Series. Penguin, 1983. 17, 203

Wrightson, Patricia. A Little Fear. Macmillan, 1983. 17

Wynne Jones, Diana See Jones, Diana Wynne.

Yolen, Jane. Children of the Wolf. Viking, 1984. 175

Yolen, Jane. The Devil's Arithmetic. Viking Kestrel, 1988. 138, 175

Yolen, Jane. The Gift of Sarah Barker. Viking, 1981. 199

Zeiger, Helane. Love Byte. Tempo, 1983. 37, 38

Zindel, Paul. Harry & Hortense at Hormone High. Harper, 1984. 44

TITLE
INDEX
to works cited